Segregated SKIES

All-Black
Combat Squadrons of WW II

SMITHSONIAN HISTORY OF AVIATION SERIES
Von Hardesty, Series Editor

On December 17, 1903, on a windy beach in North Carolina, aviation became a reality. The development of aviation over the course of little more than three-quarters of a century stands as an awe-inspiring accomplishment in both a civilian and military context. The airplane has brought whole continents closer together, at the same time it has been a lethal instrument of war.

This series of books is intended to contribute to the overall understanding of the history of aviation—its science and technology as well as the social, cultural, and political environment in which it developed and matured. Some publications help fill the many gaps that still exist in the literature of flight; others add new information and interpretation to current knowledge. While the series appeals to a broad audience of general readers and specialists in the field, its hallmark is strong scholarly content.

The series is international in scope and will include works in three major categories.

Smithsonian Studies in Aviation History: works that provide new and original knowledge.

Smithsonian Classics of Aviation History: carefully selected out-of-print works that are considered essential scholarship.

Smithsonian Contributions to Aviation History: previously unpublished documents, reports, symposia, and other materials.

Segregated SKIES

All-Black Combat Squadrons of WW II

Stanley Sandler

Smithsonian Institution Press   *Washington, D.C., and London*

Copyright © 1992 by the Smithsonian Institution

All rights are reserved

This book was edited by Initial Cap Editorial Services and designed by Janice Wheeler.

The paper used in this publication meets the minimum requirements of the American National Standard for Permanence of Paper for Printed Library Materials Z39.48–1984.

Library of Congress Cataloging-in-Publication Data

Sandler, Stanley, 1937–
    Segregated skies : All-Black combat squadrons of World War II /
Stanley Sandler,
        p. cm.—(Smithsonian history of aviation series)
    Includes bibliographical references and index.
    ISBN 1-56098-154-7 (alk, paper)
    1. World War, 1939–1945—Aerial operations, American. 2. World War. 1939–1945—Participation, Afro-American. 3. United States. Army Air Forces. Fighter Squadron, 99th—History. 4. United States. Army Air Forces. Fighter Group, 332nd—History. 5. United States. Army Air Forces. Bombardment Group (Medium), 477th—History. 6. United States. Army Air Forces—Afro-American troops.
    I. Title. II. Series.
    D790.S26   1992
    940.54′4973—dc20   91-39452

A paperback reissue (ISBN 1-56098-917-3) of the original cloth edition.

Printed in the United States of America
  8   7   6   5   4   3   2   1
  05 04 03 02 01 00 99 98

For permission to reproduce individual illustrations appearing in this book, please correspond directly with the owners of the images, as stated in the picture captions. The Smithsonian Institution Press does not retain reproduction rights for these illustrations individually or maintain a file of addresses for photo sources.

Publisher's note: The descriptions of otherwise undocumented personal incidents and the recollections of episodes and persons are entirely the author's. Every effort has been made to verify details and insure correctness; inaccuracy if it occurs is regretted.

Contents

Preface and Acknowledgments

While in an elevator ascending to a hotel reunion of the East Coast chapter of the Tuskegee Airmen, I noticed a fellow passenger scrutinizing my name tag. He seemed puzzled, for I was obviously of the "wrong" race and age to have been a black Army Air Forces pilot in the Second World War. Overcoming his initial hesitation, he asked if I had, somehow, been a Tuskegee Airman. "No," I replied, "but I am writing a book about them, and that's why I'm here." The questioner, a middle-aged white man, declared that as a bomber pilot in World War II in Italy he wanted very much to tell the Tuskegee Airmen that he and his buddies always felt safe when they saw the "Red Tails" on their flanks.

From all evidence, this veteran bomber pilot's gratitude was not unique. Rather, it is an indication of how well the pilots of the all-black 332nd Fighter Group did their job, on numerous occasions passing up opportunities to score enemy "kills" in order to shepherd faithfully the "big boys" over some of the most dangerous skies in the world. In 1,500 missions and something like 15,000 sorties, the "Red Tails" never lost a bomber to enemy aircraft, a record unique in U.S. Air Force history.

But for the historian of twentieth-century American military history, it is the blackness of the 332nd Fighter Group, the 99th Fighter Squadron (Colored) (Separate), and the 477th Bombardment Group (Medium) that gives them such interest. These were the pioneers in an Air Corps that had not segregated blacks before; it had simply refused to admit them.

This work attempts to tell their story, drawing on personal oral interviews, squadron, group, wing, and air base official records, Army and Army Air Forces records, and federal government archives, as well as secondary sources. It also tells their story in the context of a U.S. civil society that, to a large extent, made them what they were, strictly limiting their opportunities, yet instilling in so many of them an inextinguishable determination to change that system, starting with the U.S. Army Air Forces.

I am grateful to the East Coast chapter of the Tuskegee Airmen, Inc., and to the R. R. Moton Foundation for their financial and personal support. I am also indebted to the many Tuskegee veterans who gave of their time: to C. Alfred "Chief" Anderson of Tuskegee; to the late J. C. Evans, counselor to no less than ten secretaries of defense; to Lt. Gen. Benjamin O. Davis, Jr.; the late Brig. Gen. Noel F. Parrish, former commanding officer of Tuskegee Army Air Field; to Dr. Forrest Pogue, formerly director of the Eisenhower Institute, Smithsonian Institution, as well as of the George C. Marshall Foundation, for his insights and encouragement; to Lawrence Paszek, formerly of the Office of Air Force History; to the staffs of the Modern Military Field Branch of the National Archives, the Office of Air Force History, and the National Air and Space Museum. All photographs not otherwise credited are from the U.S. Air Force. A particular note of gratitude is in order for Felix Lowe, director of the Smithsonian Press, and Dr. Alan L. Gropman for their perseverance, encouragement, and insight, to Mrs. Catherine Adams for her impeccable secretarial skills, and to Therese Boyd, editor.

A final acknowledgment of appreciation is due my wife, Marion Sandler, for her support through the years.

Abbreviations

AAF	Army Air Forces
AGCT	Army General Classification Test
ASF	Army Service Forces
C.O.	Commanding officer
CAA	Civil Aeronautics Authority
CPA	Communist Political Association
CPTP	Civilian Pilot Training Program
DFC	Distinguished Flying Cross
EFTC	Eastern Flying Training Command
ETO	European Theater of Operations
F.O.	Flight officer
M.O.	Medical officer
MOS	Military occupational specialty
MP	Military police
MTO	Mediterranean Theater of Operations
NAACP	National Association for the Advancement of Colored People
NCO	Noncommissioned officer

OCS	Officers Candidate School
POW	Prisoner of war
PX	Post exchange
RAF	Royal Air Force
ROTC	Reserve Officers' Training Corps
SEAACTC	Southeastern Army Air Corps Training Command
SEAAFTC	Southeastern Army Air Forces Training Command
TAAF	Tuskegee Army Air Field
USAAC	U.S. Army Air Corps
USAAF	U.S. Army Air Forces
USAF	U.S. Air Force
USO	United Service Organizations
WAVES	Women's branch of the U.S. Navy
WPA	Works Progress Administration
WTS	War Training Service

Introduction

Traditionally, black Americans have looked upon entry into the armed forces of their nation as one of the most effective ways to open doors to their fuller participation in American life.

However, they could find little to encourage them in the 1930s, despite a national administration perceived as generally sympathetic to blacks and other minorities. At the bottom of the economic and social ladder, they faced rigid and nearly unchallenged racial segregation, in law as well as custom, in much of the United States. Even the burgeoning defense effort of 1939–41 seemed to affect them only minimally. And blacks in pre–World War II America still lived with the terrible knowledge that they might be the only people left in the civilized world who ran some risk of being burned at the stake.

It might be interpreted as a sad commentary upon the times and the nation that this people had to look to military service as a way to improve their lives. Certainly for most white Americans, military service (except in certain areas of the South) was equated roughly with servitude, and the

Army traditionally had replenished its enlisted ranks with the young misfits of society.

But with the approach of war and with the entry of the United States into global conflict, the defense of America became almost glamorous, and black Americans soon realized that participation in the war could result in benefits both immediate and postwar. Conversely, failure to enter combat would undoubtedly be interpreted by white America as further proof of black cowardice and incompetence.

With the nation gearing for war by 1940, and the subsequent advent of conscription, it might be presumed that the American military would welcome blacks. Such was not the case, and throughout the war inter- and intraservice disputes raged over the question of which branch was "absorbing" its fair share of blacks. Yet there was no alternative; how could whites be accepted or drafted into the military and face death or mutilation while blacks escaped? Here, indeed, was the rationale for black participation in each of America's conflicts since at least the time of the Civil War. However, the military persistently viewed black soldiers as poor fighters and a source of trouble. The military "thinkers" who propounded such theories never bothered to look seriously at any causes for such poor results, contenting themselves with cracker-barrel Darwinian philosophizing and half-baked conclusions about "innate characteristics" and "observed facts."

Military planners were somewhat closer to reality when they feared that the large-scale introduction of black servicemen would touch off bloodshed among citizen soldiers and in surrounding communities. The uniform lent a certain prestige, the gun a certain authority, and the military could well worry about the impact of uniformed, armed blacks upon an America habituated to black subservience—not to mention the impact upon blacks themselves.

The military solution, as in previous wars, was to segregate black soldiers in two ways. First, they were restricted, as much as possible, to the most menial positions. This solution was not entirely satisfactory, for the menial positions were frequently noncombatant and could prompt resentment among whites facing a disproportionate burden of battle. The second solution was to segregate blacks by unit from white servicemen, thus forestalling racial friction. This tradition of military racial segregation, having its roots in earliest American history, could thus be justified as a simple adherence to American mores.

Perhaps surprisingly, the youngest of the armed services held the most obdurate and conservative position on the subject of race; the Army Air Corps (later, Army Air Forces) simply closed its ranks to black Americans. But the Air Corps was the glamour branch of the services. If blacks could break into military aviation, they would reap immediate and widespread publicity—publicity that would prove that blacks could master the most complex and dangerous machinery and hearten black Americans everywhere. Thus, from the start of the American defense effort before Pearl Harbor, the Army Air Corps offered a prime target for black pressure. Of course, individual black Americans attempted to enlist in the Army Air Corps for the same reasons as whites: love of flying and adventure, desire for increased prestige and respect, self-challenge, and patriotism. But in most cases blacks had the additional incentive of a desire to prove that they, as a people, could do it.

The first break in the all-white complexion of U.S. military and—for the most part—civilian aviation came in 1939 with the opening of the government-sponsored Civilian Pilot Training Program (CPTP) to blacks. The CPTP provided momentum for the limited and totally segregated opening of the Air Corps to blacks in the following year.

Predictably, black participation in the Army Air Corps was confined for the most part to the same noncombatant roles, such as supply, transport, and housecleaning, open to them in the parent U.S. Army. But the focus of black pride would be pursuit or fighter aviation—particularly the 99th Pursuit Squadron (changed to the 99th Fighter Squadron in May 1942), whose members were the first of their race to enter American military aviation. Later, three more fighter squadrons and a medium bomber group would be formed solely for blacks, and these formations would represent the total of U.S. black combat aviation in the Second World War.

With some exceptions, almost all flight training was concentrated near the tiny town of Tuskegee, Alabama, home of Tuskegee Institute. Some evidence exists to suggest the Tuskegee location was deliberately chosen and expanded throughout the war in order to isolate black airmen, and because the Air Forces's hierarchy believed that Tuskegee still exemplified the accommodationist philosophy of its late founder, Dr. Booker T. Washington. Furthermore, the isolation and environment of Tuskegee supposedly would discourage "agitators" or "radical ideas."

The 477th Bombardment Group was so delayed in its training that it almost ceased to be a combat unit and earned its fame for its disciplined protest of military racial segregation policies. But the pioneer 99th fought in North Africa and, with the 100th, 301st, and 302nd fighter squadrons grouped into the 332nd Fighter Group, served throughout the Italian campaign, southern France, Austria, Yugoslavia, Greece, and Germany. The records document a good average group, but one whose efficiency was warped by the demands of racial segregation.

The Air Corps seems to have made an effort to apply the "separate but equal" doctrine of official civilian segregation to its new black units, but this theory often broke down in practice. A major problem remained in fine-tuning the cadet pilot flows; with only five black units, at most, to absorb successful black cadets as well as a limited number of qualified candidates, often large numbers of officers sat idly around Tuskegee for months, or pilots of the 332nd wound up putting in far more missions than their white counterparts due to a lack of replacements.

Perhaps the most oppressive result of racial segregation in the service was the blacks' awareness that every action was under unremitting scrutiny; their triumphs emblazoned by the press, black and white, out of proportion to any effect on the war effort, and their failures meticulously documented by the Army Air Forces. Certainly no white squadron had its combat efficiency monitored almost daily throughout the war by the secretary of war, the undersecretary of war for air, the chief of the Army Air Forces, and the chief of staff of the Army. All of this, of course, was in addition to the normal hazards faced by any fighter group operating in the Second World War.

In many respects the 99th and the 332nd were in the classic position of "damned if they did and damned if they didn't." Evidence of excellence, particularly in the fledgling 99th, was assumed to be due to the fact that the squadron was somehow an "elite" outfit, representing the "cream of the race." The unspoken assumption was that only such a select black outfit could be committed to war in the air. And if even an elite black organization had its problems, then the admission of blacks to the Army Air Forces could be viewed as merely a temporary wartime measure.

In many ways the Army Air Forces's program of segregated black participation in the war could be termed a failure, from the viewpoint of both the military and the participants themselves. At the end of the war the AAF asserted that at best the 332nd Fighter Group had been a mediocre outfit, not worth the extra time and effort required to bring it to minimal acceptable standards. The idea that unsegregated black entry might have proven less difficult apparently was not seriously advanced. Yet an objective study of official records documents an average-to-good unit.

Many of the participants also felt that the program, if not a failure, had at least hindered their development as airmen as well as the mission of the group. Although they were thrown almost entirely on their own resources, unable to transfer laterally to any other air unit or to rise above the level of their own group, flying far more missions on average than comparable white combat pilots, and aware of living in a goldfish bowl that one serious mistake could shatter, the veterans of the 332nd still look back with pride on those days of training, monotony, and combat. They had fought their own two-front war—against an enemy abroad and against racism at home—and they had enjoyed some measure of success. But their greatest source of pride lay in the knowledge that the struggle to open the armed forces to black Americans produced a momentum that could not be reversed even in the postwar era. Within five years of the end of the Second World War, far in advance of civilian America, equality of opportunity and treatment, and then racial integration, had become official U.S. defense policy.

Segregated
All-Black SKIES
Combat Squadrons of WW II

Beginnings 1.

I t was not much of a machine even by the private plane standards of 1924. Yet there was excitement in the air and on the ground as the fragile homemade biplane dipped low over the rolling wooded hills of east-central Alabama. At the controls was J. C. Robinson, a black pilot. The location was as significant as the flight itself, for Robinson was flying over the center of black education, Tuskegee Institute. This flight marked the earliest beginnings of a heritage of black aviation that, twenty years later, would put four squadrons of black fighter pilots into action, and, even more significantly, pioneer in the breaching of the age-old walls of racial segregation and subordination.

Although J. C. Robinson went on to fly and fight against fascist aggression in Ethiopia, as a black pilot in combat aviation he had been preceded by Eugene Jacques Bullard, an American who flew with the Lafayette Flying Corps (Lafayette Escadrille) during World War I. But James Peck, a Pittsburgh native, was undoubtedly the foremost pre–World War II black military aviator. Peck was also a veteran of the Spanish Civil War, an "ace" with five victories to his credit in less than four months of bitter aerial combat in his sub-nosed Soviet-built Polikarpov fighter. None of these experienced combat aviators, Robinson, Bullard, or Peck, was ever admitted to the U.S. Army Air Corps.

Although blacks were represented in American civil aviation in the 1920s and 1930s in minuscule numbers, those few left impressive accomplishments. Of course, only a handful enjoyed the financial resources necessary to obtain and maintain a pilot's license. Yet there were those who persevered. But the 1930s witnessed the first black air show and tours of the Bessie Coleman Aerocircus through the West and Southwest. William Brown entered the 1932 National Air Races with an ancient, secondhand machine and did well enough, ending up near El Paso, about halfway through the course, when bailing wire and improvisation could do no more.

The first black transcontinental flight also took place in 1932. Charles Alfred Anderson showed what could be accomplished with decent equipment by completing, with Dr. A. Forsythe, a round-trip transcontinental flight without incident in a modern Fairchild cabin monoplane. "Chief" Anderson, as he was to become known, had purchased his first airplane in 1928 for $3,000, and was fortunate enough to find a willing white instructor near his hometown of Bryn Mawr, Pennsylvania. In 1932 he was awarded a commercial pilot's license, and by 1939 was operating a commercial air service from a seaplane base on the Potomac River in Washington, D.C., and a land plane facility from a field in nearby Virginia. To put Mr. Anderson's achievement in perspective, it is worth noting that in 1939 a grand total of 125 black Americans held licenses as pilots: four commercial, four limited commercial, twenty-three private, and ninety-four amateur or student.

This year, 1939, was the end of the most significant decade in the history of aviation development, in which commercial and military aircraft had passed from the mostly wood and fabric structures of the 1920s to the low-wing, internally braced monocoque monoplane, equipped with retractable landing gear, flaps, variable pitch propeller, enclosed cabins, and vastly more efficient power plants. Services such as navigational and airport facilities had also improved markedly, and an internal network of domestic airlines began to emerge.

And yet how little had black Americans shared in all of this. Not only were blacks excluded from military aviation, but they were barely represented in the ranks of civilian pilots; the entire civil aeronautics field was, in the words of one authority on the subject, "originally the most racially restrictive" of all the transportation industries. It should be noted, however, that black locomotive engineers, merchant-ship officers, motorbus drivers, or long-distance truck drivers were as uncommon as black pilots. The aviation industry, with its aura of chic and glamour, entailed light, relatively clean, skilled or semiskilled work that was just not associated with black Americans in those years. For example, as late as the national emergency year of 1940, 0.2 percent of blacks were employed in aircraft manufacturing, almost exclusively in menial work. Any hope entertained by the handful of black private pilots that they could rise to the status of airline flight deck officer was blocked by the simple fact that the Air Line Pilots' Association excluded black Americans from its membership throughout the 1930s.

By the end of the decade, rumblings of war were heard once again in Europe, and once again Americans, black and white, debated America's role in that continent's conflicts. For black Americans the racial doctrines of the Nazis were offensive, and the Italian fascist onslaught against Ethiopia had mobilized black opposition. Spain seemed the one nation offering armed resistance to the tide of totalitarian aggression, and black and white Americans of varying political persuasions had enlisted in the Abraham Lincoln Battalion of the International Brigade to defend the Spanish republic. (This conflict may have been the first on which black and white Americans fought unsegregated on any scale.) But the republic was overwhelmed in April 1939, and James Peck returned from Spain to warn the Army Air Corps that the new German pursuit plane he had tangled with in the skies of Spain was markedly superior to America's front-line model, the Curtiss P-40. Peck was shown the way out of the U.S. Army Air Corps Headquarters by an orderly for his impertinence. The Air Corps would carry on for well over a year of battle with the P-40, suffering unnecessary losses in the process, both in the Pacific and in the Mediterranean theaters of war, before newer pursuits (or fighters, as they came to be called by 1942) rolled off the U.S. production line.

The United States was taking its first tentative steps toward rearmament by 1939 and, as in all previous wars excepting the Mexican, black Americans would be called upon. They had a proud military legacy, but one that white America hardly knew. Since the Civil War, in which over 37,000 black troops gave their lives, black pride and aspiration had focused upon the four excellent Regular black regiments established by federal law in the Reconstruction era. These two infantry and two cavalry regiments had performed outstandingly on the western frontier—and away from population centers, where their presence, it was felt, might foment violence.

The regiments were officered almost exclusively by whites, although blacks did make determined efforts to secure Army commissions. Twenty-two black appointments were made to the U.S. Military Academy between 1870 and 1889. Of these, twelve passed the entrance examinations, but only three survived "The Point." Of these hardy three, one was dismissed from the service in circumstances still controversial, and one continued in obscurity, acknowledged only as someone who "knew how to stay in his place." The third, Charles Young, surmounted almost overwhelming obstacles to forge a distinguished career that was blighted as he stood on the verge of receiving his general's star.

Black volunteer and militia regiments with black officers fought the Spaniard in 1898, and all four of the black Regular Army regiments fought in the Spanish-American War's Cuban campaign. The 24th Infantry Regiment, for example, charged to the top of San Juan Hill simultaneously with Teddy Roosevelt's far more famous Rough Riders.

After the war, however, black troops still had to face random bullets—this time from fellow Americans as their troop trains rolled through Mississippi and Texas. At the end of this war a few black troopers were awarded commissions in the Regular Army, the most notable of these recipients being Benjamin O. Davis, Sr., who in 1940 would succeed where Colonel Young had failed and acquire his general's star.

Black Regulars and volunteers soldiered on through America's Age of Empire in the Philippine Insurrection and on the Mexican Punitive Expedition under Gen. J. J. Pershing. But this era also witnessed the infamous Brownsville Affair when, on the shakiest of evidence of riot, three companies of the 25th (Regular) Infantry were dismissed from the service.

The record of the U.S. Navy proved even more dismal. Despite the fact that blacks and whites had messed, berthed, fought, and died together in the dank confines of ironclad Union monitors during the Civil War (fifteen to twenty black seamen remain entombed in the monitor *Tecumseh*, beneath the murk and mud of Mobile Bay), that twenty-five black seamen were lost in the blowing up of the *Maine*, and that a black chief gunner's mate fired the opening shot of the Battle of Manila Bay, no black American was commissioned in the U.S. Navy or Marine Corps until well into the Second World War.

In the wake of the Brownsville Affair, Secretary of War William Howard Taft summarized the predicament of the black American soldier:

> The fact is that a certain amount of race prejudice between white and black seems to have become almost universal throughout the country, and no matter where colored troops are sent there are always some who make objection to their coming. It is a fact, however, as shown by our records, that colored troops are quite as well disciplined and behaved as the average of other troops . . . The records of the Army also tend to show that white soldiers average a greater degree of intemperance than colored ones. It has sometimes happened that communities which objected to the coming of colored soldiers have, on account of their good conduct, entirely changed their view and commended their good behavior to the War Department.

Yet apparently even superior performance and demeanor would not bring about acceptance on any scale. World War I, which seemed to open the promise of fuller black participation and advance, closed with black Americans, if anything, more embittered than before. Colonel Young, instead of receiving his merited star as a brigadier general, was forced into retirement on the very eve of America's entrance into its "War to Save Democracy." Although General Pershing had recommended the promotion, a mere second lieutenant, raising the chilling specter of a black general commanding white subordinates, complained to a Southern congressman, who brought up the matter with the secretary of war, Newton Baker, who, in turn, carried it to President Wilson. Colonel Young was retired from the Army on the grounds of ill health, his horseback trip from his home in Ohio to Washington, D.C., to prove his health to no avail. Colonel Young was indeed a sick man, suffering from a kidney disorder, high blood pressure, Bright's Disease (which killed him within a few years), and Blackwater Fever. Yet the question of Young's health had not come up until General Pershing had recommended him for his star. This was, after all, an era of increasing racial animosity, when the film *The Birth of a Nation* (1915) could be acclaimed by the president as "history written in lightning," despite the featuring of Klansmen as the heroes of the film, and when a black man could be slowly burned to death as far north as Coatesville, Pennsylvania.

The U.S. Armed Forces, as they entered the Great War, were no exception to the prevailing racial climate. Of 380,000 blacks enrolled, only 42,000 were assigned to combat units. The remainder were given the menial assignments so familiar to them in civilian life: stevedoring, road building, general fatigue work, and graves registration. The Army's rationale was that the low educational attainments of blacks precluded them from the demanding and skilled work of combat. Yet other Allied nations were able to utilize illiterate tribesmen and peasants with good success throughout the war and on almost every front.

Those blacks deemed fit for battle were organized into two infantry divisions, the 92nd and the 93rd. The former, composed mostly of draftees who received the sketchiest of training under officers primarily Southern and white, suffered under a hostile scrutiny from the start, its failures magnified and its achievements ignored. A festering hostility between the division's commanding general and the 2nd Corps commander did not help matters. On the other hand, the 93rd Division (Provisional), composed mainly of National Guardsmen, was attached piecemeal to the French army, which used its experience with black French Colonial troops to treat the 93rd fairly. The French command professed itself perfectly satisfied with them, awarding three regimental Unit Croix des Guerres. The 369th Regiment of the 93rd, a New York National Guard outfit, had the distinction of having served the longest time in combat after the shortest period of training of any U.S. Army unit during that war.

But the 92nd was the black military unit remembered after the Armistice, not the 93rd. At worst, the performance of the former could be termed unexceptional, yet it would be singled out for decades as a cautionary example of the results to be expected from putting black Americans into combat.

A supposed "failure" of that war was the black officer, allegedly inferior to his white counterparts and distrusted by his men. A black Officers Candidate School had been established at Fort Des Moines, Iowa, but not one successful black officer candidate received a permanent commission either during the war or for almost two decades following. At the most, the military seemed to prefer, and usually got, what one observer termed "a traditional kind of Negro officer, past the stage of youthful daring and initiative, short on education, without self-confidence or any reason for it, poorly selected and inadequately trained for his job." One black officer supposedly "earned" his commission by singing plantation songs for his superiors. As a postwar Army study declared, the black officer was "still a Negro, with all the faults and weaknesses of character inherent in the Negro race, exaggerated by the fact that he wore an officer's uniform."

The Army would soon enough reap the bitter fruit of its almost willful disregard of its own principles of leadership, its refusal to go beyond the most superficial of analyses of the "race question," and its catering to local racial mores. In August 1918, troops of the black 24th Infantry, goaded beyond endurance by harassment from local citizens and police in Houston, Texas, marched into the city, firing on anyone crossing their path and being fired upon in turn. Before the shooting died down, seventeen whites and two black troopers had been shot dead. This was mutiny and murder in a time of war; thirteen of the mutineers were hanged within less than four months, and the following year six more paid that penalty. (The first of the condemned soldiers had been in their dishonored graves for two months before their trial records even reached the Army's judge advocate general's office for review.)

The U.S. Navy continued its policy of weeding out blacks from skilled seamen's ranks. Even during the war, black enlistments were confined to the Mess Branch. The fledgling U.S. Army Air Service admitted practically no blacks throughout the war. Even the black pilot of the Franco-American Lafayette Flying Corps, Eugene Jacques Bullard, was dropped when the Corps was absorbed into the U.S. Army Air Service in 1917.

On the home front, blacks heartily supported the war effort, spurred on by Dr. W. E. B. Du Bois's extremely influential editorial, "Close Ranks," in the journal of the National Association for the Advancement of Colored People (NAACP), *The Crisis*. Secretary of War Newton Baker had appointed Emmett J. Scott, former associate and personal secretary to Booker T. Washington, as special adviser to the secretary on black matters. Blacks registered some gains in war production employment, and the reports of black troops in the press were almost uniformly laudatory. When the famous and decorated 369th returned to New York, it marched up Fifth Avenue to the cheers of the city.

But what did black veterans return to? Lynchings rose sharply after 1918; ten black veterans, some actually in the uniform of their country, were victims. One federal agency ordered separate plaques for white and black war dead, and the War Department sent black and white Gold Star mothers to France on separate ships to view their sons' graves. Apparently only in France was any monument erected to the memory of black American soldiers.

The tenuous gains made by blacks during the war were not retained; in fact, there was retrogression. Not only were no new Regular Army commissions awarded to blacks, but the four Regular Army regiments, which had been kept at home during hostilities, were gradually reduced to service, almost servant, status. In the 1930s, in the wake of the Depression, the regiments were further reduced until, in the words of Judge William Hastie, "they were but skeletons of their former selves." Still, there was no shortage of applicants, for "life in Negro regiments during this period was easy, and pay was good compared with opportunities for Negroes in civil life. Discipline was good and was sustained by dependable NCO's of many years' service . . . Privates waited years to become corporals, and corporals to become sergeants." These regiments had no need to recruit; a potential enlistee had to find out which post had a black element, inquire of its commanding officer of any vacancies, and, in the unlikely event of an opening, present himself at his own expense for an examination. Unfortunately, this lotus-land backwater of the U.S. Army bore little relation to the stern art of war and, as late as 1944, the combined 9th and 10th Cavalry Regiments were returned to service duty after two years of combat training.

A black reserve and National Guard presence was retained, numbering an average of four thousand reservists. Howard and Wilberforce universities provided the bulk of black reserve officers, less than three hundred in 1939. Hampton Institute carried a coast artillery unit and West Virginia State a field artillery element. North Carolina Agricultural and Technical State College, Prairie View State (Texas), Lincoln University (Pennsylvania), and Tuskegee also supported smaller infantry training units. By that time no active U.S. Army unit carried any black officer (aside from the chaplains of the black regiments), and many black ROTC cadets had lost interest and dropped out. As late as two months before Pearl Harbor, only 150 reserve officers were black.

The Army believed that the black contribution to the Great War had been minimal. In no fewer then ten postwar studies dealing with the employment of black troops in any future conflict, a number of "lessons" seemed to emerge, few of them complimentary to blacks.

The most influential study was probably that conducted in 1925 by the Army Central Staff College (now the Army War College). Using the pseudoscientific Darwinism prevalent in the officers' clubs of the time, it concluded that "in the process of evolution the American Negro has not progressed as far as the other subspecies of the human family. As a race he has not developed leadership qualities. His mental inferiority and the inherent weakness of his character are factors that must be considered with great care in the preparation of any plans for his employment in war." Even physically the black American was inferior; "his normal physical activity is generally small due to his laziness." Not surprisingly, this "study" was not buttressed by one scrap of scientific evidence. The only positive note was found in the call for the better training of black troops and their officers (predominately white, of course), and for an integrated Officers Candidate School.

The question might well be asked then, why should blacks be utilized at all in war? General Pershing, in 1922, and the assistant chief of staff, in 1940, agreed in similar words: in order that whites not bear the full brunt of battle losses. Thus it came to be accepted War Department policy that in a future emergency black troop strength should be in roughly the same proportion as the black population of the country. All but one of these studies excluded black participation from the Army Air Corps.

Nonetheless, the first recognition of the aspiration of many black Americans to fly came in 1938. The Civilian Pilot Training Program (CPTP) of the Civil Aeronautics Authority (CAA), announced by President Roosevelt at the end of 1938, authorized the flight training of twenty thousand college students per year. The program was to be financed by the munificent sum of $100,000 from the National Youth Administration. The CPTP would make use of existing facilities in those institutions equipped to teach the seventy-two-hour ground course and the thirty-five to fifty hours of flight instruction required for a private flying license. The program was, in its early days, a tentative and "civilianized" part of the national defense program embarked upon under the leadership of President Roosevelt in the wake of the deteriorating world situation. The military implications of the CPTP were obvious: the students would form part of a flying reserve that could be mobilized if needed in war or emergency. Surprisingly, some military officers remained dubious about the program from the start. When President Roosevelt called for a fifty-thousand-plane Air Corps, many officers "realistically" demanded to know where the pilots were to be secured. Yet an almost unbelievable 400,000 pilots would be trained and licensed through the CPTP—and roughly 2,700 of them would be black.

Originally the CPTP, like the rest of American aviation, ignored blacks. But within three months of its inception, James C. Evans, director of trade and technical education at West Virginia State College, who had excellent connections in civil aviation circles and good political contacts in West Virginia, presented a training program to the CAA which resulted in the approval of predominantly black West Virginia State for CPTP training. Soon after, five other black institutions, Tuskegee Institute, Delaware State College, Hampton Institute, Howard University, and North Carolina Agricultural and Technical State College entered the program. As well, a scattering of blacks took their training at predominantly white institutions.

A handful of whites trained at the black schools, and black and white women were also enrolled. After the first year of operation the CPTP graduated ninety-one of one hundred black candidates, a score that equaled that of white candidates. In spite of this, the Air Corps refused to accept any for enlistment.

Robert A. Lovett, the assistant secretary of war for air, opposed the entry of blacks into the CPTP, apparently basing his resistance on a belief in the inherent physical inability of blacks to fly. Later, when informed by flight training officers that there was no scientific basis for this belief, the perplexed Lovett then replied that "there must be some emotional reason."

Aside from Secretary Lovett, the Air Corps thought little enough about the CPTP and seems to have all but ignored black participation. Of more direct concern to the Air Corps was Public Law 18 (passed in April 1939), which provided for the contracting with civilian schools of aviation for the elementary and primary phases of military aviation cadets. The act was in response to the threatened swamping of the established Air Corps flying schools at Randolph and Kelly fields. As a result of an amendment to the bill proposed by Sen. Harry H. Schwartz of Wyoming, the secretary of war was authorized to lend aviation equipment to one or more schools approved by the CAA for the training of black pilots.

Here the Air Corps found itself facing a dilemma. From its inception, the newest armed service had rigorously excluded blacks. But Public Law 18 might be interpreted as mandating black pilot participation in the Air Corps. After considerable soul searching, the Air Corps's position emerged by the end of the year: The North Suburban Flying School, Glenview, Illinois, had already been designated by the CAA for black pilot training, but since we are having difficulty in finding twenty qualified students needed to begin instruction, and, now that the War Department is funding and financing the program, and it is the policy not to mix colored and white men in the same tactical organization, and since no provision has been made for any colored Air Corps units in the Army, colored persons are not eligible for enlistment in the Air Corps, so there is no need for additional facilities.

Through this tortuous official circumlocution, the Air Corps dashed any immediate hopes for black participation. In fact, the chief of the Plans Division of the Air Corps asserted that even the training of blacks was not mandated specifically, only the lending of aircraft and aeronautical equipment to a school designated by the CAA for the training of black pilots. "Therefore the law is complied with when the school has been designated." Presumably, those cadets who had made their way through the Glenview School would be thanked for their time and sent on their way back to civilian life.

The CAA was a little more sanguine about the Glenview School's purpose, turning it into a demonstration of "the adaptability of the Negro to flying instruction." The school cooperated closely with the black Coffey School of Aeronautics, also in suburban Chicago. This school was operated by the dynamic Willa Brown, holder of a limited commercial pilot's license and a CAA ground-school instructor's license. Her school and the Glenview School were the only two noncollege institutions to offer the CPTP and, later, the War Training Service courses. Yet neither was ever offered a contract for military pilot training.

Tuskegee Institute, however, would emerge as the prime site for the CPTP and the Public Law 18 contract programs for the training of black pilots, and Tuskegee Army Air Field (TAAF) would be the only source of black military pilots. Tuskegee was late in securing CPTP certification due to the lack of a suitable airfield within the required ten miles of the contracting institution. But Dr. Fred Patterson, president of the Institute, was able to secure an exception, thanks to the efforts of G. L. Washington, Tuskegee's director of mechanical industries. Washington drove from Tuskegee to Washington, D.C., to plead personally with the CAA. The Montgomery, Alabama, commissioner of public works quickly backed him by assuring the CAA that the Montgomery Municipal Airport would be made available for the training of Tuskegee CPTP students—no small concession for a white Alabama official in the 1930s. On Friday, October 13, 1939, Tuskegee Institute's application was finally approved. Two days later the institute was issued, jointly with Alabama Air Service, CAA Certificate No. 119 as an elementary flying school. Elementary instruction entailed 240 hours of ground school and 35 to 45 hours of flight instruction. Under the assumption that its application would be accepted, Tuskegee Institute had already begun publicizing the CPTP among its students, and had instituted physical examinations.

In the same month as the receipt of accreditation, G. L. Washington was able to secure the cooperation of the Alabama Polytechnic Institute at Auburn (now Auburn University) for ground instruction. Two months later, the first flight instruction of Tuskegee students, by Polytechnic instructors, began at the Montgomery Municipal Airport. However, the situation proved very difficult, as each student was obliged to make a total of seventy to eighty forty-mile round trips between the Institute and the airport. Consequently, federal, state, and Institute officials met at Tuskegee in February 1940 and settled upon a plot of land nearby for an airfield for primary instruction. The Institute donated about $1,000 and students volunteered their labor. The result, Kennedy Field, boasted a wooden hangar (capacity: three Piper Cubs), a raised platform for aviation fuel, sanitary facilities, and "a small structure for record keeping and to get out of the rain." But Kennedy sufficed to transfer instruction from Montgomery and to put a stop to the endless commuting.

The satisfaction felt in the granting of certification and in the completion of Tuskegee's first airfield was topped by triumph: in the CAA examinations of the first Tuskegee CPTP class 100 percent passed, and passed in many cases with marks that evoked national interest and the commendation of the CAA. In May 1940, the first Tuskegee CAA class completed their flight tests and received their private pilot licenses. The seriousness with which they had pursued their studies must have been intensified by news of the course of the war in Europe, as France tottered to catastrophe and England stood alone in that frightening year. On July 1, 1940, Tuskegee Institute was approved by the CAA for secondary flight instruction (240 hours of ground school and 35 to 50 hours of flight instruction), and until a new field could be constructed at Tuskegee, the use of a second airfield would be needed. Once again Alabama Polytechnic proved helpful, permitting the use of its small Works Progress Administration–built strip for flying in the new program. On July 29 Tuskegee's new secondary trainer, a Waco, buzzed the Institute ("To us it sounded like a bomber," recalled Washington) and landed at Kennedy

Field. Out climbed Tuskegee's first aviation instructor, Charles "Chief" Anderson.

Secondary training commenced on July 29 with the full quota of ten students, even before Anderson's arrival. The trainees were dressed in a uniform closely resembling those of Air Corps aviation cadets; aviation-minded black Americans had their eyes on higher challenges. As the sole center for secondary CPTP training for blacks, Tuskegee now enrolled elementary graduates from other black institutions, and, by mid-August 1941, "Chief" Anderson and his staff were instructing students from all of the black CPTP colleges, plus Lincoln and Langston universities. Advanced flying instruction took place at Auburn before a large and usually appreciative audience of local whites, who, on occasion, would express their admiration—and perhaps astonishment—at a perfect landing with such ejaculations as "Did you see that nigger land that plane?" The Tuskegee CPTP was well underway.

Suddenly and unexpectedly, the War Department announced on September 16, 1940, that "the Civil Aeronautics Authority, in cooperation with the Army, is making a start in the development of colored personnel for the aviation service." This was not a change of heart on the part of the Air Corps, but a response to a provision of the Selective Service Act of the same month, which mandated black inductions into the armed services in proportion to their population ratio to whites. In fact, just four months prior to this announcement a memo from Gen. Henry H. "Hap" Arnold, chief of the Air Corps, had determined that blacks could indeed be utilized in the air service "in labor battalions or labor companies to perform the duties of post fatigue and as waiters in our messes." These openings were for enlisted men only, of course. "Negro pilots cannot be used in our present Air Corps units since this would result in having Negro officers serving over white enlisted men. This would create an impossible social problem." Yet plans seemed to exist in all armed services to cover the remotest contingency, and a 1938 Air Corps study, never publicized, provided for a black pursuit (fighter) or observation unit, preferably the latter, with black pilots and enlisted technicians gradually worked in.

The announcement of the opening of the previously all-white Air Corps received widespread publicity, along with the racial provisions of the Selective Service Act, and was circulated in a White House press release. After all, 1940 was a presidential election year, with Franklin Roosevelt facing the strongest challenge of his political career, running against the no-third-term tradition and a dynamic candidate, Wendell Willkie, who enjoyed some black support.

On the eve of the election, the Roosevelt administration moved to ensure the black vote. President Roosevelt nominated Col. Benjamin O. Davis, Sr., as brigadier general, and another black officer, Maj. C. C. Johnson, U.S. Army Reserve, was appointed executive assistant to the director of the Selective Service system to deal with racial matters. William H. Hastie, dean of Howard University, was appointed civilian aide on Negro affairs to the secretary of war. Those black Americans who could remember Emmett Scott's relative helplessness in the War Office in World War I, and the denial of a general's star to Colonel Young in 1917, could only hope that better days had arrived.

In its haste to assure black voters of its benign intentions, the administration overreached itself in that pre-election month. The War Department announced on October 9 that "Negroes are being given aviation training as pilots, mechanics, and technical specialists." The natural public interpretation of this release was that the *military* aviation training was now being given to blacks. Of course, this was not the case. Only the CPTP was open to blacks, and no black technicians were being trained at government expense anywhere. The September announcement, noted above, was also misleading, but it did emphasize the civilian component of black pilot training. Knowledgeable blacks immediately spotted the fallacies in the announcement. James Peck pointed out that no blacks were in training for any branch of military aviation, either as pilots or ground crew.

A. Philip Randolph, head of the largest black union in the nation, the Brotherhood of Sleeping-Car Porters, and leader of the planned massive March on Washington for equal participation in the defense effort, demanded of the president proof that "even one Negro is now being given aviation training in the Army Air Corps." No direct or public answer was ever forthcoming.

A fascinating glimpse into the racial thinking of high administration leaders with military responsibilities is afforded by a fragmentary account of a meeting the president held with Assistant Secretary of War Robert Patterson, Secretary of the Navy Frank Knox, NAACP secretary Walter White, T. Arnold Hill, assistant to Mary Mc. Bethune of the National Youth Administration, and A. Philip Randolph, to explore black participation in the armed forces. The president opened by expressing his pleasure on learning that "Negroes would be integrated into all branches of the armed services as well as service units." But "integrated" was hardly the word to describe what the armed services' civilian heads had in mind. Secretary of the Navy Knox forthrightly voiced his belief that "undemocratic segregation" had no place—in the Army. As for his own service, Knox pointed to the "impossibility" of "Southern ships and Northern ships," thus intimating that the Navy would continue to exclude blacks. The president, breezy and vague, then threw out the suggestion of black regiments assigned next to white regiments, or a similar grouping of artillery batteries in an Army division, and thus to "back into" some unsegregated military outfits. Assistant Secretary of War Patterson understandably responded that the War Department had never thought of such an idea, but would look into it. The president appeared more definite in his suggestion that each service appoint someone "to handle matters pertaining to the Negro." Knox immediately interpreted this to mean someone without authority, in an advisory capacity only, an interpretation unchallenged by the president. Although Walter White probed to find the limits of military racial segregation, he must have been frustrated with the elusive answers he received from Patterson. The conference broke up under pressure of time, its only tangible result the subsequent appointment of a civilian aide on Negro affairs to the secretary of war.

No mention had even been made of the Air Corps, and agitation continued for the admission of blacks to more than simply the CPTP. In a very limited and grudging way, admission had already been granted to Air Corps ground units. Toward the end of 1940, the Air Corps began organizing black ground units "solely to take care of the colored selectees allotted to the Air Corps," in the frank words of the Air Corps G-3 (Operations). This was the response of the Air Corps to the Selective Service Act mandate that all branches of the armed services absorb all races in proportion to their representation in the general population. The majority of blacks throughout the war who served in the Air Corps/Forces were thus organized into Aviation Squadrons (Separate), as these units came to be termed.

Unlike other military units, these squadrons never had a defined function. The newly appointed civilian aide on Negro affairs to the secretary of war, Judge Hastie, wrote to General Arnold that "General B. O. Davis will verify the fact that no one seems to know what these units are supposed to do." What they wound up doing almost exclusively were airbase house-keeping and fatigue duties. On one occasion an Aviation Squadron (Separate) participated in an Air Corps parade in a nearby town—bringing up the rear behind the town's sanitation workers. There were even rumors that the squadrons would be used to pick cotton, but fortunately this rumor proved to be without foundation.

The Army Air Forces later pointed out that whites of low Army General Classification Test (AGCT) scores were also assigned to the aviation squadrons, but of a total of 250 such units, only 32 were white, and these did not carry the burden of "(Separate)" on their guidons, logos, and letterheads. Understandably, morale was not of the highest in either white or black aviation squadrons, and individual as well as group indiscipline was common, culminating in a large-scale riot (or mutiny) at MacDill Air Force Base, Florida, in 1943 (see chapter 4).

From the beginning, the Air Corps made it quite clear that its "experiment" of admitting blacks to combat aviation must remain strictly within the boundaries of racial segregation. And despite Judge Hastie's best efforts, the Air Corps would adamantly resist all attempts even to modify this segregation. Here the Air Corps missed an opportunity; as a service that had never imposed segregation upon blacks for the simple reason that it had never really knowingly admitted blacks, it was to some extent free of the dead weight of racial "tradition" and might have made at least a beginning toward racial integration in a war fought ostensibly to secure freedom. But it was not to be, and there is no evidence that the argument was ever used within the Air Corps. The nation's newest armed service would thus adopt the racial "traditions" of the Army and the Navy.

In 1940–41, the Air Corps was simply and unimaginatively following precedent endorsed by the highest authority. The secretary of war, Henry L. Stimson, used those 1925 and 1937 Army studies on the employment of blacks in future wars to justify military racial segregation, confiding awkwardly in his diary that "in the draft we are preparing to give the Negroes a fair shot in every service, however, even to aviation, where I doubt very much if they will not produce a disaster there." Stimson later despaired that the "problem [is] almost impossible of solution."

Somewhat more positively, Army Chief of Staff Gen. George C. Marshall informed Sen. Henry Cabot Lodge (R.-Mass.) that "the existing policy of military racial segregation has proven satisfactory over a long period of years. It provides for a full percentage of colored personnel and a wide variety of military units." Actually, that policy provided for exactly two nonchaplain active-duty black officers, and the barring of blacks from all but a handful of armed service branches. General Marshall based his defense of military racial segregation upon two points that he later explicated to Stimson: first, civilian custom and habit had established racial separation in that sphere, and second, that "either through lack of educational opportunities or other causes the level of intelligence and occupational skill of the Negro population is considerably below that of the white. . . . " Consequently, "experiments within the Army in the solution of social problems are fraught with danger to efficiency, discipline, and morale."

Assistant Secretary of War for Air Robert Lovett's attitude toward blacks in aviation has already been noted, while General Arnold, although striving for fairness of treatment throughout the war, seemed to resent the presence of blacks in his service. The War Department's Operations Division prepared an influential study for the chief of the War Plans Division, Brig. Gen. Dwight D. Eisenhower, entitled (significantly) "The Colored Troop Problem." Its conclusions were that an "apparent lack of inherent natural mechanical adaptability" and an absence of leadership would cause severe problems if any mixing of the races in the Army was permitted.

These attitudes were reflected down the chain of command to the enlisted men of the Army and Army Air Forces. No less than 90 percent of Army white enlisted personnel and 50 percent of blacks favored segregation (it should be noted that black figures were undoubtedly inflated by the Army's use of only selected units and Southern troops); the U.S. military used these figures to verify preconceived attitudes. The Army Air Forces (AAF) asked enlisted men for their response to the statement, "Negroes are now being trained as pilots, bombardiers, and navigators." The responses were somewhat mixed; although military racial segregation was overwhelmingly approved, less than one-half of respondents said they objected to working alongside blacks in AAF ground crews. Forty-five percent believed that blacks should even be in the AAF, and a little over 2 percent favored unsegregated blacks in the AAF. (Significantly, the closer white respondents worked with blacks, the more their resistance to military racial integration weakened, a phenomenon ascribed by one authority to the thought that "misery loves company.")

Not surprisingly, the mass citizens' U.S. Army of World War II reflected the majority of U.S. citizens' attitudes. An Office of War Information survey of July 1943 found that an almost incredible 90 percent of civilian whites favored military racial segregation, as did 18 percent of civilian blacks. Few regional differences were perceived. Although 57 percent of white respondents believed that blacks could make a contribution to the war effort, 29 percent would have continued the pre-1941 policy of excluding them from the AAF altogether. In fact, a survey of a year earlier indicated that blacks themselves believed the AAF was all but closed to them. Even in the Northeast and Northwest, 50 percent of whites believed in racial segregation, and a majority from around the nation felt that any deficiencies in black accomplishment were simply the faults of blacks themselves.

Thus the military could and did assert that they were just following the dictates of their civilian masters in pursuing military racial segregation. Walter White sardonically pointed out that the only exceptions were to be found among those outside the mainstream of American military life, in conscientious-objector camps and in military hospitals. He simplified somewhat; other exceptions included varying medical detachments, some Officers Candidate Schools, the WAVES, the Merchant Marine, and prisoner-of-war camps. Perhaps the acting chief of the Army Service Forces summarized most accurately the racial attitude of the military, as late as the end of the Second World War:

For the moment and the foreseeable future, special intermingling of Negroes and whites is not feasible. It is forbidden by law in some parts of the country and not practiced by the great majority of the people in the remainder of the country . . . To require citizens while in the Army to conform to a pattern of social behavior different from that they would otherwise follow would be detrimental to the morale of white soldiers and would tend to defeat the effort to increase the opportunities and effectiveness of Negro soldiers.

Or, in the words of one undoubtedly distracted officer speaking on the day after Pearl Harbor to a conference of black newspaper representatives, "The Army is not a sociological laboratory." This argument has a surface logic, yet it could have been noted that the armed services do indeed change or at least modify the living patterns of their members. It can be safely assumed that very few enlistees or inductees in their civilian lives had been accustomed to being awakened at 4:30 A.M. by a whistle or a screaming sergeant, to shaving in cold water from a helmet liner, or to facing the daily possibility of mutilation, disability, or death. But the argument never seems to have been advanced at the time.

Finally, on January 9, 1941, the War Department approved Army Air Corps plans, drawn up in the wake of Public Law 18 of 1939, for an all-black pursuit squadron. The formation of the first black combat unit in Air Corps history was officially announced at a press conference on January 16. A few days later funding was approved for the training of 460 enlisted personnel at the Air Corps Technical School, Chanute Field, Rantoul, Illinois. Pilot preflight and primary training were awarded to Tuskegee Institute, and basic and advanced training would be given at a new Air Corps field to be built seven miles northwest of the town of Tuskegee. It is not clear from the record whether the Air Corps was speeded on its way by the threat of a lawsuit filed by the NAACP in the name of Yancy Williams, a Howard University student anxious to join the Air Corps, but the suit was withdrawn soon after the press conference.

Predictably, black spokesmen were not gratified at the announcement of a "Jim Crow Air Corps." Within the hierarchy of the War Department, William Hastie made his opposition known, calling the Air Corps's plans "a serious mistake" in a memo to Robert Lovett, and adding that "I cannot over-emphasize the catastrophic effect of the arrangement upon morale." In a memo to the secretary of the Army's general staff, Hastie called for "at some place in the Army a beginning of the end of racial segregation." Outside the services the black pilots of the National Airmen's Association argued logically that "in the Air Corps there is no tradition either favorable or unfavorable to complete racial integration. If we permit the establishment of a Negro unit it will be establishing a precedent which will be hard to break down." *The Crisis* called the establishment of the 99th Pursuit Squadron "a step in the right direction . . . but it is by no means the answer to the demand of colored people for full integration into all branches of the arms and services of the nation," and concluded that the association "can be forced to accept it, but we can never agree to it." Tuskegee officials agreed to the segregation policy as simply better than having no black aviation at all.

Judge Hastie later detailed some of the major inconsistencies inherent in a separate squadron. First, millions of taxpayers' dollars would have to be expended simply in a duplication of existing facilities. This duplication and the fact that all black military aviation was to be confined to one squadron meant a delay of at least six months before pilot training would even commence. It would be difficult to explain to qualified black applicants how, in a time of a supposedly desperate shortage of skilled manpower, they would be kept waiting for months before being accepted into the one Air Corps unit that would give them the technical or pilot qualification with which they could serve their country. Furthermore, as Hastie pointed out, pilots move about a lot, flying in and out of military and civil airfields, and requiring a host of services that could hardly be given on a segregated basis. If racial segregation was as essential to good discipline and morale as the Air Corps insisted, what would happen when a black detachment flew into an airfield in the Deep South and required the fuel and services that were its due as a regular component of the U.S. Army Air Corps? (Of course, this could and did happen regularly, usually without incident, which perhaps could be perversely used to prove that segregation did "work" during the war.) In a wartime situation that stressed unity and cooperation against a common foe, what were black Americans to make of a program that stressed separation?

Apart from segregation, other questions were raised by critics of Air Corps racial policy. First, why only pursuit aviation? Hastie remained convinced that the reasons were primarily racial. If the Air Corps were to train black bomber or transport pilots, the possibility might arise of black officers giving orders to white enlisted men or officers, such as ground crew, navigators, bombardiers, and copilots. A pursuit pilot would have no one else in his plane to command, and the support requirements of a pursuit squadron could probably be filled by black personnel. Hastie further believed that the Air Corps, realizing that pursuit pilot qualification was the most exacting of aviation training, hoped that blacks would be that much more likely to fail. Paradoxically, he also felt that the Air Corps may have believed that if blacks could fly pursuit aircraft, they could probably fly anything. From the evidence, it seems that most prominent in the minds of Air Corps planners was the consideration that a bomber or transport squadron would require a much larger number of black technical personnel than a pursuit squadron, and the Air Corps was not satisfied that the nation had a sufficient number of blacks who could meet the required educational and technical standards. The Air Corps was also aware that pursuit aviation was the glamour branch of the service; anything else offered to blacks might be interpreted, rightly or wrongly, as "second best."

The other question was why Tuskegee? Certainly the Coffey School near Chicago had strong claims upon the Air Corps's attention, including its own airfield and $100,000 worth of military equipment for ground instruction. But the Air Corps objected to the anticipated high costs of land there, ground and air congestion, and the possibility of flooding for any Chicago area site. The Air Corps had also objected to the use of Chanute Field for the training of enlisted black aviation technicians, convinced, for uncertain reasons, that disturbances and riots would ensue at the field, and within the nearby communities. Presumably the same argument was advanced against the Coffey School.

The use of regular Air Corps training facilities was out of the question, according to General Arnold, due to heavy congestion and the discontinuity in the training process that would result from the influx of significant numbers of blacks to these fields. Yet General Arnold had earlier assured Sen. Harry Schwartz of Wyoming that it would be possible to train black cadets at a civilian school or at Randolph or Kelly fields "without trouble." But, of course, General Arnold would never have permitted this significant breach of segregation.

James C. Evans, later a successor to Judge Hastie, suggested that of the dozens of Texas training fields at least one could be turned over for black aviation training. Evans anticipated little racial trouble because, he noted, a "tripartite culture existed at least in the San Antonio area—black, white, and Spanish." Judge Hastie's immediate successor, Truman Gibson, pointed out that a separate aviation training program would prove unnecessarily expensive, but such arguments went unheeded. Not only was Tuskegee supposedly "riot proof," but nearby Tuskegee Institute, in the words of one Air Corps planner, "furnished many precepts and examples in conduct and attitude." Perhaps an example of the "conduct and attitude" that appealed to the military then could be found on the cover of an earlier issue of the Institute's journal *Service*, in which black vocational opportunities were depicted—waiter, cook, and railroad porter. Yet the "accommodationist" philosophy of the Institute's founder, Dr. Booker T. Washington, was already discounted on the campus. The current president, Dr. Fred Patterson, apparently originally objected to the segregated training of black fliers and "later regretted having given in on the matter of Tuskegee." Although he believed in total support for the war effort, Dr. Patterson also went on record to declare that "to label and denounce compulsory segregation is necessary and right."

Dr. Patterson came to accept the segregated Tuskegee organization because he realized that wherever blacks would be trained in America they would be segregated, that Tuskegee was a beginning, and that at least blacks were now in the Air Corps. Perhaps optimistically, he also felt that "integration would take care of itself."

An early commanding officer of TAAF, the segregationist Col. Frederick von Kimble, was under no illusions concerning Dr. Patterson's stand, reporting that "from time to time there were other complaints from white Army personnel concerning Dr. Patterson's attitude, which was believed to encourage the Negroes in their fight for social and political equality."

The presence of the Institute and a nearby black veterans' hospital were further deciding factors for the Air Corps's Tuskegee decision. That service may well have overestimated, nevertheless, the amount of goodwill toward blacks in the surrounding white community. The town of Tuskegee was characterized by Colonel von Kimble's successor (Colonel Parrish) as "openly hostile to *all* Negroes throughout the war." Dr. Patterson agreed that local whites did not like the black aviation programs, but did appreciate their money-spinning potential. In fact, relatively minor but potentially explosive racial incidents did take place on at least two occasions, one at the air base, the other in the town, during the war years. Certainly local Air Corps officials did not regard Tuskegee as a racial Nirvana; the Southeastern Army Air Forces Training Command (SEAAFTC), in which Tuskegee Army Air Field was to be located, later reported plaintively that "everything was done to avoid racial strife, to treat the Negro as a military, not as a social or political problem, and to keep the command out of difficulty. It was sometimes felt that Washington was not always fully aware of these difficult problems."

One month after the announcement of the formation of the first black pursuit squadron, the Air Corps notified the Southeastern Army Air Corps Training Command (SEAACTC) of the authorization of a primary flying school at Tuskegee Institute for the training of black aviation cadets, under the provisions of Public Law 18. The Air Corps dropped its proposal to utilize the Tuskegee CPTP facilities, because this would be a deviation from the method of training white cadets, and could cause political trouble. Originally, a quota of thirty cadets was established, but in early April this figure was reduced to fifteen per class, and later to ten.

Tuskegee was now well into the flying training business, but a serious financial problem loomed. Although as an Air Corps contractor the Institute received $17.50 per hour per cadet (for a total of ten hours) and the cadets themselves paid one dollar per day for mess and sixty-six cents for quarters, the costs of constructing a new airfield for contract pilot training would have to be borne by the Institute. The Air Corps had simply presumed that any school bidding for a training contract would already have an airfield.

Tuskegee administrators were in a quandary, for the Board of Trustees was hesitant to commit the large sums of money needed for a project that might be canceled on short notice. After turning unsuccessfully to the Reconstruction Finance Corporation, the General Education Board of New York City, and the Carnegie Corporation, the administrators approached the Rosenwald Fund of Chicago as a last resort. Two fortuitous events made the Fund receptive. First, the Fund's annual meeting for 1941 was held at Tuskegee Institute. The second was that Eleanor Roosevelt was a member of the board and, upon her arrival on campus, was quickly made aware of the Institute's problems in aviation training. Mrs. Roosevelt was so responsive that she even requested that she be taken aloft on a flight in one of the Institute's CPTP Cubs to study the situation. "Chief" Anderson served as pilot on that historic flight as Secret Service men held their breath. Soon after, the Fund loaned $175,000 of the $200,000 required to construct the primary field. And from that time until the end of the war, Mrs. Roosevelt remained a steady friend of black aviation, questioning and prodding the Air Corps/Forces for fair treatment of the "Tuskegee Airmen."

As noted, the training program arranged by SEAACTC/SEAAFTC would be the same as that for other schools contracting for primary flight training under Public Law 18. Classes of about ten cadets would receive five weeks of preflight processing and training, after which they would undergo a ten-week course of ground and flight instruction. Any shortages of cadets would be made up from graduates of Tuskegee's CPT Secondary Pilot Training Program. The graduates of the contract primary flying school would then be channeled into the Air Corps's Basic Flying School for continued military pilot training. The annual output of black pilots was set at forty-five. All that remained was to begin the training, and the deployment, of the first black U.S. military pilots in the nation's history.

Training 2.

Now the focus would shift to the first black Air Corps squadron, the 99th Pursuit Squadron. Although the enlisted cadre of the new squadron was assembled from personnel of the old black 24th Infantry Regiment, in response to widespread publicity other enlistees streamed in from all over the nation. They were given instruction in technical specialties in the Air Corps Technical School at Chanute Field, preparatory to transfer to Tuskegee as ground crew for the fledgling 99th. The temporary commanding officer (C.O.) of the 99th was a white officer, Capt. Harold Maddux.

July 19, 1941, will always be remembered as the moment when blacks first officially entered the U.S. Army Air Corps. For on that day, with appropriate ceremonies, the first eleven black CPTP graduates and one black Army officer were inducted into military aviation training. The chief speaker was Maj. Gen. Walter Weaver, commanding officer of SEAACTC, and the officer most responsible for locating black aviation at Tuskegee. Congratulatory telegrams were read from generals Marshall and Arnold, while Signal Corps photographers preserved the scene at the foot of the

Booker T. Washington Monument in still and motion-picture photography. Preflight training for the twelve initial cadets of Class 42-C commenced the same day at the CPTP airfield, Kennedy Field. Training would continue at Kennedy Field until September 1941, when the primary field, Moton Field (so named in honor of Booker T. Washington's successor as Tuskegee Institute's president), was finally completed, after numerous construction delays.

On the platform with the dignitaries on July 19 sat the only member of Class 42-C who was not a CPTP graduate. He was Capt. Benjamin O. Davis, Jr., son of Gen. Benjamin O. Davis, Sr. General Davis and Captain Davis then were the only nonchaplain Regular Army black officers, a situation almost ludicrous, given the number of blacks by then in the armed forces.

Appointed to the U.S. Military Academy from Ohio in 1932, Benjamin O. Davis, Jr., endured four years of the infamous "silent treatment" from his "fellow" cadets. Iron must have entered his soul then, for he became a master at subordinating his emotions to his duty and his profession. Davis refused interviews by the black press and would not allow himself to be used as a "symbol" of either black oppression or black success, for, in his words, "I didn't want to play that game." Possibly, not playing "that game" saved his career. By the end of his plebe year, Davis had amassed enough demerits for such infractions as imaginary dust on his spit-shined shoes to warrant his dismissal, but the commandant of cadets, Lt. Col. Simon Boliver Buckner canceled half of the demerits, and Davis remained. Had Cadet Davis been perceived as a "troublemaker," his time at the Point might well have been cut short.

While in his fourth year at West Point, Davis applied for Army pilot training, and was rejected solely and specifically for his race. In fact, the acting chief of the Air Corps, Gen. Oscar W. Westover, went further than mere rejection. Davis's rejection, General Westover noted, "if accomplished, might be considered a precedent in like cases until such time as the War Department sees fit to constitute colored flying units in the Army." This was a hard blow to Davis, who later noted that "black people have always had to endure more than their white counterparts if they are to achieve."

Interestingly, Davis did not seem to be a natural flier, and had to receive special attention from "Chief" Anderson while in flight training. Apparently Davis's almost rigid perfectionism was a hindrance to him here. But the youthful captain had obvious leadership qualities, and was called from his duties with the Tuskegee Army ROTC to serve as commandant of cadets. He was destined to rise to lead the 99th Pursuit Squadron into battle, to command the 332nd Fighter Group, and to retire from the Air Force as a lieutenant general.

Both Davises, father and son, endured criticism for supposedly not speaking out against military segregation, but the record is clear that they did not avoid the topic. They fought at least the more obvious iniquities and inequities of the system, as much as was possible for active-duty officers. Benjamin O. Davis, Jr., personally desegregated the base theater at Fort Patrick Henry, where his men of the 99th awaited shipment to combat overseas. After the war he was quoted as asserting that "segregation is inefficient in operation and in some instances impossible in application." His father went even further, at about the same time declaring pointedly, "The colored man in uniform receives nothing but hostility from community officials . . . In fact the Army by its direction and by action of Commanding Officers, has introduced Jim Crow politics in areas at home and abroad where they have not hitherto been practiced." But for both officers performance came well before agitation.

By the summer of 1941 two airfields were simultaneously under construction at Tuskegee. Moton Field was hurried to completion with the aid of Institute students (as had been the case with CPTP Kennedy Field), and the efforts of its black general contractor, Archie Alexander. (Alexander went on to become a Tuskegee Institute trustee, a Republican National Committeeman, and, in 1954, governor of the U.S. Virgin Islands.) Tuskegee Army Air Field (Airport No. 3), to be used for the combat training of primary graduates, was also planned and built by black contractors, and the work was more or less completed in three months. SEAACTC pushed the construction of the bases, noting that "the project is considered by the War Department as Number 1 priority due to political pressure that was being brought to bear upon the White House and War Department to provide pilot training for colored applicants."

In line with the "separate but equal" racial philosophy that the Air Corps had adopted once its efforts to exclude blacks had failed, the service was determined to ensure that the two bases and their training personnel and facilities were, in the words of General Arnold in his orders to General Weaver, "fully equivalent . . . to that provided for white personnel under similar conditions." Blacks deserved a fair trial, if for no other reason than to ensure that if the "experiment" failed the service could not fairly be blamed. The Air Corps may have had in mind the consideration that it might well have lost any court case brought by blacks protesting inferior facilities. Yet the official history of SEAACTC/ SEAAFTC conceded that "no one at Maxwell Field [SEAACTC headquarters] is supposed to have taken the project very seriously," and, in fact, treated it with "amused detachment." The equally official history of TAAF summarized the opinion of blacks on the scene: "First of all, the majority of troops on the station know that their presence in the Air Forces is permitted reluctantly, and that they are a source of embarrassment to the War Department."

The officer who had the greatest impact upon the Tuskegee training programs, Col. Noel F. Parrish, remarked after the war that no one in the U.S. Air Corps was pushing the idea of black participation, but that no one could afford to be seen as opposing the idea either. Undersecretary Lovett and some of the civilian personnel in USAAC headquarters were more helpful in forwarding the program, however. Informally, SEAACTC's commanding officer, General Weaver, told Parrish that he needn't worry about standards: "Just keep 'em happy. Your job is just to keep 'em happy." Another officer on General Weaver's staff saw matters decidedly less casually: "There will be a world war between blacks and whites, and you and I by getting this school going are probably contributing to the power of the blacks in this war. That's something we can't foresee, we just do our job."

In accordance with an Army Air Corps plan drawn up in December 1940, TAAF consisted of a base group detachment and facilities, four hundred personnel, and equipment for the training of thirty-three pursuit aircraft pilots at any one time. The backbone of the base was its fourteen training aircraft: six PT-13s, four BT-13s, and four AT-6s. Later a varying number of P-40 fighter planes was added for combat training.

The 66th AAC Primary Flying School (as the Tuskegee primary operation was designated) was singularly fortunate to have as its commanding officer Capt. Noel F. Parrish (later colonel and then brigadier general), a white Regular Air Corps officer from Kentucky who had previously been assigned to the Glenview School. Parrish was later termed by one authority "a man of insatiable curiosity and interest in all kinds of people." Before leaving for his supposedly temporary assignment at Tuskegee, Captain Parrish sought out and talked to every anthropologist he could find at the University of Chicago to hear their views on race, and during his assignment at Tuskegee (which would be "for the duration"), he consulted with newspaper editors and reporters of both races as well as Northern and Southern politicians. In fact, Parrish became a personal friend of Claude A. Barrett, director of the National Negro Press Association. Not coincidentally, TAAF (which Parrish was soon to command) enjoyed, with a few exceptions, a good press "image." At Tuskegee, Parrish fostered cordial relations with Tuskegee officials such as Dr. Patterson and G. L. Washington, and with black personnel on the bases such as Benjamin Davis, Jr.

Parrish combined his theoretical knowledge of the American racial situation with a practical, almost offhand, manner of dealing with race and its convoluted permutations in the South. Constantly asked by whites, "How do Negroes fly?" he replied that "Negroes fly very much like everyone else flies." But even Parrish was without a ready answer when Southern novelist Carson McCullers asked him if blacks might not make better fliers "because they're closer to nature." Easier to answer was the question posed by one white local: "Are those really Negroes up there or are you doing it for them?"

Like Davis, Parrish was primarily interested in performance; the nation was in a state of national emergency and would be at war before the year was out. But Parrish came to despise racial segregation, and by the end of the year was bluntly outspoken, asserting that "segregation is discrimination," and that "a segregated unit is always slightly phony." Finally, Parrish proved himself a leader, consistently easing the more egregious anomalies of racial segregation and personally becoming involved as much as a command situation would permit; one pilot remembers Parrish up to his elbows in swamp mud at the scene of a particularly grisly nighttime air crash site.

All of Captain Parrish's tact, good humor, and concern were needed in the Tuskegee environment. Although the Institute was a center of black culture in the midst of the old Black Belt (the center of the black population), it was surrounded by hostile whites, who, although in a minority, controlled the town, county, and state. And those whites were particularly fearful of large numbers of armed blacks on the Tuskegee bases.

Perhaps, almost as provoking as the racial attitudes and patterns in the area, was the singular barrenness of the town of Tuskegee and its environs. The town and county were officially "dry"; eating places were segregated and unsavory, with the exception of the local hotel, which served no food at night. There was no decent place to dance although, in the words of TAAF's official history, some "dens of iniquity at varying distances from Tuskegee" could be found by the more enterprising or reckless. As in almost every other wartime boom town, Tuskegee's main problem, however, was that of housing; the cadets could be put up at the Institute, and later in barracks, but officers, civilian instructors, and base employees had to fend for themselves in a wartime housing situation exacerbated by racial patterns.

As some compensation for such a bleak environment, TAAF and the Institute sponsored some outstanding entertainment, the most prominent featuring Louis Armstrong, Joe Louis, Lena Horne, Eddie "Rochester" Anderson, the Camel Caravan orchestra and singers, and opera stars Grace Moore and Richard Crooks. Football, basketball, and baseball teams were great successes, as were music appreciation, singing, glee clubs, an excellent training detachment band, the post orchestra (The Imperial Kings of Rhythm), and a military personnel art exhibit. The Institute also provided some diversion with its dances and female students; there was some student resentment at the aviators' girl-getting abilities, but cadets were somewhat frustrated by the school's "six-inch rule" (six inches apart) for couples. After the war, Parrish could report that "Tuskegee Air Field operated for five years with many hundreds of Negro women and several white women. During this time almost every conceivable interracial complication arose except one—sex."

In the meantime, reflecting the militarization of the CPTP in the wake of accelerating rearmament, the Tuskegee Primary Contract Flying School was renamed the 66th Army Air Corps Training Detachment. Already, by the summer of 1941, students entering the CPT secondary program were required to pledge to serve in the Air Corps if qualified. Less than a week after Pearl Harbor the CPTP was directed into the war or war-related efforts.

Black Air Corps cadets were selected in the same manner as white, and pilots of both races who had graduated from the CPT secondary program could be assigned to basic flying school, bypassing preflight and elementary. Unfortunately, the earliest classes at the 66th AAC Primary Flying School experienced an attrition rate well above that of comparable white units. Of the thirteen cadets of 42-C, only six completed primary and five advanced training. Class 42-D, consisting of eleven cadets, had only three complete the training cycle through advanced, while Class 42-E of ten cadets lost six by the end of advanced. Captain Parrish, not one to speculate about blacks being "close to nature" or whether they suffered from emotional or physical disabilities that made it difficult for them to fly, instead studied the situation as he found it, and noted the dearth of familiarity with aviation among entering black cadets. He recommended that such cadets be drawn exclusively from CPT secondary rather than on the basis of priority of application. Parrish reported that "of the last class of ten to report to this flying school, five have never been in an airplane in their lives. Of the five who have flown, three had their first flight as students in the CPT course. This situation is typical."

SEAACTC approved Parrish's proposal, but it was turned down by Air Corps headquarters since the proposal would result in the selection of black cadets in a different manner from white. Air Corps training officers also noted perceptively that in such a small group as the classes of 1942, percentages would be misleading. But a little over a year later, because of the slow pace of the 99th's activation, the service reversed its decision by calling graduates of the CPT secondary directly into basic flying training.

In October 1941, the initial ground crew for the 99th, having completed their training at Chanute, arrived at the still uncompleted TAAF. While at Chanute, they had to accomplish in nine to twelve months what the Air Corps G-3 (Operations) had asserted usually took from five to nine years of training and experience (specifically, five to seven years for a crew chief, and five to nine years for a line or hanger chief).

On November 8 the remains of the pioneer Class 42-C completed primary flying school and were transferred for basic flying training to the TAAF. There they found a "muddy, congested" facility, that, in the words of a contemporary, "could hardly be dignified by the term 'organization.' " The base intelligence officer claimed to have spent his first two weeks on duty at TAAF simply trying to locate a desk. A certain amount of confusion is understandable and was not that unique to TAAF; the nation was undergoing rapid mobilization, and Tuskegee was in almost every way a "first."

Air Corps skepticism and a refusal to take the project too seriously persisted. Colonel von Kimble, the second C.O. of TAAF, believed that high authorities in Washington wanted the program killed outright. But closer to the scene, General Weaver, who had pressed for the Tuskegee project, forthrightly reported to Air Corps headquarters that "these Negroes are wonderfully educated and as smart as they can be, and politically they have behind them their race composed of some eleven million people in this country."

It seems obvious that the higher ranking officers in the SEAACTC with one egregious exception did not allow racial prejudice to overcome their professionalism. The attitude of Maj. James Ellison, the first C.O. of TAAF, is instructive. The official history of the base stated that "Major Ellison was extremely anxious to make a 'go' of the project. He often stated that his ambition was to fly across the country with a Negro squadron and prove to the nation that it could happen . . . he received a good deal of censure and kidding about the project. His fellow officers made statements that sounded like pages from Hitler's *Mein Kampf.*" While some of Major Ellison's attitudes could be considered as somewhat patronizing, they were positively enlightened in comparison to those predominant in Air Corps headquarters.

Yet there were two significant differences between the Tuskegee project and the training of the white military pilots, differences that were to affect Tuskegee adversely, and that were based upon racial considerations. First, the lack of any alternative commissioned slots for black Air Corps washouts meant that they all went immediately back into the pool of A-1 potential draftees. Later, in 1943, a small number could enter bombardier and navigator training schools, but never enough to make much of a reduction in the figures of eliminees. After 1943 the remainder were made privates and more or less hung around Tuskegee, depressing morale. In fact, to make matters worse, the AAF began to forward newly commissioned black officers to Tuskegee simply because there was no other place to send them, at least until the activation of the black 332nd Fighter Group. Signal officers, quartermaster officers, and graduates from the integrated Miami Beach Officers Candidate School piled into TAAF. Colonel Parrish could only complain to himself, "Why do they all come to Tuskegee?"

White eliminees, on the other hand, could qualify as bombardiers, navigators, or ground officers. Consequently, Tuskegee eliminees could be very bitter, asserting that they were deliberately washed out for racial reasons, that higher standards of proficiency were demanded of black cadets, and that a secret quota existed to keep the number of black pilots low. Those who did win their wings were sometimes given the Tuskegee name of "sandmen" ("Uncle Toms," "suck-ins"). There is no evidence for any of these assertions, and much to the contrary. The chief of the Air Staff, Gen. Barney Giles, for example, complained to his assistant of the "present and most extreme difficulty in obtaining technically qualified black personnel." The fault lay not in any artificial quotas or standards, but in the entire distorting concept of racial segregation. Until the services' technical and training facilities were open to all qualified personnel, and until their graduates could be assigned on the basis of need rather than race, "technically qualified black personnel" would remain either in short supply or concentrated at one location, usually Tuskegee. Considering how few black cadets possessed aviation backgrounds, the elimination rates at Moton and Tuskegee fields do not seem unduly high. While individual Tuskegee veterans differ on the subject, Benjamin O. Davis, Jr., and Judge Hastie conceded that facilities and treatment were equal to that found on "white" bases.

Another problem encountered exclusively at Tuskegee was the interminable amount of time that could elapse between receipt of an acceptance notice and the actual orders to proceed to Tuskegee. In those early days of the program pilots were needed for only one pursuit squadron. Furthermore, a correlation did not always exist between acceptance into pilot training and an actual opening for a trainee. Some acceptees had to wait so long for their orders that they began to feel pressure from their local draft boards. Judge Hastie in September 1941 wrote bluntly, "It is inexcusable that the Army invests in national advertising for aviation cadets, organizes units in college communities to stimulate recruiting, relaxes educational requirements for flying cadets, and inaugurates plans for noncommissioned pilots, all to meet the increasing need for Army flyers, and at the same time requires a Negro to wait *three years* to begin his pilot training" (emphasis added).

According to Roy Wilkins a year later, the situation was still one which bred "discouragement, despair, and cynicism." The files of the War Department Advisory Committee on Negro Troop Policies and those of Hastie are filled with anguished letters from young acceptees facing unwelcome attentions from their draft boards. Their plight led to bitter comments in the black press, and as a result of such unfavorable publicity and of pressure from Hastie, a small beginning was made toward the procurement of black nonflying officers with the establishment of an integrated Officers Candidate School at Miami Beach, Florida. Finally, in late 1943, Tuskegee eliminees were given the opportunity to qualify as navigators at Hondo Field, Texas, and as bombardiers at Keesler Field, Mississippi, thus providing alternate commissioned nonpilot careers to blacks—alternatives available to white eliminees from the beginning.

The hectic year of 1941, which had seen three Tuskegee aviation programs either founded or flourishing, came to a dramatic end with the entry of the United States into global war as a result of the Japanese attack on Pearl Harbor. The first year of war saw the transfer out of Major Ellison as C.O. of Tuskegee Field. Ellison, as noted, had been enthusiastic about the Tuskegee program and had, in fact, accompanied Dr. Patterson and G. L. Washington to War Department headquarters and lobbied Alabama congressmen to ensure that black military aviation would begin at Tuskegee. He was a decent, sincere, blunt, old pilot who had apparently even opposed some of the segregation policies prevailing in surrounding Macon County.

Major Ellison's successor, Col. Frederick von Kimble, would not make the same "mistake." Colonel von Kimble, provoked by the entrance of two Tuskegee airmen into the white section of the Tuskegee PX, had festooned Tuskegee Air Field facilities with "Colored" and "White" signs, which segregated most facilities on base by race. Although von Kimble hailed from Oregon, he had obviously imbibed the racial attitudes of the surrounding Black Belt. (G. L. Washington noted how Southerners often proved courteous and accommodating to black Tuskegee personnel, while Northerners tended to bend over backward to cater to what they perceived as the "Southern way of life.") In fact, Colonel von Kimble even complained that segregation policies were contravened at some *Northern* bases, and called upon SEAAFTC (formerly SEAACTC) to enforce these policies uniformly. Although von Kimble's professionalism was strong enough to make him work hard for the success of the Tuskegee program, he was a complex, brooding man, who believed that "Negroes did not have the necessary administrative preparation nor temperament for leadership to fit them for superior positions." He allegedly expressed this belief by asserting that no black would rise about the rank of captain as long as he was in command. And yet Colonel von Kimble, according to Parrish, also expressed the wish to be the "Great White Father" to his charges.

Von Kimble's segregation-within-segregation at Tuskegee Field was patently illogical, for the entire black flying program was predicated on racial separation. Understandably, morale at TAAF was low by the end of

1942, just before Colonel von Kimble's transfer out; many black base personnel were Northerners and, in the words of one contemporary, were not used to "colored water and white water." The Army Air Corps (after June 1942, the Army Air Forces) had a way to deal with black troops unused to military racial segregation. The air adjutant general reported that the command staff "can handle the situation by a brief explanation to the personnel after they report." The riot-torn summer of 1943 would demonstrate just how fatuous, even disastrous, this advice would prove.

Fortunately, in the case of Tuskegee Field, although several racial confrontations occurred, none resulted in injury or loss of life. It is significant that the most serious incident, that of April 1, 1942, came in the midst of Colonel von Kimble's imposition of segregation within segregation (see chapter 4).

Perhaps with knowledge of the Tuskegee Field situation in mind, Gen. Benjamin O. Davis, Sr., the supposed "accommodationist," told a meeting of the Advisory Committee on Negro Troop Policies that blacks would "rather train in 40 degree below zero weather than in the South." (Not long before his death, General Marshall would tell a biographer that "I might say here that one of the greatest mistakes I made during the war was to insist that the colored divisions be trained in the south.")

Quite probably the one positive outcome of Colonel von Kimble's concern with Southern racial mores was his institution of indoctrination classes particularly designed for the Northern black arriving at TAAF. Von Kimble's program went well beyond the "brief explanation" ideas of the air adjutant general noted earlier, and seems to have eased matters. Early in March 1942, the arrival of a large contingent of black airmen from New York and New Jersey made such a program imperative, if distasteful to the new arrivals.

The need for more than a "brief explanation to the personnel after they report" was emphasized by an incident in which black aviation cadets hazed four white cadets at Orangeburg, South Carolina. The "hazees" were from the North and inclined to endure the ordeal as normal, but the situation could have turned ugly, considering the location. Immediately after this incident, von Kimble put his indoctrination into Southern racial mores classes into effect.

Civil authorities in Alabama and throughout the Deep South were profoundly concerned about the stationing of large bodies of armed blacks in their areas. An almost frantic correspondence flowed among

Gov. Frank M. Dixon of Alabama and Alabama senators Coke Stevenson and Lister Hill, and officials from other Southern states on the stationing of armed black guards at Southern airfields and installations. Governor Dixon was active in discouraging the stationing of more blacks in the Deep South. One fellow Alabaman wrote congratulating the governor that it was "due to your bold, outspoken, and unhesitating stand in matters of this kind that White Supremacy and all that it stands for still controls in Alabama." On the other hand, the commanding general of the Army 4th Corps Area plainly told the governor that "the Negro in the uniform of the United States has not always received the equitable treatment that is due him by virtue of the fact that he is a soldier."

In the midst of this racial tension, on March 6, 1942, the first class of black aviation cadets, the survivors of 42-C, graduated at TAAF. With Gen. George E. Stratemeyer, commanding general of SEAACTC, as the graduation speaker, the pioneer fliers, Capt. Benjamin O. Davis, Jr., and lieutenants Lemuel R. Custis, George S. Roberts, Charles DeBow, Jr., and Mac Ross received their wings as military aviators and were commissioned into the U.S. Army Air Corps.

By mid-1942 the CPT program was being phased out in favor of the CAA War Training Service (WTS), which was closed to civilians, and which would continue to the end of the war. By V-J Day the CPTP and the WTS could look back upon an impressive and unprecedented record that not only had supplied an enormous number of pilots for civil and military aviation, but also represented a step toward the entry of women and blacks into flying. From the start of the Tuskegee CPT program, G. L. Washington had viewed it not as an "experiment" (the common white attitude), but as a "demonstration" of something that should have been fairly obvious to the informed: that is, that blacks could fly in about the same proportion as whites if given the opportunity. The record backed Washington's assertion, for it shows that blacks had done as well or slightly better than whites in CPTP flight instruction, and had excelled in ground training.

But the CPTP was the thin edge of the wedge, indeed. A quota of only ten elementary graduates was allocated to enter Tuskegee Secondary, which was the key to appointment for blacks as aviation cadets. Washington calculated that fully nine years would have to elapse before all qualified elementary graduates (who, it should be noted, were licensed private pilots) would have entered Air Corps cadet training. Again, according to

Washington, assuming a washout rate in secondary of 30 percent (which is probably high), at least two hundred qualified pilots were lost to air cadet training for the service. The Air Corps, which had quadrupled elementary and secondary quotas between 1939 and 1942, was still operating within 1940 quotas for blacks. Attempts by G. L. Washington to expand black CAA training to other black institutions beyond the original five were fruitless and, of course, this was a time when the Air Corps and, later, the U.S. Army Air Forces were expending large sums to recruit desperately needed aviation cadets.

Just how lackadaisical the service could be in its recruitment of blacks is illustrated by the experiences of Herman "Ace" Lawson, a city council-man in Sacramento, California, after the war. Lawson might have become an original member of the 99th, but when making inquiries was ordered by an Air Corps major, "Get the hell out of here, boy, the Army isn't training night fighters!" When Lawson discovered that blacks were in-deed being accepted for Air Corps training, he immediately applied—and waited five months for a reply. With none forthcoming, he wrote to his congressman, his senator, and finally his president. After a further wait of two months, he received word that he had been accepted. (So eager was Lawson for military flying training that he left $1,000 worth of photo-graphic equipment in the trunk of his 1935 Dodge at the railroad station. The Dodge and equipment were never seen again by Lawson.) The startling aspect of Lawson's experience was that he was already a licensed pilot, having earned his certificate at the Fresno State College CPTP.

But more positions were finally opening for blacks; on May 23, 1942, the second black AAF squadron, the 100th Pursuit Squadron, was acti-vated at TAAF. Lieutenant Mac Ross was appointed commanding officer. Ross already "enjoyed" the distinction of becoming the first black mem-ber of the "Caterpillar Club" (restricted to those who had to make an emergency exit from an aircraft in flight). While flying a P-40 in fighter transition training he had suffered an engine malfunction and was forced to bail out, landing safely in a cotton patch. Ross worried that the inci-dent, common enough, would be used to prove that blacks could not fly.

Expansion continued, with the activation of the black 332nd Fighter Group, under the original command of a white officer, Lt. Col. Samuel Westbrook. As in the past, the AAF had responded to black pressures, rather than from the perception of any need for black manpower.

The 332nd, which would comprise the 100th, 301st (activated early in 1943), and the 302nd (activated in March 1943) fighter squadrons, was soon transferred to Oscoda AAF, Michigan, for its training, because TAAF facilities were inadequate to handle further training at the time. The move represented a break with the AAF's "tradition" of racial separation, for, of course, Oscoda was a "white" base.

But interminable training seemed the fate of the 99th; training in fighter tactics with the P-40, training in navigation, training in aerial combat, and training in gunnery. Even in such technical pursuits the 99th found that it was not to be treated like other squadrons, that it was indeed part of an "experiment." For example, gunnery scores were very high, with one cadet scoring the highest marks in the SEAACTC/SEAAFTC. But soon local headquarters banned the 99th's firing practice during the generally calm hours of dawn and dusk, because the squadron's high scores were "misleading." And each accident in the "quite low" accident rate was "very conscientiously reported by training officers."

Despite such intrusions, training proceeded smoothly enough, with not only a low accident rate, but maintenance and technical inspection that was rated as respectively "very satisfactory" and "excellent" by SEAAFTC.

These favorable evaluations are the more impressive as morale seems to have been low by the end of 1942, as noted, not caused only by Colonel von Kimble's racial policies, but perhaps even more by the fear that the 99th might never get into combat, that it would suffer dry rot or become muscle-bound from all its unfulfilled training. To exacerbate the situation, the 99th found itself enduring the old armed forces "hurry-up-and-wait" syndrome: standing to alert for embarkation, canceling all furloughs, confining everyone to post, then standing down just when anticipation was at its highest.

A bright spot in this wearying time was the transfer out of Colonel von Kimble, and his replacement by newly promoted Colonel Parrish. Parrish had earned the respect of all who had worked with him in his capacity as director of the primary program at Moton Field.

Apparently Colonel von Kimble's segregation had not been rigidly enforced toward the end of his tenure at TAAF. Many of the obnoxious "Colored" and "White" signs had been torn down, and the base military police had refused to replace them. Colonel Parrish was thus able to change policy unobtrusively, having witnessed firsthand the debilitating effects of his predecessor's racial obsessions. Parrish could claim, with justice, that he was simply following War Department policy, which banned segregation by race but permitted it by unit. As Colonel Parrish reported to the commanding general of SEAAFTC shortly after taking command:

1. Strict compliance with the spirit and the letter of War Department policies mentioned in basic communications is a policy of this station.
2. White and Negro officers are not separated in official assemblies. Insofar as facilities permit, officers living on the station are provided with quarters of their choice. There are no signs or regulations at this station requiring the use of separate toilet facilities for Negro and White officers.
3. There is on this station one (1) officers' mess. Membership in this mess is optional for all officers.
4. It is the policy to place Negro officers in posts of administrative responsibility whenever qualified Negro Personnel is available.

Every effort is being made to comply with War Department policies expressed in basic communications and at the same time to prevent misunderstanding, difficulties, and demoralizing incidents from occurring due to friction with customs obtaining in the surrounding communities.

Morale at TAAF was further sustained as rapidly promoted Col. Benjamin O. Davis succeeded Harold Maddux, the first, white, C.O. of the 99th. Captain George Roberts may well have been the best flier in the squadron, but Lieutenant Colonel Davis had the seniority, of course, and his qualities of leadership had become evident to Dr. Patterson and G. L. Washington from his first day of training.

All of the abilities of colonels Parrish and Davis would be needed to the utmost, as the apparently endless training of the 99th continued, and as TAAF began to fill up with the odds and ends of other black AAF detachments. Normally, a training airfield of the time had either primary or advanced flying training, but TAAF carried both, as well as the training (and retraining) of the 99th, the 96th Service Group, the 83rd Fighter Control Squadron, and the 689th Signal Warning Company. By the middle of 1942 approximately 217 officers and 3,000 enlisted airmen were crammed into the base; yet the AAF continued to add technical training schools at TAAF for blacks. Understandably, in the words of one contemporary, "confusion reigned supreme." Finally, in August 1942, the Air

Corps Technical Training Command admitted that the facilities at TAAF were inadequate for an expanded program. This realization, plus Judge Hastie's representations, led to the decision to remove the 100th Fighter Squadron to Oscoda Army Air Field, Michigan. Enlisted specialists were to be scattered throughout the United States for training that was becoming partly integrated, in that black and white students were on the same bases, even if they were usually instructed separately. But crowding remained a severe problem throughout the war years at TAAF, as the Army Air Forces continued to establish new programs at the base and to send blacks there individually or in groups.

Training, practice, and more training continued for the 99th throughout the latter part of 1942 and well into 1943, with fighter transition the most important phase. While obsolete and inferior to enemy fighters, the P-40 Warhawk was forgiving, had few vices, and proved an effective introduction to combat training. The 99th was soon earning commendations for proficiency and precision in its flying. According to one source, the 99th's precision flying remained unmatched until the advent of demonstration flight teams after the war. Ground crews excelled as well, performing engine changes in one-third the time usually required. To no one's surprise, the inspecting general of Third Air Force reported in October 1942, the 99th "in excellent condition and ready for immediate departure overseas shipment." The report added that morale would "suffer should its departure be delayed." But its departure would be delayed.

The 99th was indeed proud of its excellence, but spit-and-polish was not its purpose. Probably no one of the 99th was aware of the German term for spit-and-polish units that never left for the front—*asphaltsoldaten*—but many remembered that the commanding officer of Chanute Field had wished to retain the enlisted men of the 99th for a permanent drill team.

The interminable delay in committing the 99th to battle was the last in a series of frustrations in military racial matters that prompted the resignation of Judge Hastie from his position as civilian aide on Negro affairs to the secretary of war. In the year of his resignation Hastie published a bitter attack on AAF racial policies, "On Clipped Wings," which, coupled with the unfavorable publicity resulting from his resignation, impelled the Army and the Army Air Forces to reconsider some of its racial assumptions and to inaugurate some changes in this area (see chapter 4).

But at Tuskegee these events seemed to have little effect. As a result of an abortive alert in September, morale was recorded as "very poor" by March 1943. Eleanor Roosevelt wrote to the Air Staff expressing her surprise at the lack of utilization of black aviators, inquiring, "Does this mean that none of those trained are being used in active service?"

The AAF labored under some legitimate difficulties in the transfer of the 99th overseas. A long memorandum drawn up by the Army assistant chief of staff, Brig. Gen. Dwight D. Eisenhower, in March 1942, outlined the objections voiced worldwide to the stationing of black groups in particular nations or colonies. One of the first theaters considered for the 99th was the China-Burma-India theater, where the squadron might fly with Gen. Claire Chennault of "Flying Tiger" fame. But the AAF reconsidered when it was pointed out that the inexperienced 99th, flying obsolete aircraft, would probably be annihilated by the Japanese. Outside of the Pacific, only in North Africa was there large-scale combat with Germany, and that campaign was coming to an end by March 1943. Definite plans were drawn up for the 99th to join the Liberian Task Force, but the receding Axis threat to Dakar, shipping shortages, and the reluctance of Liberia to accept black troops, canceled the option. While the Liberia plans were drawn up primarily from considerations of military effectiveness, those 99th personnel aware of this possibility wondered if they were to be sent to an African backwater for primarily racial reasons.

During this trying period Secretary of War Stimson visited Tuskegee and counseled patience to colonels Parrish and von Kimble (the latter not yet having departed for his new assignment), pointing out how long it had taken "our little brown brothers" in the Philippines to achieve civilization and self-government. Von Kimble, deeply pessimistic, said that the black fliers were doing poorly, although unlike Parrish he had never flown with them. Parrish replied, as he had on other occasions, much to von Kimble's annoyance, that the percentages of good and bad black fliers was about the same as for whites. Perhaps influenced by Parrish, Stimson reported that the 99th was "outstanding by any standard."

On April 1, 1943, the final word came to TAAF and raced through the town of Tuskegee and the Institute: the 99th was moving out! For the next two days the squadron boarded troop trains at the tiny Chehaw depot for the New York Port of Embarkation, combat, and the only "first" that now really mattered—the first enemy aircraft to fall to the guns of the 99th Fighter Squadron.

Testing and Proving 3.

Colonel von Kimble, on hand to assist the men in loading up, asserted that "all of the men were very close to me," a surprising statement in light of his racial attitudes. Less surprising was the presence of the TAAF commanding officer, Colonel Parrish, also assisting in the loading.

After a slow troop train trip, the 99th arrived at Camp Shanks, New York, where they remained for eleven days for shots and paperwork during the embarkation processing. They then embarked upon the USS *Mariposa*, a former luxury liner pressed into troop transport service. Colonel Davis was appointed executive officer of the ship, and other officers of the 99th served as ship adjutant, provost marshal, and police officer. Since white troops were also embarked, this arrangement may well represent the first time in American history that black officers commanded white troops.

The eight-day crossing was cramped, tense, and uneventful, but on April 24, 1943, land was sighted—Africa! After disembarkation at Casablanca and temporary bivouac just outside that exotic city, the men of the 99th endured another tedious rail journey, across French Morocco to their first base, located at OuedN'ja, a little town near Fez. At least psychologically the 99th was off to a good beginning. Relations with nearby white Army Air Forces units were cordial, and impromptu dogfights were staged between the 99th's P-40s and the A-36s of a neighboring fighter-bomber group. The town of Fez proved delightful, enhanced by the presence of Josephine Baker, the famous 1920s expatriate black American entertainer, who introduced officers to prominent local French and Arab families. Merely being in Africa was a source of wonder and excitement for many.

Most exciting of all was the thrill of flying for the first time brand-new equipment, as twenty-seven fresh P-40 Warhawk Model Ls arrived. Colonel Davis asserted that "our equipment was of the best," but the 99th's commanding officer was undoubtedly here speaking for public consumption; the P-40, even its L model, was distinctly inferior in every significant respect to all front-line German pursuit aircraft. Before the Advisory Committee on Negro Troop Policies, Colonel Davis later noted more accurately that his men "liked the P-40, but would like something better."

However, the 99th did enjoy the benefit of instruction from experienced Air Force combat veterans, including the famous Lt. Col. Philip Corcoran, immortalized as "Flip Corcoran" in the enormously popular comic strip of the time, "Terry and the Pirates."

After a month of intensive combat training, the squadron moved to Fardjouna on the Cape Bon Peninsula, Tunisia. There the 99th, which was attached to the 33rd Fighter Group, operated under the XII Air Support of the Northwest African Tactical Air Force.

Operational sorties commenced on June 2, 1943, with a ground strafing mission against the fortified Italian island of Pantelleria. There in a moment of "indescribable beauty," in the words of one witness, two squadron P-40s roared into African skies. All of the months of training, of waiting, of fears that the 99th might never have the chance to prove itself and might be relegated to convoy patrol or worse, seemed to dissolve in the roar of the two Allison aero engines. The pilots assigned to this historic mission, lieutenants Charles B. Hall and William Campbell, at that moment must have considered themselves the luckiest men in Africa. Later that day two more squadron P-40s were flown off from Fardjouna—and both missions sighted no enemy. This anticlimax is not surprising; Axis armies had just been cleared from all of North Africa, and the Allies dominated the skies. In fact, not one enemy aircraft was sighted for a week following the two pioneering sorties. But, finally, on June 9, four German Bf 109s were spotted taking off to intercept twelve American A-20 bombers attacking an airfield on Pantelleria. Eight escorting P-40s from another squadron turned to the attack. However, the enemy broke off contact and fled. Two days later, the Pantellerian campaign, the first reduction of significant enemy territory solely by air power, was over.

On June 18, enemy aircraft were again encountered and the first aerial combat of black Americans was about to begin. Although warned by radio of unidentified aircraft approaching Pantelleria, a flight of 99th P-40s, led by Lt. Charles Dryden, was surprised by German Bf 109s skillfully dodging in from the sea among the Americans at speeds approaching 450 M.P.H. Lieutenant Dryden's flight broke formation and a melee followed. Lieutenant L. Rayford was set upon by two enemy who would have shot him down were it not for the timely intervention of Lt. Spann Watson, who opened fire at long range and scored hits on the Bf, which then broke off combat. Lieutenant Willie Ashley had meanwhile lost considerable altitude and attached himself to what he presumed was a friendly fighter. It turned out to be an inattentive FW 190, and the alert Ashley opened fire. Lieutenant Ashley pursued the radial engine enemy fighter, now smoking and losing altitude, until intense enemy ground fire forced the American to break off pursuit. Ashley thus lost the opportunity to become the first black American to down an enemy aircraft while in U.S. military service. He was fortunate as well as cool-headed, having survived an encounter with skilled and experienced enemy pilots flying superior equipment. Had the FW's pilot proved more alert, Lieutenant Ashley might well have become the first black American pilot to die in aerial combat. The FW was the latest and best of the Luftwaffe's fighters, superior to the Bf 109, and, of course, far outclassing the U.S. P-40. Still, the 99th had performed creditably, seeking and tenaciously holding combat with the enemy. And its pilots would learn.

On July 2, 1943, the first enemy aircraft fell to the guns of the 99th. Operating now with the 324th Fighter Group and based at El Haouria, the squadron was assigned to escort sixteen medium Mitchell B-25 bombers to the Castleveltrano area on the Sicilian coast—a typical mission.

Rendezvousing with their charges without incident, they tested their guns over a startlingly blue Mediterranean Sea, and moved into the protective position they were now coming to know well. Over the target the bombers unloaded their explosives to the accompaniment of inaccurate antiaircraft fire. But almost immediately a group of German fighters came boiling up to the attack like aroused hornets from an overripe kicked pear. Breaking formation to deal with the Jerries, the American flight charged into battle. Lieutenant Charles Hall, of Brazil, Indiana, headed for the space between the enemy fighters and their bomber targets, and turned inside the enemy formation, firing a long burst that penetrated the second enemy aircraft, an FW 190. Lieutenant Hall had executed a textbook attack with verve, and was rewarded by the sight of the FW falling off and heading straight for the earth, crashing in a cloud of dust and debris, for a confirmed "kill." Lieutenant W. I. Lawson claimed a probably destroyed FW and a damaged Bf 109, but these claims were unconfirmed. Lieutenant Charles Dryden's P-40 was severely damaged in the battle before the Germans broke combat.

Lieutenant Hall's victory roll was greeted with boisterous celebration, although joy was tempered by the loss of two pilots killed in a takeoff collision earlier on that day. But no such consideration inhibited the "brass" who descended upon the dusty military airfield with their congratulations. No less than the commander of American forces in North Africa, Gen. Dwight D. Eisenhower, as well as Army Air Forces Lt. Gen. Carl Spaatz and Maj. Gen. James "Jimmy" Doolittle, made their appearances. The men of the 99th could be forgiven for wondering if the first kill of a white squadron would have produced such a gathering of the mighty.

The fame of the Tuskegee Airmen reached into the heart of Dixie, and in purple prose, but without a trace of condescension, the Birmingham *News* trumpeted:

When the screaming P-40 Warhawks, piloted by the first Negro fighter squadron in the history of the world, roared through the Mediterranean skies to aid an allied offensive concentrated on the Italian island of Pantelleria, the Tuskegee trained pilots faced their acid test and came through with flying colors to prove that they had the necessary mettle to fly successfully in combat.

The invasion of Sicily on July 10, 1943, provided the background for the 99th's blooding. While the squadron flew escort for the Allied invasion fleet, they claimed no kills and suffered only one aircraft lost (although the pilot was rescued). With an Allied lodgement secured, the 99th could move to Sicily itself. Twenty-seven C-47 transports airlifted the combat elements to their new base at Licata, Sicily, while ground services followed by sea and truck. By July 23 the 99th was heavily engaged, flying thirteen missions daily, a good indication of efficiency, considering that the service echelons did not arrive at Licata until July 28. By August 17, 1943, the 99th was a veteran of two campaigns, Pantelleria and Sicily. Unfortunately, the bulk of the German forces had escaped across the Straits of Messina to the mainland, and the frustrating Italian campaign loomed ahead.

The most common assumption among Allied planners was that an Italian collapse would impel a German evacuation of most of the peninsula. The Italian military did indeed collapse, but Allied forces still had to engage the enemy in a weary battering of successive German defensive lines that would go on to almost the final collapse of the Reich itself.

The black squadrons of the U.S. Army Air Forces would also remain in Italy until V-E Day, but their sorties would carry them to nations and cities that remained mere names to the footsoldiers in the Italian mud: Vienna, Athens, Ploesti, Bucharest—and Berlin. Their greatest contribution to the Allied cause was undoubtedly their vital role of bomber escort and ground support.

In the skies of Europe the 99th found a challenge that was taxing and dangerous but straightforward. But there was another enemy for the 99th, one subtle and insidious, that could have destroyed their squadron as completely as any devastating Luftwaffe strike from the skies. This enemy was racial prejudice and was located in, among other places, AAF headquarters in Washington, D.C. At the moment when the 99th was poised for large-scale combat, forces were gathering and an attitude coalescing that, if not breaking up the 99th, would at least have relegated it to the backwaters of coastal and convoy patrol. The effect upon the expanding black American military aviation program would have been equally destructive.

This time of testing coincided with the relief of Colonel Davis and his return to the United States to assume command of the new all-black 332nd Fighter Group. *Time* magazine had used the occasion for a news story on the 99th entitled, "Experiment Proved?" Utilizing a characteristically laconic interview with Colonel Davis, plus rumor and hints, the national newsweekly in its September 20 issue vaguely noted that the 99th "had seen little action, compared to many other units, and seems to have done fairly well; unofficial reports from the Mediterranean Theater of Operations (MTO) have suggested that the top air command was not altogether satisfied with the 99th's performance, there was said to be a plan some weeks prior to attach it to Coastal Air Command, in which it would be assigned to routine convoy cover." Ten days later, the New York *Daily News* reported that the squadron had already been broken up and returned to the United States for training! Publicly, all was mere rumor and supposition. But behind the façade of official reticence and impartiality, the entire concept of significant black participation in the AAF was in jeopardy.

The command questioning of the 99th began at the lowest level, with the commanding officer of the 33rd Fighter Group (to which the 99th was then attached), and continued up the chain of command in Washington, to stop just short of the commander in chief, President Roosevelt. Major General Edwin House, C.O. of XII Air Support Command, reported to Maj. Gen. John Cannon, C.O. of the Northwest African Tactical Air Force, that while visiting the Licata Air Field on the very day that the 99th first encountered the enemy, "I happened to be on the airdrome and was very complimentary and encouraging to the personnel I met." But despite this encouragement from on high, the 33rd's C.O., Col. William Momyer, had reported to him that the 99th "seemed to disintegrate" when jumped by enemy aircraft, although ground discipline and the ability to execute orders were excellent. As an example, Colonel Momyer related that the 99th had allowed itself to be drawn into battle with those six Bf 109s escorting a flight of twelve Ju-88 medium bombers attacking Pantelleria. He then accused the 99th of a "lack of aggressive spirit," although the incident he offered would seem to indicate just the opposite, albeit it might have shown a lack of air discipline. Momyer continued by accusing the 99th of avoiding heavily defended targets in dive-bombing missions, of averaging fewer sorties per man, and of withdrawing frequently from combat for rest.

Based on the performance of the 99th Fighter Squadron to date, it is my opinion that they are not of the fighting caliber of any squadron in this group. They have failed to display the aggressiveness and daring for combat that are necessary to do a first class fighting organization. It may be expected that we will get less work and less operational time out of the 99th Fighter Squadron than any squadron in this group.

General House believed that he knew the cause of the problem: "the

Negro type has not the proper reflexes to make a first class fighter pilot." His solution was to send the 99th back to Africa for coastal and convoy protection duties, and to replace their obsolete P-40s with the even more inferior P-39s. The 99th's P-40s would go to some more "aggressive" squadron.

General Cannon endorsed General House's critique completely, and the reports were pushed even higher up the chain of command, to Gen. Carl Spaatz, commander of the North African Air Force. General Spaatz cautiously commended the "fairness" of generals House and Cannon, and merely stated that the 99th had "excellent" ground discipline and conduct, and that no squadron had "a better background of training" than the 99th, which had been introduced to combat "very carefully." Spaatz, in his turn, forwarded the Momyer-House-Cannon criticism along with his own observations to Gen. Henry H. "Hap" Arnold, commanding general of the AAF, in Washington, D.C. Arnold had already written to Spaatz by special courier that

We have received from very unofficial sources second-hand tales of the fact that the Negro pilot tires easily and that he loses his will to fight after five or six missions . . . I am sure that you also realize the urgency required for the information, in view of the fact that we contemplate building additional Negro units at once.

Thus Spaatz's reports were welcomed in AAF headquarters. Arnold apparently ordered studies made of the question of black pilot qualities. A report of the acting chief of the Air Staff for training noted that the 99th required eight months of training time, compared to only three months for a comparable white squadron. This criticism was hardly valid, in that the 99th was a pioneer military organization, an outfit of exceptions and beginnings, suffering from the unorthodox training organization method that saw every phase of flight training, from CPT elementary to AAF combat training, all at one base, a base that did not even exist before 1941. A shortage of P-40s had further delayed training for the 99th. An evaluation from the Operations Division of the War Department was more cautious, merely citing a report from General Eisenhower to the effect that through early August the 99th had creditably carried out difficult strafing missions in Sicily.

The critique of the 99th was laid before the Advisory Committee on Negro Troop Policies, and on October 16 Colonel Davis, now back in the

States to command the 332nd Fighter Group, was called before the committee to answer the criticisms of his former squadron. Davis logically pointed out that the 99th was a novice among veterans. Candidly admitting mistakes in the early missions of his command, Colonel Davis noted the complete lack of combat experience of his men. The accusations of a lack of aggressiveness were met head on; according to Davis the 99th met enemy fighters on 80 percent of its missions, even though enemy fighters were relatively rare at that point in the European campaign. And while a white squadron could muster from thirty to thirty-five pilots for missions, the 99th had only twenty-six. As a result, on many days of combat Davis's pilots flew from three to six missions per day. Davis could discern no difference between the stamina of his men and of comparable white squadrons, even though the 99th had been in combat for two months before receiving any replacements.

The Special Committee, which included Colonel Davis's father, Brig. Gen. Benjamin O. Davis, Sr., had already heard evidence from Colonel Parrish that due to segregation the 99th could not benefit from the combat experience of white units, for the 99th fought alone, and not as a part of an AAF fighter group. Davis did not mention this point before the Special Committee, probably deeming the question as too political, but many years later noted that "we operated in a vacuum." But he did yield to one cry from the heart; if all the time and effort spent on the 99th had produced only a mediocre-to-poor outfit, then "there is no hope."

General Arnold was nonetheless determined to end the combat career of the 99th Pursuit Squadron and ordered a draft memorandum for President Roosevelt asserting, "It is my considered opinion that our experience with the unit can lead only to the conclusion that the Negro is incapable of profitable employment as a fighter pilot in a forward combat zone," and proposed reassigning the 99th to a rear defense area.

The memo never reached the president. Colonel Emmett O'Donnell of the Air Staff, later to rise to high rank in the postwar U.S. Air Force, completed a revised draft of the Arnold memo as directed. But Colonel O'Donnell sent a cover memorandum stating that *"I urgently recommend that this entire subject be reconsidered."* Colonel O'Donnell's cover memo should be noted in some detail, not only because the entire volatile subject was indeed reconsidered, but also for the cogency of O'Donnell's arguments, far more sophisticated and aware than those of his superiors.

Colonel O'Donnell did not argue the point of the combat efficiency of the 99th. Instead, he noted:

Every country in this war had had serious trouble in handling disaffected minorities . . . to recommend at this time any action which would indicate the relative inferiority of the colored race would be really "asking for it."

O'Donnell pointed out that one to four squadrons could hardly make much difference in the total war effort, and that the squadron or squadrons might improve with time and under white leaders.

Can we say they are any worse than the Chinese, on whom we have spent millions; or the Mexicans or South Americans? The loss in combat efficiency through their utilization is all out of proportion to the possible loss in productive effort at home, which may result in bringing this subject to a head now. Race riots, strikes, and cries of "discrimination" would surely follow the wide publicity such actions would receive in the yellow press. Further, I feel that such a proposal to the President at this time would definitely not be appreciated by him. He would probably interpret it as indicating a serious lack of understanding of the broad problems facing the country.

General O'Donnell concluded that "it might be far better to let the entire matter drop, without writing *any* letter to the President."

The matter *was* allowed to drop. Ultimately, it made little difference either way to these high-ranking AAF officers since the 99th comprised so small a fraction of resources and personnel. Most of those same officers remained unconvinced of the value of the 99th or of blacks in the USAAF generally, as can be seen in their testimony before the Gillem Report and in the Nippert Report, both of 1945 (see chapter 8).

The last word on the quality of the 99th at the time should undoubtedly rest with the Statistical Control Division, Office of Management Control of the Army Air Forces. Its report of March 30, 1944, compared the 99th to other P-40 squadrons in the MTO from July 1943 to the end of January 1944. The report began by asserting that "an examination of the record of the 99th Fighter Squadron reveals no significant general differences between this squadron and the balance of the P-40 squadrons in the M.T.O." During this seven-month period, the 99th was inferior only in the category of objective bombing (12 percent less than comparable squadrons) although it flew 10 percent more armed patrol and reconnaissance missions. From October 1943 on, the 99th flew only 79 percent of the number of sorties flown by other P-40 squadrons, but destroyed twelve enemy aircraft for a loss of two P-40s, while comparable squadrons in the same period averaged three enemy aircraft for a loss of 0.3. The report concluded that General House's critical memorandum, General Cannon's and General Spaatz's endorsements be studied in the light of the detailed statistical material presented in the report.

This analysis indicated, if anything, some superiority for the 99th. The lower number of sorties and missions in certain categories, and the higher losses of aircraft were indicative of a problem that plagued the 99th and its successor black squadrons to the end of the war—maintenance. This weakness was undoubtedly a result of few blacks having had peacetime mechanical experience.

The 99th had survived its most dangerous challenge. No threat from the enemy throughout the war would pose so great a menace to the very existence of black military aviation as this nonviolent assault on the squadron by higher AAF commanders.

Of course, the 99th was engaged in combat throughout the weeks of their greatest peril, and the overwhelming majority of the men remained ignorant of the hostile forces gathering against them. The men of the 99th were apparently also too busy with the routine of battle and military life to ponder the fact that, almost two years after Pearl Harbor, they were still the only black unit in the Armed Forces of the United States to engage America's enemies in air combat.

On September 2, 1943, Lt. Col. George S. "Spanky" Roberts assumed command of the 99th, as Colonel Davis was transferred back to the United States to organize the 332nd Fighter Group. Early on the morning of the same day, advance elements left Licata to set up a base on the Italian mainland in what was presumed to be a routine operational movement in the wake of the Allied landings at Salerno. But landing in the Battapaglia area, the advance group came under enemy fire for twenty-four hours as the Germans broke through Allied lines. The group beat a hasty retreat and was thrown in with the British Tenth Corps, with orders to fire only on enemy footsoldiers and to let the German tanks pass. Fortunately, the airmen-turned-footsoldiers were spared putting these frightening instructions to the test, as the German onslaught was stanched just short of Tenth Corps's lines.

The advanced echelon of the 99th continued its odyssey southward to the Paestum area, passing between German and Allied lines, only to discover that the landing field it was to occupy was at least temporarily under German management. Conditions seemed hardly better at the second field to which the weary pioneers were assigned; for five days and nights they were bombed and strafed by the Luftwaffe thrice daily. Nonetheless, ten fighters of the 99th were able to mount fourteen sorties and four patrol missions, although temporarily based on yet another base in Sicily, near Barcelona.

Finally, the advance party was reunited with the rest of the squadron at the great Foggia Air Field complex, occupying Foggia No. 3 on October 17, 1943. At this time the 99th was assigned to the 79th Fighter Group, Col. Earl E. Bates, C.O. A period of mutually beneficial cooperation followed. Contemporary opinion appears unanimous that Colonel Bates was conscientious, fair, and highly competent. Walter White, in Europe on a fact-finding tour for the NAACP, noted the "total obliteration of consciousness of differences in skin color among both white and Negro fliers of the 79th Group." Further proof may be found in the 79th Group's unofficial war record, in which the pigmentation of the 99th component is never mentioned. The evidence is also strong that Colonel Bates avoided the pitfall of the white liberal of the 1940s, the urge "to do something for the Negro," which could often be translated by blacks as doing something *to* them. The squadron historian noted,

With the Pantellerian and Sicilian Campaigns we thought of ourselves as veterans. That belief was short-lived. The 79th Fighter Group was an experienced organization. [The 79th taught the 99th more effective takeoff and flight tactics.] With these changes comes more experience and with the experience comes confidence. These attributes are precisely what pilots of the 99th Fighter Squadron are getting.

Morale was high throughout October. Early in the month the advance echelon had chipped in to buy a pig and hold a barbecue. The night of the open-air barbecue and sing-along made the war and loneliness bearable. On the thirty-first, the squadron held its first formal church service in months, an improvised affair with the pulpit sited in front of a wrecked German Dornier 217, the Luftwaffe markings standing out incongruously in the spiritual setting.

As always, the men of the 99th were primarily concerned with combat proficiency, and this was where Colonel Bates earned their respect, mixing black and white squadrons in combat and training missions. The 99th still had a lot to learn, for their initial two months of combat had occurred at a time of quiescent enemy air activity. On only fifteen missions during that period did P-40 squadrons of the MTO encounter enemy aircraft; ten of these missions were over Sardinia, where the 99th did not operate, and the 99th had been dispatched elsewhere on the other five occasions of enemy encounters. In fact, from July 20 to October 16, when the 99th was engaged exclusively in beach patrol with occasional escort and bombing missions, they did not encounter a single Axis aircraft. On October 2, the 99th resumed combat operations as the fourth squadron of the 79th Fighter Group. They bombed and strafed ground and shipping targets in the Isernia-Capionone area, and later the road network northwest of Sangro, always on the lookout for targets of opportunity.

The men of the 99th were learning the ways of aerial combat, as well as dedication and persistence, which could perhaps be considered as good a definition of courage as any. Flight leader Lt. H. Clark might serve as an example. Brushing a P-38 of another squadron with his landing gear on takeoff, Lieutenant Clark continued his mission, safely crash-landing his P-40 at its conclusion.

On October 22, the 99th was sent into battle from Foggia No. 3 for the first time, with ground-attack missions on ammunition dumps. Although two Warhawks were hit by flak, no enemy aircraft was sighted, and all of the squadron's fighters returned safely.

The month of November was particularly trying for the men of the 99th; most days of that month saw missions canceled by foul weather that also blew down tents and turned the ground into a particularly tenacious mud, remembered with a curse by ground crews, as well as by all infantrymen who have had to fight in Italy in any November. The squadron, fearing that even Thanksgiving might bring no surcease, turned its thoughts to camouflaging its rations for the occasion. Happily, turkey with all the trimmings was there on time. Another bright spot was the visit of General Cannon early in the month to distribute medals to several of the pilots.

But most of the days of November passed in the dreary round detailed by the squadron historian:

We are up to our necks in mud. Here and there are fallen tents, blown down the night before by the wind. No one soldier has a complete uniform. Every man has a different idea regarding which of his clothing to wear in order to keep warm. It is very difficult to keep clothes warm [*sic*].

Almost in despair, the writer noted how the bleak mountains and the surrounding skies seemed on most days "to merge into a huge mass of blackness."

Such thoughts apparently did not affect combat missions, and as the weather finally cleared, the 99th averaged forty-eight sorties per day in close support missions in aid of the British Seventh Army in its crossing of the river Sangro.

Between November 19 and 22, the 79th Fighter Group moved to Madna, a coastal airstrip near Termoli on the Italian east coast. And on the latter date the first "fifty-mission crush" was pounded into the garrison cap of a 99th pilot, Lt. James Wiley.

December brought weather little improved from that of the previous month; many missions were canceled or aborted, and those missions that were completed consisted of the unglamorous but essential duties of bombing and strafing.

But December brought relief to thirty-two enlisted men of the squadron. They were the first to be granted rest leave to the Sipento Albergo Ciolella, a hotel in Manfredonia operated by the American Red Cross as a rest camp. There good food, good hunting, sailing, sightseeing, and simple rest restored spirits to men who had not had more than one day off-duty since their arrival from the States.

On December 9, General Arnold and assorted AAF brass visited Madna Air Field. General Arnold gratuitously observed that "the eyes of Negro America were upon the 99th Fighter Squadron," an observation that must have grated on the men of that squadron. Would they ever see the day when they would be evaluated like any other military outfit, where their successes and shortcomings would be evaluated in terms of personal and unit worth, rather than in racial generalizations?

Morale was beginning to slip. Christmas Day, overcast, cold, and drizzly, was endured more than celebrated. And despite the squadron's respectable total by the end of the year of 255 missions and 1,385 sorties, Lieutenant Hall's victory, so long ago in June of 1943, remained the squadron's only kill. As one contemporary noted: "This was disheartening and the morale of the squadron was far from high. To make matters worse, the ground crewmen had just about lost faith in their pilots' courage to engage the enemy." This attitude was indeed disheartening, for the pilots of the 99th were painfully aware that they had to "prove" themselves as no white squadron had ever had to. Now, apparently, they had to prove themselves to their own men. The lack of kills could hardly be blamed on pilot pusillanimity or ineptitude: from October 1943 to the middle of January 1944, the 99th, operating from the east coast of Italy in its familiar role of ground attack, had encountered not one enemy aircraft.

Early on January 16, 1944, the squadron left Madna for Capodichino Air Field, near Naples, crossing from the east to the west coast of the Italian "Boot" to support the Allied landings at Anzio. The fortunes of war were about to change dramatically for the 99th.

On January 27, while on morning patrol, a formation of sixteen of the squadron's Warhawks, led by Lt. Clarence Jamison, spotted fifteen German FW 190 fighters dive-bombing Allied shipping off St. Peter's Beach in the Anzio beachhead. Diving into the enemy the P-40s maintained strong flight and fire discipline. With short and effective bursts from their six .50-caliber machine guns, lieutenants Howard Baugh and Clarence Allen ripped into the enemy, sending one down quickly and slowly disintegrating another. Lieutenant Willie Ashley caught another FW on the deck and chased him to within a few miles of Rome, where his gunfire finally caused the German to burst into flame and crash. Lieutenant Leon Roberts also jumped an enemy fighter at low altitude, causing him to flip over and dive into the ground. Lieutenant Robert W. Diez, with a 60-degree deflection shot, closed another enemy fighter and watched him crash into someone's backyard. Lieutenant Henry Perry caught an FW coming out of a dive and raked it from nose to tail. The enemy fluttered and fell off on one wing to the earth. All this was at no cost to the American flight.

The ground crews craned their heads upward as Lieutenant Jamison's first flight roared over the mud, pierced steel plating, and forlorn tents of Capodichino Air Field. *Five victory rolls.* Was it true? Could it possibly continue? It was, and it did; January 27, 1944, was only half over.

That afternoon, at 1425 hours, Lt. Lemuel Custis, a charter member of the 99th, downed an FW 190 in low-level close combat. Lieutenant Charles Bailey caught another FW with a 60-degree deflection burst, which forced the enemy pilot to bail out, and Lieutenant Wilson Eagleson spotted a third FW on the tail of a flight mate and sent the enemy flaming into the ground. Three probable hits were also claimed. But now these victories exacted for the first time their price. Lieutenant Allen G. Lane was shot down in a scramble with an undetermined number of enemy FWs, but parachuted to safety. Lieutenant Samuel Bruce was lost in action, the first of the 99th to be killed in air combat, and thus the first black American to die in aerial battle with an enemy. (Six of his mates had lost their lives in ground-attack missions.) But a total of eight victory rolls in one day produced an almost ecstatic sense of pride.

Squadron commander Major Roberts had a hand in the day's fighting. While engaging enemy FWs attacking Allied shipping at St. Peter's Beach, Roberts was hit by flak after damaging an enemy fighter. His three right wing guns and the right side electrical system were put out of action, and Major Roberts headed for home. But on the way back to Capodichino, the commander spotted an enemy machine-gun position and, with his three remaining guns and the aid of his wing man, silenced the nest.

The exciting momentum continued the following day, with four more of the enemy brought down in intense fighting over the Anzio beachhead. Lieutenants Diez and Lewis C. Smith each brought down an FW (Diez's second in as many days), and Lieutenant Hall shot down two of the enemy, an FW and a Bf 109, for his third kill. All of the 99th fighters returned, with only one Warhawk damaged. In two days, twelve enemy fighters had been downed, three probably destroyed, and four damaged. The squadron could also take some pride in the realization that their victories had been gained with something less than first-class equipment. Further, Luftwaffe pilots may have been at the peak of their skill at the time; lack of fuel for training and heavy casualties were not yet apparent.

Not surprisingly, General Cannon paid a surprise visit to the 99th the next afternoon to congratulate the victorious pilots. He left with a laconic "keep shooting."

Early in February 1944, Allied air forces in Italy noted increased enemy air activity over the Anzio-Nettuno area. The Allied bomb line on the beachhead dropped back considerably, and German ground activity increased. Pilots also discovered that they could no longer chase damaged German aircraft to the vicinity of Rome with relative impunity.

In action over the Anzio area on February 5, two Warhawks of the 99th were shot down, although one pilot, Clarence Jamison (now a captain), made his way back to Capodichino. Lieutenant Elwood Driver, who scored a probable on that day, described aerial combat over Anzio-Nettuno:

About ten-plus FW-190's dove from 16,000 feet from an easterly direction and flattened out on deck over Anzio. At the time I was headed west at 6,000 feet. Before the FW-190 reached a position beneath me, I made a diving left turn and pulled out about 300 yards behind him and began firing. I continued to fire in long bursts even though he was pulling away. As my tracers straddled the cockpit, a sheet of flames burst from the right side. I last saw the plane burning and headed towards Rome at 50 feet from the ground. The firing was done from 500 feet down to the deck. I was slightly above at all times. During the time I was firing, a clipped wing Spitfire was also firing. He was to my right and ahead about 50 yards. I claim one Focke Wulf 190 destroyed.

Two days later the 99th bagged three more FWs without loss, their last victory for many months to come. Increasingly, the pilots of the squadron were discovering the inferiority of their fighters. On several missions in February 1944, they reported chasing Luftwaffe Messerschmitts only to discover "the ME-109's outdistanced them." And the Me (Bf) 109 was actually a slower fighter than the FW 190.

There were compensations: Special Services was more frequently on hand with coffee and doughnuts, and enlisted men could be trucked into Naples for a film. But the month of February, following January's glory, was depressing. Many of the men had been in combat long enough to begin to figure and worry about the "percentages," the supposedly increasing chances of death, mutilation, or captivity as their combat missions lengthened. And the Warhawks were wearing out.

The squadron historian, typing hurriedly and ungrammatically noted, "Sickness played havoc with the flying personnel. The nerves of the pilots was on edge. For some reason, pilots was on edge and no longer laughed and joked as they sat around operations waiting for takeoffs," adding ominously, "Some little difficulty always arose during each mission. Pilots and mechanics talked in whispers about the dreaded 'percentage system' catching up with the squadron. We have eluded this parasite of Fighter Squadrons for many months."

March was to bring no change. In that month no enemy aircraft fell to the guns of the 99th and the squadron lost no pilots, although one was slightly injured by ground fire on a mission. Certainly the 99th was not idle, although rainy weather in the first half of the month played havoc with maintenance. But, as usual, the squadron found itself in the familiar ground-attack role, with enemy opposition now light in the air. Many missions were flown in support of the controversial Allied air assault on the venerable Monte Cassino Abbey.

But March 1944 had its memorable moments; on March 15 the Luftwaffe mounted one of its most violent air attacks of the Italian campaign. Although German aircraft "raised hell," in the words of the squadron historian, over Capodichino for thirty minutes the squadron suffered no loss. Coincidentally, Mount Vesuvius erupted, spewing a flow of lava that crested at fifty feet and traveled at the rate of nine hundred feet per hour. Scores of Allied aircraft were destroyed by lava and ash. Airmen of the 99th who still craved excitement after all this could be trucked into Naples for some genuine Italian opera, a diversion now competing with Special Services activities.

A "typical" March 1944 mission of the 99th would be the one mounted on the 19th. It made no headlines, no news bulletins, and can be found only in the squadron record and in the memories of its participants. But it had its place as a contribution to the wearing down of Hitler's war machine. As such it, and so many others like it, are far more typical and probably more significant than those more spectacular slam-bang dogfights that caught the eye of Allied journalists and their air forces's public relations machines.

Eight Warhawks took off at 10:30 to dive-bomb a troublesome gun position east of Anzio. They made four direct hits, but four one-hundred-pound bombs overshot the target. The position was then strafed. Anti-aircraft fire over the target ranged from moderate to heavy, and was somewhat inaccurate. One Warhawk was damaged by flak, but all aircraft returned to base. Mission accomplished.

The 99th was flying an average of two patrol and dive-bombing missions per day during this period as part of "Operation Strangle," a continuous attempt to interdict Axis rail traffic between the Po Valley and the front. As a consequence, the enemy was forced to rely almost entirely on road transport and coastal shipping for supplies.

The squadron was busy even on those days on which no missions could be flown due to weather conditions. Planes had to be test-flown and slow-timed. Cross-country flights were sometimes required for official business, and new pilots had to be trained. And, of course, the steady work of the ground crews went on. Engines were overhauled in the field, guns cleaned, calibrated, and test-fired at the butts; sheet-metal men cut, filed, patched, and riveted, while the electronic and hydraulic personnel practiced their arcane crafts on the aircraft insides.

April opened with the officers and men of the squadron hoping that rumors predicting the separation of the 99th from the 79th Fighter Group would prove false. But the scuttlebutt, for once, was true, and the 99th moved out of Capodichino to Cercola Field on April 2, where it was now attached to the 324th Fighter Group. The parting was sweetened by a farewell party thrown in downtown Naples by the 99th's C.O., Capt. Erwin B. Lawrence, and attended by Colonel Bates, the 79th's C.O., and top officers of the component squadrons of the 79th—the 85th, 86th, 87th, and 99th.

The abrupt change of base did not transform the squadron's mission—still patrol and ground attack—or its luck: still no further enemy kills. And the promise of bomber escort work remained just that, as the new P-47s failed to arrive in any numbers.

Still, April was not "the cruelest month." General Ira C. Eaker, C.O. of the Mediterranean Allied Air Force, inspected the squadron on April 20, and told assembled personnel that "by the magnificent showing your fliers have made since coming to this theater, and especially in the Anzio beachhead operations, you have not only won the plaudits of the Air Force, but have earned the opportunity to apply your talents to much more advanced work than was at one time planned for you." General Eaker was presumably referring to early attempts to confine the 99th to convoy and coastal patrol work. His comments must have stirred some bitter memories from old timers in the squadron.

May 1944 saw the opening of an Allied spring offensive. The Mediterranean Allied Air Force and the 99th were assigned the interdiction of German transportation, particularly motor transport. Within a week the town of Cassino finally fell to the Allies, and Fifth Army commander Gen. Mark Clark and General Cannon had both complimented the 99th on its contributions. General Clark had specifically called for the 324th to help with the close-in air support vital to the Cassino Battle. The 99th was in the thick of furious fighting as it pounded German positions and supply lines with incendiary and fragmentation bombs. The C.O. of XII Tactical Fighter Group noted that "eternal credit is due to the 324th Fighter Group for the manner in which it carried out this assignment and it is an example in really close support operations."

The squadron on June 2, 1944, could look back on one year's combat service: 500 missions and 3,277 sorties, fifteen enemy aircraft downed at a cost of two aerial combat deaths. Equally important as a morale booster, Sgt. Thomas Fuller, the first enlisted man to replace another rotated stateside, joined the squadron. An even more important fillip to squadron spirits was the news that the 99th would be trading the last of its battle-weary warhorse Warhawk P-40s for more modern fighters.

Finally, after brief moves to Ciampo Field, and then on to Orbetelo with the 86th Fighter Group, the 99th relocated to Ramitelli Air Field on June 28 for permanent assignment to the new black fighter group, the 332nd Fighter Group, Col. Benjamin O. Davis, Jr., commanding.

Home Front / Battle Front 4.

W hile the Tuskegee Airmen were proving themselves in battle, another struggle was waging unremittingly on the United States home front, a struggle that in a surprising number of cases spilled over into military indiscipline, violence, and death. Black Americans, military and civilian, fought their own two-front war in the Second World War. Their "Double-V" battle cry stood for victory over Jim Crow at home and victory over their nation's enemies abroad.

On the home front in this war there would be no "close ranks" sentiment save, perhaps, briefly in the patriotic aftershock of Pearl Harbor. *The Crisis*, organ of the NAACP, asserted plainly that "a Jim Crow army cannot fight for a free world." Adam Clayton Powell, Jr., demanded to know, "Is this a white man's war?", and Roi Ottley replied that it was indeed a "white folks' war." The "Double-V," popularized by the Pittsburgh *Courier* as far back as 1938, implied an uncompromising struggle, despite the national emergency. As Charles Himes proclaimed, "Now is the time, here is the place." Less public forums revealed more bitter and negative sentiments, as witness the well-known wartime graffito, "Here lies a black man, killed fighting a yellow man for the glory of the white man." Walter White was shocked to witness the tumultuous applause that greeted a black student's cry, "I hope Hitler wins!"

But aside from fringe black groups upon which military intelligence and the FBI devoted an unwarranted amount of attention, in the words of one authority, "By and large, however, the militance of most Afro/Americans was directed to insure equal participation in, not withdrawal from the war effort."

A full 88 percent of blacks in one poll felt that there should be no soft-pedaling of demands for full rights of citizenship at home, while 42 percent of blacks polled in New York City felt that victory at home was actually more important than overseas (although only 34 percent said so to a white pollster). The Office of War Information found considerable dissatisfaction among blacks with their participation—or lack of participation—in the war effort, although regional differences were significant, with Southern blacks almost consistently more optimistic, possibly to white interviewers. Yet black Americans also generally looked upon the Second World War as a great opportunity for improvement, if they kept up their pressure. The distinguished black psychiatrist, Dr. Kenneth Clark, perhaps best summarized the contemporary attitude of educated and articulate black Americans:

The Negro hopes that out of the present war will arise such conditions as to make mandatory the fuller participation of Negroes in the political and economic life of America. This may come about, he hopes, in either one of two ways. First, this being primarily a "white man's war," a long and destructive war may so weaken all combatants that they will be unable to subjugate the darker races. Second, a victory for the forces of democracy may actually result in the development of a more liberal treatment of minority peoples. The feeling is widespread that the inevitable disturbances of the usual social patterns—sometimes bordering even upon disintegration—may be the source from which a positive, dynamic, and honest attitude toward them will arise.

This attitude was encouraged by the perception that the Roosevelt administration was sympathetic to black aspirations. High federal government figures, such as Vice-President Henry Wallace and Undersecretary of State Sumner Welles, made no secret of their commitment to nothing less than black equality. Eleanor Roosevelt, of course, occupied a special place in black affections, while FDR himself at least sounded as though he were sympathetic. On the other side of the political aisle, the 1940 Republican presidential candidate, Wendell Willkie, eloquently pointed out the glaring anomaly created by the administration's high wartime principles and America's keeping about a tenth of its population in a servile status.

The more prominent national journals had, by the early 1940s, practically ceased to publish derogatory material about black Americans, and generally pursued a more enlightened policy in racial matters. *Collier's* May 1941 issue prominently featured Willkie's plea for racial understanding, "Americans Stop Being Afraid!" while the *Saturday Evening Post* carried Walter White's forthright "It's Our Country, Too: The Negro Demands the Right to Fight" as early as 1940. *Time,* hardly in the forefront of "social experimentation," could nevertheless insist that "since World War I, the Negro's status as a U.S. fighting man has gone backward . . . The 13,500,000 Negroes of the U.S. remained semi-citizens who wanted to be allowed to do their share of working or fighting to keep the U.S. free." In all, the overwhelming majority of black Americans expressed in polls, journals, newspapers, and speeches, their desire for greater participation in the war effort.

These were the glory years of the American black press. Army studies estimated a circulation of two million copies, that about three-quarters of all adult blacks read at least one black newspaper, that, startlingly, about 56 percent of black troops read the very influential Pittsburgh *Courier,* and that 76 percent read at least one paper in the Afro-American chain.

The black press filled an enormous gap. A perusal of white newspapers of the time shows blacks featured almost entirely in the realms of entertainment, sport, and crime, with the occasional reference to race relations, usually in the wake of racial disturbances. Conversely, an Army study late in the war revealed that three-quarters of white troops had not read or heard of any accomplishment of black Americans in the war (although those who had run across such news reacted favorably). Incredibly, one-half of black troops surveyed had supposedly heard or seen nothing of war news concerning their race! Thus it fell almost exclusively to the black press (in the absence of black radio stations) to report black American news in an unstereotyped fashion, to mold black attitudes toward the war effort, and to provide detailed coverage of blacks in battle. Not surprisingly, the 99th and the other black Army Air Forces squadrons to come featured prominently in the black press, and a representative of that press was almost continuously on duty with the 99th and, later, with the 332nd Fighter Group.

Hollywood films of the 1940s retained earlier racial stereotypes in their treatment of blacks. A wartime Army study found that one-quarter of black roles featured domestics inferior in intelligence, or entertainers rarely at work, and "lazy, shiftless, no good, slew-footed, happy-go-lucky, razor-toting, tap-dancing vagrant[s]." This almost uncannily perceptive study, which could well take its place among the later, more academic studies dealing with blacks in American films of the 1940s, concluded that the stage Irishman, bibulous, maudlin, and occasionally violent, "changed about the [time of the] advent of the talkies," but not the "stage Negro." The Army study concluded that commanders of black troops should avoid stereotypes in dealing with their men. But any commander of average susceptibility would have had his faculties taxed indeed to have purged his mind of such racial stereotypes embedded in the majority press and feature films.

The American Red Cross compounded the problem when it announced early in the war that although it would now, for the first time, accept black blood, "In deference to the wishes of those for whom the plasma is being provided, the blood will be processed separately so that those receiving transfusions may be given plasma from blood of their own race." The Red Cross, of course, was perfectly aware that there is no difference for transfusion purposes between the blood or the dried plasma of the races, but had to bow to the prejudices and pressures of those who apparently had no objection to receiving serum and antitoxins from horses and cows. Even more bitterly ironic was the fact that a pioneer in blood preservation, supervisor of the Blood Plasma for Britain project and director of the First American Red Cross Blood Plasma Bank, Dr. Charles R. Drew, was a black medical doctor of the Howard University Medical School. Dr. Drew resigned from the American Red Cross after its blood segregation decision.

Few black Americans graced the local boards of the Selective Service System, although blacks were conscripted in only slightly less than their proportion of the nation's population. Only three Southern states permitted blacks to sit on local boards, and they had jurisdiction only over their racial fellows. The rational for this restriction, as provided by several Southern governors, was that to give blacks what could amount to a life-

or-death decision over whites would lead to trouble. Apparently this logic worked one way only: no trouble would follow the giving of whites this power over blacks.

Galling as was this official segregation, anecdotal tales of degradation dramatized the paradox of a nation ostensibly fighting against "alien theories" of inferior races and peoples while maintaining either legally or socially such theories on the home front. A sample included a Jim Crow air raid shelter in the nation's capital, textbooks for black children in Mississippi omitting material on voting, elections, and democracy, or of enemy POWs eating in restaurants and railroad cars while uniformed black guardians of American liberty ate in the kitchen, behind partitions, or not at all. An Army counterintelligence report noted that in Salt Lake City some black troops had discovered that the only establishments that would feed them were a Japanese restaurant and a German tavern!

A new generation of better educated and informed black Americans in and out of uniform would not accept such insults passively, even in the name of patriotism; in fact, they now argued that it was indeed patriotic to fight for democracy at home as well as overseas. And white intransigence in the face of such assertion would soon lead to what one authority termed a "harvest of disorder."

Previous "race riots" almost invariably were the result of white aggression growing from some supposed black outrage, and quite often took the form of "burning the niggers out." But the outbreaks of the 1940s resulted in most cases from violent black reaction to real or perceived white offenses. While black rage was nothing new, this new generation of blacks now felt confident and assertive enough to do something about their condition.

That condition was improving; during the war the number of skilled and semi-skilled black craftsmen and foremen doubled, while black average income climbed from $400 to more than $1,000 by the end of the war. Black union membership more than doubled from 500,000 in 1940 to 1,250,000 by 1945. Further, the general climate of opinion had changed somewhat, and the war presented opportunities for strong pressure upon white America.

But improvement could not come fast enough to erase the years of repression; despite economic gains, a black family income was still one-half that of a white family. As late as 1942 blacks represented a mere 3 percent of workers in the usually better-paying war work. In the South, economic and social improvement moved at a snail's pace in the South. Just before the riots of the summer of 1943, Dr. Kenneth Clark asked. "Does the young Negro American, deprived of the right to earn a living in industry, limited and segregated in the armed forces of the nation—does he think the American way of life is worth fighting for and perhaps dying for?" Even Dr. Clark and other prominent black Americans, however, did not foresee the violent eruptions soon to come, but rather emphasized the "apathy and indifference" among black "industrial serfs and sharecroppers" to whom uncommunicativeness to strangers "had become a condition for their very survival."

But in that summer of 1943 fatal racial riots and violent protest erupted in Harlem and Detroit, with lesser disturbances in Houston, Charleston, Richmond, Virginia, Washington, D.C., Philadelphia, and Pittsburgh, to note only the most significant.

Although these riots and disturbances numbered ultimately in the hundreds before V-J Day, they represented an almost infinitesimal loss to war production. But the intangible costs were literally incalculable. The tales of brawls, mob attacks, police brutality, and military indiscipline received full coverage in journals, newspapers, radio, and newsreels. Blacks were enraged by photos of bloody members of their race being escorted from the Detroit combat zone, while rangy transplanted hillbillies struck them in the face. Even that master of racist propaganda, Dr. Joseph Goebbels, piously deplored the condition of blacks in America.

The black military was not immune to the rage that issued in violence. In fact, significant military racial incidents far outnumbered those in civilian life, although often the two areas overlapped, with violent consequences. From early in the war the black public and black troops shared the often justified belief that the black soldier faced constant danger and threat long before he might face combat overseas. And the white public, particularly those near concentrations of black training areas, constantly feared a takeover or at least a wild rampage by armed blacks. In July of 1943, Army chief of staff Gen. George C. Marshall warned in a memo to all commanding generals that "disaffection among Negro troops continues to constitute an immediate and serious problem." It is unclear whether General Marshall actually meant "disaffection" in the sense of disloyalty, or simply confused that word with "dissatisfaction." But he was quite perceptive when he asserted:

All of the reported racial disturbances follow a fairly definite pattern. Unrest and disaffection begin with real or fancied incidents of discrimination and segregation. No positive action is taken to overcome the cause of irritation and unrest. Gossip or rumor of a nature designed to excite the men circulates among the units and a major incident brings on a general outbreak.

It should be noted that the chief of staff asserted that *all* of the reported military racial incidents followed this pattern.

The record seems clear that military racial outbreaks of violence began more often with "real" than with "fancied" grievances. The vast majority of such incidents took place in the South, a few in border states, and a very few in the North and West. In the South in the 1940s, of course, patterns of segregation had the sanction of law. One could be arrested for *not* enforcing such law as well as for not conforming to it, a powerful rationale for military commanders.

The earliest recorded military racial incident occurred even before Pearl Harbor, in April 1941, when white Civilian Conservation Corps youths and black Quartermaster troops fought each other over the use of a diving platform at the YMCA lake at Fort Jackson, South Carolina. Black troops were already aroused over the death earlier in the month of a black private found hanging from a tree at Fort Benning, Georgia. The death was ruled a suicide, although the trooper's hands had been tied behind his back. Racial incidents continued at Fort Jackson and in nearby Columbia until well into 1942.

As 1941 progressed, the incidents grew more savage. In Fayetteville, N.C., near the giant Fort Bragg army post, a shootout between white military police and a "cursing, jostling bus load" of black troops left two dead and five wounded, more or less evenly divided by race. In the North, a later racial military gun battle, again between white MPs and black soldiers, this time over a public telephone booth at Fort Dix, New Jersey, in April 1942, claimed one MP and two troopers dead. (Fort Dix, for some reason, seems to have been plagued by violence. A disturbance with no interracial overtones erupted among black troops at a USO dance hall, and resulted in the death of one soldier, the wounding of two others, and the beating of a black MP. And on Thanksgiving night 1942, a shooting affray between black troops and black MPs left no less than three dead and twelve seriously wounded.)

But, oddly, the incident that provoked the most national attention in the early war years resulted in no deaths or even serious injuries. In August

1942, something resembling a reign of terror was directed against black troops around the Arkansas town of Gurdon. There state troopers beat, cursed, and ran off uniformed black American soldiers, making a particular point of assaulting and abusing their white officers as "Yankee nigger lovers." Wire services took up the story, which then appeared in the Chicago *Tribune* and the New York *Times*. The episode seems to have been unprovoked. Months later, the battalion that had been on the receiving end of Arkansas law enforcement suffered from extremely high rates of such military pathology as poor morale, indiscipline, desertion, sickness, and slovenliness.

Such violence was making nonsense of the assertion by the Operations Division of the Army General Staff, in the very month of the first Fort Dix racial shootout, that current Army policies had "practically eliminated the colored problem, as such, within the Army." The proof: "The lack of any serious troubles between white and colored soldiers within the confines of military stations."

Despite the recent commitment to military segregation, some AAF officers were at least aware of the real situation. A Colonel Cooke from the inspector general's department noted:

Biracial incidents in the Army [of which the Air Forces were a component] were not premeditated and most of them could have been avoided through proper education, leadership, and discipline . . . Some local law enforcement agents in the South not only welcome the slightest excuse, but actually seek the opportunity, to shoot down Negroes.

Far more common among the high-ranking officers and civilian officers in the military was the tendency to blame most military racial trouble on the black press as well as on "agitators." Secretary of War Henry Stimson denounced most black journals as "shockingly biased and unreliable." John J. McCloy, assistant secretary of war, went further, labeling the black press as "subversive." A study of the black press yields almost no incitement to violence and little disaffection, but indeed shows a definite "bias" toward their own people. It hardly made sense for black editors to crusade for the rights of white people, who at any rate enjoyed far more opportunities for the redress of their grievances than did blacks. If the black press sometimes proved "unreliable," certainly the charge could be levied fairly on occasion against the white press, as witness the publication of top secret war plans by the Chicago *Tribune* on the eve of Pearl Harbor, or the premature reporting by a wire service reporter of the German surrender, despite his personal pledge of silence. More often, the black press could be fairly accused of sometimes garbling stories or of jumping to unsubstantiated conclusions. Again, the majority press could hardly plead innocent here. Perhaps the attitude of the World War II black press toward that war was best summarized by the black Amsterdam *Star-News* in the wake of the Fort Dix incident:

They [black soldiers] cherish a deep resentment against the vicious race persecution which they and their forbearers have long endured. They feel that they are soon to go overseas to fight for freedom over there. When their comparative new found freedom is challenged by Southern military police and prejudicial superiors, they fight for freedom over here.

Closer to home, the men of the 99th remembered the incident on the night of April 1, 1942, in which a black Tuskegee MP had retrieved, at gunpoint, a black military prisoner from a white town policeman. Town police, reinforced by a deputy sheriff, two Alabama state policemen, and about fifteen armed local citizens severely beat an MP and disarmed the MP patrol as they retrieved what must have been a terrified prisoner. White soldiers from Tuskegee Army Air Field, led by Colonel Parrish, managed to round up most of the black military personnel and return them to base, a base which many of the troops were preparing to defend against a suspected local white onslaught. Army Air Forces investigators, led by Gen. B. O. Davis, Sr., concluded that the black MP had been in the wrong in demanding custody of the prisoner, but implied that excessive force had been used by police. The prompt efforts of Colonel Parrish defused a potentially explosive situation that had been building since the beginning of the year. As noted above, the town of Tuskegee was hostile to blacks, and the local sheriff had earned a name for himself for his antiblack actions and attitudes. A riot of the Fort Jackson, Fayetteville, or Fort Dix magnitude could well have closed down the Army Air Forces's entire "experiment" in black military pilot training. Further town-base clashes were avoided by a peculiar arrangement recommended by Eastern Flying Training Command (EFTC), by which two lieutenants, one black and the other white, were promoted to captain with the promotion of the white to predate that of the black by one day. Both men would work in the provost marshal's office, but the white, by reason of "seniority," would become the provost marshal.

The year 1943 witnessed the worst national military racial violence of the war, just as that year also saw the worst civilian race riots since the "Red Summer" of 1919. Violent black-white violent confrontations erupted at Camp Van Dorn (Mississippi), Camp Stewart (Georgia), Lake Charles (Louisiana), March Field and Camp San Luis Obispo (California), Fort Bliss (Texas), Camp Phillips (Kansas), Las Vegas, Camp Breckinridge (Kentucky), and Camp Shenango (Pennsylvania).

The violence at Camp Van Dorn demonstrated how even a well-trained unit could turn aggressively defiant. In fact, in all of the incidents noted, blacks either initiated the particular violence or responded aggressively to provocation, a distinct change from previous years. The 364th Infantry Regiment had been trained at Fort Jackson during the period of the Columbia violence, and one battalion, the 367th, was later involved in a shooting with black MPs in Phoenix. Upon transfer to Camp Van Dorn, Mississippi, the reconstituted 364th, composed of a majority of Northern blacks, chafed under the unfamiliar, complex, and humiliating local seg-regation regulations and became aggressively unmilitary. A black trooper, without a pass and in improper uniform, was shot and killed by the county sheriff. An uproar ensued, quieted only by black MPs firing into a mob of 364th troops, wounding one. After a further incident in a dance hall, the 364th was finally sent off to the Aleutian Islands to wait out the war.

The Camp Stewart and Camp Shenango violence could have proved more serious, for there troops actually broke into military stores and seized arms and ammunition in the wake of civilian provocation, either to defend their areas or to "fight it out." In confused nighttime firing at Camp Stewart, one died and four were injured. In Camp Shenango, black prisoners broke out of the guardhouse and, joined by other soldiers, seized guns and ammunition. Before black and white MPs could restore control, one trooper had been shot dead and five wounded.

Random, individual violence scarred many black units. One died and three were wounded in the clash in Las Vegas, while the officers of the battalion slept in a nearby truck park. Previously, during the battalion's training period, several men had been shot by guards, or by accident while "playing around," and shortly before embarkation overseas a mess sergeant was hacked to death by three troopers intent on robbery.

A particularly unpleasant episode occurred at Fort Lewis, Washington, in August 1944, when a large group of black troops attacked Italian Service Unit ex-POWs. One of the Italians was "attacked outside of his barracks and carried away by at least five colored soldiers" and lynched. Army investigators blamed black resentment over supposedly better treatment of their former enemies, and agitation by "a Mulatto soldier." Two months later, a large-scale brawl between a black light-tank company and white paratroopers at Fort Patrick Henry, Virginia, left a civilian bystander dead of gunshot wounds.

Many black military units seemed to have no fear of the military police, white or black. During the last half of 1944 alone, "Negro soldiers cursed M.P.'s, wrecked a Post Exchange wall telephone, cut wires and overturned a juke box, at Camp Pickett, Virginia." At Columbus, Georgia, "seven colored soldiers forcibly took one soldier from the hands of the Military Police . . . and then returned later in a commandeered government truck and continued to fight with military police." At Camp Shelby, Louisiana, a particularly defiant truck company ensconced in the PX manhandled white company officers, refused to obey orders given in person by the post provost marshal, beat an assistant PX manager, and drove a black MP into the street with thrown beer bottles when he tried to restrain a trooper from looting the PX jewelry counter. Other black MPs were assaulted with fists and beer bottles. The fracas was only ended when MPs fired shots through the roof. When no less than two-thirds of the company defiantly admitted to involvement in the disorder, the division commander simply sent the mutinous company off to Fort Rucker, Alabama, the next morning. And earlier, in December 1942, two hundred black servicemen vowed to "clean up" Vallejo, California. Some of them charged hurriedly mobilized MPs, who opened fire with "tang [stun] guns." Two black soldiers were wounded, although neither seriously.

Black troops, of course, could in reply point to the authenticated cases of their fellows shot dead in uniform as a result of some infraction of the complex code of racial segregation and subordination then in effect throughout large areas of the nation.

The catalyst that impelled a significant change of racial attitudes and policy in the military establishment, however, was not this violence but the resignation of the civilian aide on Negro affairs to the secretary of war, Judge William Hastie, on January 5, 1943. Well before racial outbreaks had reached their crescendo in the summer of 1943, Judge Hastie had become increasingly alarmed and despondent over military racial attitudes and policies, particularly in the AAF. General Arnold he found "entirely out of sympathy with my efforts" and Assistant Secretary of War for Air Robert Lovett "politely disinterested." Specifically, Hastie, in his letter of resignation, protested: the AAF's establishment of Aviation Squadrons (Separate), a separate black clerical school, the refusal to train and utilize black service pilots and other officer technical specialists, the inadequate program of black flight surgeon training, the refusal to assign blacks to positions of responsibility at Tuskegee, the reluctance to continue the successful black enlisted training at Chanute Army Air Field, and the proposal for yet another segregated black training facility at Jefferson Barracks, Missouri.

Although the Army had, rather daringly, established integrated Officers Candidate Training facilities from the earliest days of the prewar defense program, the AAF, true to its mindless policy of extending military racial separation even to those areas where it had not previously existed, proposed a segregated OCS at Jefferson Barracks.

This last proposal may well have been the last straw for Judge Hastie. Four days after learning of the proposal from the press, he gave notice of his intent to resign. For Hastie, "the Air Forces are deliberately rejecting the general practice of unsegregated Officer Candidate Schools which has proved so eminently successful throughout the Army and which has been so hopeful an augury."

While it was not one of his stated reasons for resigning, the fact that Judge Hastie was not even informed of the formation of the Advisory Committee on Negro Troop Policies must also have rankled. Once again, as with the Jefferson Barracks proposal, the civilian aide on Negro affairs to the secretary of war was finding out about a development of primary concern to his office from the press.

As for Tuskegee, Judge Hastie asserted that the training there was so out of balance with the supporting specialist and combat assignments that "the entire future of the Negro in combat aviation was in jeopardy." Finally, Hastie warned that he would "give public expression to my views." The judge was as good as his word. His official statement of resignation on January 16 had merely stated his intention to resign and to request his two assistants, Louis Lautier and Truman Gibson, to remain at their posts. But after his resignation Hastie poured out his feelings in statements to the press, statements that were soon edited into a pamphlet entitled, "On Clipped Wings: The Story of Jim Crow in the Army Air Corps."

Arguing bluntly and accurately that the "Air Command did not want Negro personnel" in the first place, Hastie perceptively continued that "the tragedy is that by not wanting the Negro in the first place and by doubting his capacity, the Air Command has committed itself psychologically to courses of action which themselves become major obstacles to the success of Negroes in the Air Forces." "On Clipped Wings" outlined the discouraging struggle of black Americans to make their contribution to the USAAF at a time when all adult Americans were supposedly required to put themselves at the disposal of their government in a time of national peril. Hastie wryly concluded that "we Negroes are often forced to the conclusion that white men are very peculiar, so peculiar that amusement provoked by the ludicrous enables us to bear with some of our neighbors' whimsical ways."

For his dramatic gesture, Judge Hastie was awarded the NAACP's highest award, the Springarn Medal. He was succeeded in office by his assistant aide, Truman Gibson. Gibson had wished to resign along with Hastie, but had been persuaded by the judge to remain in order to preserve continuity. But the black public remained mostly unaware of Judge Hastie's confidence in Gibson, who was excoriated in an unwitting hilariously mixed metaphor by Congressman Adam Clayton Powell, Jr., as "the rubber stamp Uncle Tom who was used by the War Department."

It is undoubtedly true that Gibson enjoyed better relations with Secretary of War Stimson than had Hastie. Strong feelings carried over into the postwar years. Hastie is not mentioned in Stimson's memoirs, while Gibson is ignored in Walter White's autobiography, *How Far the Promised Land.* But the record is clear that Truman Gibson did not sell out his people. Well before Hastie's resignation Gibson had persisted, along with Roy Wilkins of the NAACP, in exposing the inequities of AAF segregation, and had early advocated that "the Air Corps be swamped with applications from young blacks who would like to be flying cadets." After Hastie's resignation, Gibson, in his new capacity of civilian aide on Negro affairs to the secretary of war, came to Tuskegee to inspect facilities, and went out of his way to assist Colonel Parrish during the numerous visits of the TAAF commanding officer to the Pentagon. The War Department would change its racial attitudes slowly, but credit for much if not most of that change must go to the black press, the NAACP, Judge Hastie, and Truman Gibson.

The Hastie resignation broke the log jam in military race relations. One later authority went so far as to assert that "since it [the Army Air Forces] was well aware of its vulnerability, it began to move with a speed and determination never observed before in the area of race relations," after Judge Hastie's resignation. The new chief of the Air Staff, Maj. Gen. George E. Stratemeyer, had personally assumed control of the AAF's faltering race relations and, as early as January 9 (even before Hastie's resignation) ordered the assistant chief of staff for operations "to collect all data and be prepared to submit a paper on our treatment of the Negro and his training within the Army Air Force[s]." The same day General Stratemeyer ordered a halt to the plan for segregated training at Jefferson Barracks, Missouri, and in fact mandated that all segregated AAF training should cease—except, of course, at Tuskegee.

Blacks would now be eligible for service pilot (e.g., reconnaissance, liaison) training and employment, and black air surgeon training would be taken with white candidates, not as previously, by correspondence course. General Stratemeyer's efforts are the more remarkable in light of his earlier apparent racial attitude, revealed in his comment while head of SEAACTC, that "commingling of white and colored races caused considerable damage to the morale of the Army personnel at Tuskegee," a comment that, incidentally, bore little or no relation to the facts.

But at least at the top of the AAF hierarchy, the attitude seems to have developed at this time that the black American was not so much biologically inferior as more likely the victim of economic deprivation, prejudice, and even institutionalized racism. Even nomenclature would change: "colored" was discouraged in favor of "Negro" (capitalized); out altogether were "negress" (with or without the capitalization), "darkey," "boy," or "uncle," not to mention "coon," and, of course, "nigger."

The formation of the Advisory Committee on Negro Troop Policies on August 27, 1942, as a means of coordinating black troop policies, might also be considered a modest step forward, although, as noted, Judge Hastie was not even informed on the matter. Assistant Secretary of War McCloy was named chairman, and the committee broadened its responsibilities to act as a clearinghouse for staff and civilian ideas on the uses of black troops. The original careful brief of the committee was that it would concern itself "strictly with military problems in the use of Negro troops and that the broader social problems" would be dealt with only incidentally. But the resignation of Judge Hastie compelled a broader outlook, exemplified by the committee's commissioning and distribution of the War Department pamphlet "Command of Negro Troops" (February 1944). However, the committee never stretched its mandate as far as desired by General Davis, who forthrightly urged "that the policy to be recommended by this committee have for its mission the breaking down of the so-called Jim Crow practices within the War Department on the military reservations." General Davis perceptively attributed military racial disorders on post and within the civilian black population to the relative inaction of the War Department.

Ironically, at the very time the AAF was planning its segregated Officers Candidate School at Jefferson Barracks, it had been operating an Officers Candidate School for over a year at Miami Beach, which was integrated in all but sleeping arrangements. Miami Beach must have been chosen by the AAF with more thought to its meteorological than to its racial climate, for at the time no blacks were permitted to dwell within the city's limits. (According to one informed source, blacks could not even pass through the town until World War I.) The owners of Miami Beach hotels commandeered by the Air Force swore they would be ruined if it ever became known that one black had spent the night in their hostelries. But the AAF persevered, and a state of something akin to racially integrated officer training prevailed. Still, no black cadet could rise to tactical officer over his squad, and none was permitted to drill white cadets, although the handful of black instructors could. Sometimes Miami Beach's racial customs could work to the advantage of black cadets. All were required to have their hair cut once a week. Since no white barber in the Beach would cut black hair, black cadets were trucked once a week into Miami—which was off limits to white cadets. Their tonsorial duties attended to, the black cadets could enjoy the rest of the afternoon on their own in Miami. On at least one occasion a staff car was requisitioned to transport a single cadet (who later rose to the Air Force rank of major general) in lone splendor to Miami for his haircut.

"Integrated" training for black medical officers could be even more traumatic. Lieutenant Vance Marchbanks, who was later to become the 332nd's group surgeon, remembered sitting in the segregated Fort Bragg, North Carolina, cafeteria, served by white waiters, but feeling with his fellows like "contaminated animals." Black medical officers there were denied Officers' Club privileges, and their request to use the adjacent base golf course was met by the baffling retort that "the people who built that course are now dead." A soft drink could be purchased at the Bragg PX only on condition that it be consumed outside. Perhaps the most disconcerting was the loon-like staring at the apparition of a black officer.

The training of black navigator and bombardier cadets initiated in 1943 proceeded smoothly in conditions of semi-segregation. At Hondo Field, Texas, black cadets lived in their own barracks and were instructed in classrooms reserved for them. But they ate in the same mess as white cadets and enjoyed equal access to the Cadet Club, cadet PX, and cadet day room. Black officers had the use of the bachelor officers' mess, and (significantly) the Officers' Club. The first class of black navigators graduated on February 26, 1944, after flying a training exercise to New York City that attracted national attention. Apparently the same general conditions prevailed at the bombardier school that trained blacks at Midland, Texas. Both the bombardier schools were in Texas, a state in which racial segregation was mandated by law. But apparently the cadets, white and black, were too busy with their training to become involved in any "incidents" on or off either base. Not all black officer trainees enjoyed such moderately benign conditions, however. Keesler Field, Mississippi, for example, was generally considered by blacks to be something fairly close to hell on earth.

Nonetheless, the War Department took vigorous steps to circulate its new military racial perceptions. Three pamphlets and three films were commissioned to familiarize commanders and their troops with the wartime contributions of black Americans and to outline approved methods of dealing with black troops. "Command of Negro Troops" seems to have been the most effective pamphlet. A no-nonsense primer for white officers commanding black troops, it could reward study by military commanders today. It plainly stated that Army general classification scores were not necessarily tests of innate intelligence. Further, men who scored in the low categories of IV and V, as did the bulk of black troops, required particular concern. Day room philosophers were laid low in the section headed "Racial Theories Waste Manpower," while the Double-V was analyzed sympathetically. Racial terms seemingly neutral for the time like "nigra," "boy," "darkey," "uncle," and "negress," were warned against, as was any retailing of dialect stories that officers might even have overheard among black troops. The pamphlet debunked theories that blacks possessed innate rhythmical, athletic, or musical abilities, and cautioned commanders against the excessive utilization of black troops in these overworked stereotypical roles. The heading "Little Expected, Little Gained" could be said to have summarized the main thrust of this unprecedented work.

"Leadership and the Negro Soldier" (ASF Manual M-5, October 1944) was a more elaborate extension of "Command of Negro Troops." It came equipped with tests and questionnaires and served as a text for a ten-hour course. Each of its eight chapters served as a lecture for a one-hour session, while another hour was to be devoted to the showing of the film, *The Negro Soldier,* and the final hour to a discussion of "Command of Negro Troops." The only significant criticism that could be made of either Army publication is that they were so late in coming. Surprisingly, the hard-hitting "Command of Negro Troops" encountered little opposition, even in the South. Perhaps the prefatory disclaimer in "Leadership and the Negro Soldier" served to disarm critics: "It is essential that there be a clear understanding that the Army has no authority or intention to participate in social reform as such but does view the problem as a matter of efficient troop utilization."

Not so fortunate was the fate of another Army pamphlet, "The Races of Mankind," prepared for a private educational organization by the distinguished anthropologists Ruth Benedict and Gene Weltfish of Columbia University. The Army Service Forces (ASF) were attracted to the work as a refutation of "master race" theories. But the House of Representatives Committee of Military Affairs investigated the pamphlet and its distribution and concluded that "wartime is no time to engage in the publication and distribution of pamphlets presenting controversial issues or promoting propaganda for or against any subdivision of the American people." Even before this rather curious piece of reasoning (the pamphlet could not, even by the most fine reasoning, be said to present a case "for or against any subdivision of the American people," but rather presented precisely the opposite), the work had been withdrawn from distribution.

The War Department made full use of film to propagate its changed attitudes. The first, and most publicized, was Frank Capra's *The Negro Soldier* (1944). Capra wrote to playwright Lillian Hellman that he intended "an emotional glorification of the Negro war effort" by tracing the history of black soldiers since the American Revolution. Emotional the film surely was, set in the framework of a well-dressed, musical black church. The film followed the progress of a black parishioner by means of flashbacks through basic training to Officers Candidate School. Reality does intrude in scenes in the soldier's outfit, which is all black, and in the Officers Candidate School, which is integrated. But how much reality can be claimed by a supposed historical treatment of black American soldiers which failed to mention slavery even while chronicling the Civil War, and ignored segregation and subjugation? Capra claimed that black publishers, editors, and writers were pleased and surprised by his confection, and the film was indeed shown with success in more than 3,500 "white" cinemas. Yet *The Negro Soldier* should be remembered as the first Hollywood film to deal with blacks at any length as more than figures of fun or menace.

More straightforward was *Wings for This Man*, a film short dealing with the Tuskegee Airmen and narrated by the well-known Hollywood liberal, Capt. Ronald Reagan, USAAF. This film was more successful in that it chose a limited theme and could ignore some unpleasant material without doing much violence to its historical integrity.

Five films can be identified as having been produced under the auspices of the War Department during World War II to improve military race relations. *The Negro Soldier* stands the test of time least well of the five, but even it was a vast improvement over the only known surviving effort along similar lines of World War I. *Training of Colored Troops* (c. 1917) featured interminable camp marching scenes, followed by a vague story line of an inducted black soldier, his "Rastus"-type father and "Mammy" mother. An almost obligatory watermelon-eating contest and a buck-and-wing dance provide the welcome ending.

All was not sweetness and enlightenment in the hierarchy of the USAAF, however. General Frank O'D. Hunter, commanding officer of the First Air Force, in a telephone conversation with Gen. Barney Giles, chief of the Air Staff, stated that he "didn't pay much attention" to "the War Department stuff" mandating the new racial policies. General Giles replied that "we were forced to do that," and approved Hunter's attitude. Giles was not simply holding Hunter's hand. A month earlier he had told the chief of staff of the First Air Force that "I reported to the Secretary of War a couple of days back that no matter what we did to those colored boys down there [Tuskegee], they would always be squawking and they're going to squawk until the war is over and probably a long time after the war."

Some supposed resistance to the War Department's new racial policies may have been simple ignorance. Just as Judge Hastie did not know about the formation of the Advisory Committee on Negro Troop Policies, neither did Undersecretary of War Patterson. Thus it is not surprising that Brig. Gen. Edgar E. Glenn, chief of staff of the First Air Force, was in ignorance of the committee as late as May 10, 1945, two days after V-E Day. General Glenn's reaction to the almost three-year-old news of the committee's existence gives the flavor of the times.

Glenn: The what?
Gen. Ray Owens (Air Staff): The McCloy Board. He is the Assistant Undersecretary of War. He has a board that is supposed to handle all colored affairs.
Glenn: Is he colored?
Owens: No, he's not, though he has one on his staff.

It is startling that a high-ranking officer of the First Air Force, of which the mostly black 477th Bombardment Group was a component, should be unaware of the race of the chairman of the Advisory Committee on Negro Troop Policies, and that another high-ranking officer would garble the rank of that chairman. (McCloy, of course, was the assistant secretary of war and a white man.)

General Arnold had to issue a letter to all AAF commanders noting that there seemed to be a feeling in some quarters "that the Army Air Forces are not complying with, and do not desire to comply with War Department policy as affects handling of Negro troops." He concluded that War Department policy "is automatically Army Air Forces policy." These changes in attitude came none too soon; in late 1943 Gen. B. O. Davis, Sr., and Truman Gibson reported, after a tour of Army camps, an increasing "implacable hatred of the Army" among black soldiers. And at the least, many black troops were performing submarginally in a war and in a nation that appeared to mean less to them than to white Americans.

The AAF were fortunate in that none of that service's personnel were involved in racial incidents leading to serious injury or death. Indiscipline there was, as at MacDill Army Air Force Base, Florida, in May 1943. An intoxicated black trooper fought with a white soldier in the base post exchange as a large and unruly crowd of blacks began to gather. Some of the black troops seized rifles from their barracks and wandered about for four to five hours before order was restored. The trouble seemed to have been the result of poor leadership. A bloody confrontation was barely avoided at Fairfax, South Carolina, when sixteen black officers from Walterboro Army Air Force Base, refused service at a "Whites Only" diner, began shouting "Go to hell!" and "Heil Hitler!," drawing a crowd of about 150 armed locals to the scene.

The AAF, like the Army, exercised a startling leniency in the face of racial incidents. In none of the confrontations noted so far was punishment meted out. And when in November 1944, an entire Aviation Squadron (Separate) mutinied at Herbert Smart Airport, Macon, Georgia, the blame fell upon their inefficient white officers. And even though the better known "Freeman Field 101" (see chapter 6) were courtmartialed for their attempt to integrate a "white" officers' club, only the "ringleader" was punished, and that was lightly.

Tuskegee Army Air Field itself was not immune to conflict on the home front, as the April 1942 incident amply demonstrated. And in August 1944 twelve black officers determined to integrate the PX cafeteria, which at the time was informally divided into "white" and "colored" sections. The interlopers were served on the other side of the invisible divide, but in a "tense" atmosphere. From then on, black personnel had the almost exclusive use of the cafeteria. Whites now "brownbagged" their lunches or drove into Tuskegee, often expressing their disgust with people supposedly keen to fly but who seemed more concerned with eating arrangements.

Yet those black officers were within their rights, for they were simply implementing a War Department directive of July 8, 1944, which stated that recreational and PX facilities were not to be denied on account of race. Nonetheless, Colonel Parrish felt obliged to explain to Tuskegee town officials that such theoretical race mixing was confined to TAAF.

For the rest of the war Tuskegee was spared further racial incidents. However, it had begun to burst at the seams by 1944 as a result of USAAF racial policies. TAAF now trained all pilot replacements for the 332nd, as well as most nonflying officers and enlisted personnel. At its peak the cadet flying school held no fewer than six hundred cadets in eleven training classes.

Although black navigators and bombardiers were now being trained elsewhere in somewhat integrated facilities without overt problems, it did seem that the considered policy of the AAF was to dump every black flying and ground program it could in TAAF. In addition to the pre-aviation, pre-flight, advanced single engine, advanced twin engine, and P-40 transition programs, Haitian and French Colonial aviation cadets (who were after all, primarily black) were trained, along with black Army liaison pilot cadets. Two dozen black Signal Corps cadets wandered forlornly about the base after one of their two aircraft warning companies was disbanded, and some remained in this useless limbo until the end of the war. The 648th Ordnance Company (Provisional) squatted at TAAF while headquarters, Third Air Force, and Colonel Parrish tried to determine who had jurisdiction over the orphan unit. This problem was finally resolved by the simple expedient of dissolving the 648th. Apparently the worst month was August 1944, when TAAF was burdened with 105 nonrated black officers, with AAF Officers Candidate School at San Antonio funneling an additional eight new black second lieutenants each month. The figures given for the ratio of enlisted men to officers averaged one officer to every four and one-half enlisted men, or, put another way, five to six officers for each job. Exacerbating the problem was the War Department's assigning of fifty liaison pilot cadets for training at TAAF. Along with these fifty cadets came fifty new aircraft of a different type and speed from those usually found at the field, enormously complicating the work of the control tower crew. Although cadets were finally trained at an auxiliary field, they were still under the control of TAAF. Undoubtedly the most depressing element was the presence at the field of washed-out cadets. These eliminees had no place to go (as noted, until early 1942 black eliminees were simply discharged to face their local draft boards), unlike white eliminees who had the option of training for other roles, such as bombardiers and navigators. Even when nonflying training was opened to black AAF cadets, it was limited in extent and did little to draw down the pool of surplus officers and eliminees. Although all of the latter were given assignments around the base, much of their employment smacked of "make-work," and their presence in large numbers at TAAF did nothing for morale.

Tuskegee Army Air Field was unique. While almost all AAF training fields specialized in one phase or another of military flying, TAAF carried the cadet from college instruction through the awarding of his wings as a combat pilot in the USAAF, and his initial assignment, all within a complex of bases and installations no more than five miles apart, and surrounded by a more or less hostile countryside. The commandant of cadets held responsibility for no fewer than eight different types of classes. Not surprisingly, the lines of command coalesced, crossed, and contradicted each other, with portions of the complex coming under Third Air Force, Air Services Command, and the Flying Training Command. The most vivid example of this confusion could be seen along the flight line, as swift Air Force P-40 fighter planes mixed with slow, hedge-hopping Army liaison craft to the consternation of control tower personnel.

Yet the AAF calmly planned to add navigator-bombardier training for blacks to the burdens of TAAF. Colonel Parrish was almost vehement in protesting the imposition, concluding that

This is certainly a waste of manpower and malassignment of personnel and a se-rious imposition on this station as these men are not needed, can serve no useful purpose at this station, and constitute a serious drain upon our personnel which has to be assigned to care for them. This office has made repeated reports of this matter and to date no relief has been forthcoming.

Higher headquarters of the AAF finally did offer relief by training naviga-tors and bombardiers at existing schools, as noted, thus breaking with the AAF "tradition" of segregating all black aviation training at the Tuskegee complex.

Tuskegee Army Air Field was driven to some rather transparent expe-diences in its attempts to find work for superfluous personnel. In the spring of 1944 the newly created position of assistant post beautification officer was announced, followed by those of assistant to the assistant mess officer, and assistant to the assistant supply officer. Colonel Parrish was well aware of this absurd situation and of the reasons for it. Not only had the man to be matched to the job, but in the AAF's policy of racial segregation, a black man had to be matched to a job that was open to blacks. The job could not put him in authority over a white man, and it had to be performed in a black unit only. And, of course, the man had to be qualified. As Colonel Parrish wrote soon after the war, "practically every policy, every directive, and every plan had its special Negro-White angle which was usually overlooked or evaded until serious difficulty resulted." For example, there could be a shortage of white combat intel-ligence officers, while a surplus of black combat intelligence officers sat around TAAF (possibly slaving away as assistants to the assistant supply officer), because there were no black combat intelligence units with open slots at the time. Parrish further noted that he had to take "scores of cross country flights to the Pentagon to secure decisions on matters that had become so involved that normal channels of command had completely failed to produce decisions."

Tuskegee Army Air Field also appears to have been something of a center for "radical" opinion. The adjutant general of the SEAACTC reported in 1942 that "it is believed that a small minority of personnel on duty at the station concerned are radically inclined and are participating in agitation to keep alive race questions and questions of social equality," but added that these personnel were being "ferret[ed] out." The official history of SEAACTC/SEAAFTC concluded that such "energetic socialists who were over enthusiastic [in its opinion] in crusading for Negro equality should not be allowed to occupy important positions in Tuskegee," but added that "if a Negro insisted on violating the segregation rules, he was transferred to Tuskegee where his disaffection would not be so noticeable among such a large number of Negroes or out of the Command entirely." Looking back through the more equable perspective of over three decades, the late General Parrish conceded that some actual Communist party members and "fellow travelers" did work in his command, but that, in those days of solidarity with "our glorious Soviet Ally" they did not interfere with the program or agitate in any way.

Despite the crowding, confusion, and make-work, the primary mission of the Tuskegee complex, military aviation for blacks, continued without interruption. The racial incidents described earlier remained the only developments that might have affected the efficiency of the base. Much of the credit for the relatively calm racial relations as well as the efficiency of TAAF must go to Colonel Parrish, who in turn attributed the situation to the "serious and concerned effort on the part of instructors and students alike, and a uniform determination not be distracted by minor issues. Negroes have proved their value and capacity far beyond the expectations of skeptics, and white personnel of varying backgrounds have developed a good humored adaptability and an easy going effectiveness which is sometimes bewildering to visitors and inspectors."

More of those "visitors and inspectors" should have come to TAAF to witness the circumstances of large numbers of armed blacks training in "easygoing" relationships with a minority of whites, a number of whom

were apparently of radical political bent. For throughout the war the AAF
and the War Department held to the belief, in the absence of convincing
evidence, that communist or Axis agents were responsible in large part
for military and civilian racial strife. For example, Army Intelligence
reported "subversive groups at work among the Negro population," but
confessed itself unable to find evidence of such groups or of their agents.
The AAF *Intelligencer,* a monthly military intelligence journal, carried
items on black subversion or anticipated black subversion in almost every
issue, again with little or no corroboration.

The reason for this lack of firm evidence of black American support of
"un-American" causes should have been obvious even at the time: Nazi
racial theories and practices, of course, were deeply repugnant to a
people traditionally victimized by racism.

Whatever appeal communism may have had to black Americans was
mobilized into total support for the war during the German invasion of the
"Socialist Motherland" on June 22, 1941. In fact, the "Communist Party
of the USA" was itself transmogrified into the "Communist Political Association" (CPA) in May 1944. Although the novel CPA continued to press
for an end to racial segregation, the effect of such efforts was largely
vitiated by the association's denunciation of the black March on Washington Movement as "too belligerent," and the refusal of the Southern Youth
Congress, a communist affiliate, meeting at Tuskegee Institute in 1942, to
endorse the Double-V. As for racial segregation in the military, a communist official admitted in 1945 that "we criticized, but seldom led, vigorous
struggles against racial segregation in the armed forces."

These efforts of the Party/Association must have borne some fruit,
however, for despite Army Intelligence suspicions of communist subversion, Capt. Robert Diez was actually dispatched to a CPA meeting as a
representative of TAAF. Captain Diez spoke a few innocuous words of
greeting and was thereupon offered a lifetime membership!

The Japanese, with their slogan of "Asia for the Asiatics," held some
initial appeal for American blacks. The assistant chief of staff, Army G-2,
believed that 80 to 90 percent of blacks were pro-Japanese in 1940, and
that such black groups as the Nation of Islam and the United Negro
Improvement Association were subversive even after Pearl Harbor. What
could the Army do? G-2 suggested the calling of attention to the rapid
gains in black conditions in the last decade, and an "effective 'smear'
campaign linking Japs with Nazis." The AAF, in turn, considered the

formation of a "special unit of colored agitators." Fortunately, this "dirty dozen" scheme was turned down by higher authority. Throughout the war, despite continued attention by military intelligence, firm evidence of subversive activity among blacks in military service was conspicuously lacking. It remained easier to speculate about "subversives" than to admit that the problem was almost entirely domestic in its origins and in its continuance. No thorough attempt was made by any federal authority to uncover the causes of military racial disturbances. For many black Americans, civilian and military, the home front had indeed become a battle front.

The 332nd Fighter Group 5.

The black 332nd Fighter Group was activated on October 13, 1942, at Tuskegee Army Air Field. Consisting of the 100th, 301st, and 302nd fighter squadrons, and later of the pioneer 99th, this group remained the sole black fighter group of the Second World War.

The 100th Fighter Squadron had been activated on May 26, 1942, at Tuskegee. The squadron was transferred to Selfridge Army Air Field, Michigan, in March 1943 to continue combat training, but within a month had moved on to Oscoda Army Air Field, Michigan. The final two squadrons of the 332nd, the 301st and the 302nd, had been activated earlier in the year at Tuskegee, and had also made the transfer to Oscoda due to overcrowding at TAAF.

The formation of an all-black fighter group had been considered by Undersecretary of War Robert P. Patterson as early as January 16, 1942. It would provide an opportunity for increased black participation in the Army Air Forces, while remaining within the framework of racial segregation. Although evidence is lacking, Judge Hastie undoubtedly muted his enthusiasm. Certainly Walter White of the NAACP recorded that "there were many of us who felt such a step would be a mistake." But in the established circumstances of the day no other course seemed possible.

When the news was first released that the black 332nd would train at Selfridge Army Air Field, the local county board of supervisors objected, but they had their knuckles rapped by Michigan's governor and both senators. Upon arrival, the fledgling group was welcomed by local authorities and citizens, as well as by blacks from nearby Detroit, all of whom were impressed by the group's esprit and precision drill. Intensive flight and gunnery training kept the airmen too busy to ponder, in the words of Judge Hastie, the "whimsies" of whites. This was wartime combat training, and lives were lost in air accidents as the group accumulated skill, experience, and confidence.

The first two commanding officers of the 332nd were white, temporary, officers. Lieutenant Colonel Samuel Westbrook, a Georgian who performed adequately, seems nonetheless to have left little impression. But his successor, Col. Robert "Get to your damn guns" Selway, was able to build the group into a disciplined unit. However, when Selway went on to become C.O. of the all-black 477th Bombardment Group (Medium), he actively carried out segregation policies that resulted in the "Freeman Field 101" confrontation and the practical collapse of the 477th as a fighting organization (see chapter 6).

All of the pilots of the 332nd had already undergone the standard twenty hours of transition P-40 fighter training at Tuskegee, but the Selfridge-Oscoda program was plagued with delays. Original equipment consisted of war-weary P-40Cs from the First Air Force. A former line chief recalled that in a few cases ground crews had to use fire hoses to spray water on the Allison engines to prevent overheating while the old crates were warming up on the flight line. Some of the P-40s were emblazoned with the familiar "shark's mouth" popularized by the Flying Tigers, who used similar equipment, giving rise to the rumor in the black press that the 332nd was forced to use leftover Flying Tigers.

It was thus a relief for the men of the group, pilots and ground crew alike, to receive their new fighters, P-39 Airacobras originally designated for Lend-Lease to America's allies. Although it was inferior even to the P-40 workhorse, at least the Airacobra's engine would not burn up. An odd aircraft, it had a water-cooled engine mounted behind the pilot, driving the prop by a hollow shaft passing through the cockpit. The pilot straddled the shaft, whose gearing made strange noises on its way to the prop and which did double duty as a cannon barrel. Altogether, quite a bit of activity could be taking place between the legs of the distracted pilot of a Bell Airacobra. Still, the aircraft was a more nimble fighter than the heavy P-40, and it won some praise from the 332nd's pilots, at first.

In June 1943, another first was established when nine officers of the 332nd were assigned to attend an air intelligence school for training in combat intelligence—the first black officers to be assigned to nonsegregated training. In October 1943, Colonel Selway was relieved by Col. Benjamin O. Davis, Jr. The grapevine had tingled with rumors of Davis's impending return to the States and assignment as commanding officer of the group. His arrival was greeted, in the words of the official history of the 332nd, with "broad grins." Colonel Davis's arrival as C.O. coincided with the end of a week-long tour of inspection of the group by Colonel Davis's father, Gen. B. O. Davis, Sr.

Dawn-to-dusk training continued, with no more than the usual number of accidents. An incident with a happy ending occurred when Lt. S. M. Ellington became separated from his flight. Having exhausted his fuel, Ellington could see only a well-traveled four-lane highway as a landing site with any promise. He found a break in the traffic, put down successfully and, aided by the P-39's tricycle landing gear, which permitted excellent visibility, bowled along the highway to the nearest filling station, opened the auto door–like cockpit, and told the startled attendant to "fill 'er up!"

General Frank O'D. Hunter, C.O. of the First Air Force, of which the 332nd was a component part, addressed all group personnel on October 17, 1943, stressing (rather gratuitously) the requirement for strict discipline. He promised that everything possible would be done to get the 332nd into combat within the next few months, and closed with the ominous and familiar observation that "the activities of the 332nd will be closely followed by everyone of the First Air Force." Would the activities of the 331st or the 333rd be followed as closely? General Hunter, like Colonel Selway, would later earn notoriety in the Freeman Field incident for his full backing of Colonel Selway's enforcement of segregation for the 477th.

By November, training cycles were coming to their close; some would claim later that, like the 99th, the 332nd was being "overtrained." A flying evaluation board weeded out those whose flight proficiency was deemed below par, and rumors of an imminent embarkation to a war zone spread quickly. On December 16 the enlisted men of the group threw their farewell party; four days later the officers and their wives and sweethearts held a similar brilliant but bittersweet affair in Detroit. The following day all personnel were restricted to base, and on December 22 the group boarded troop trains for Fort Patrick Henry, Virginia, their port of embarkation for the war.

The 332nd's "war" would begin even before they reached foreign shores, however. At Patrick Henry the men found that a roped-off section of the base cinema had been designated for black use. An immediate flare-up resulted, and all personnel were confined to quarters on Colonel Davis's orders. But the 332nd's C.O. went beyond this action. He warned the base commander that he would not be responsible for his men if the theater segregation was not ended. The ropes came down, and talk of violence ceased, but such areas as clubs and rest rooms remained segregated or closed altogether to the men of the 332nd. In the sardonic words of the group surgeon, "There were no 'off to the wars feelings of pride' and external patriotic demonstrations as exhibited by our fellow white brothers-in-arms. The wounds of our patriotic pride would take a long time to heal and, when they did heal, they left a deep and ugly scar. About the best thing that could happen would be an early departure"—to combat.

And depart they finally did, on the evening of January 2, 1944, but not before last-minute telephone calls were permitted, calls that often necessitated waiting in line, from captains to privates, for up to six hours before reaching the phone. In pouring rain the group personnel embarked upon a convoy of Liberty ships for an Atlantic voyage punctuated by only one submarine scare. (Troop ships are floating rumor mills, and the 332nd's abounded with the usual tales: "We hit a whale last night," "We're surrounded by a U-boat wolfpack," "There's a flu epidemic and the officers are secretly burying the dead at sea by night.")

The 332nd's convoy somehow made it to the southern Italian port of Taranto on February 3. The harbor was still littered with the wrecks of Italian fleet units, sunk in the brilliant British aerial torpedo attack of three years previous. The sight was of more than casual interest to the men of the 332nd. For the Royal Navy's Fleet Air Arm's surprise torpedo attack on a heavily defended shallow harbor had preceded the Japanese attack on Pearl Harbor, but Great Britain and Italy had been at war.

The 332nd's introduction to "Sunny Italy" was hardly auspicious, and contrasted sharply with the near idyllic entry to the war zone that had greeted the men of the 99th a year earlier. Rain, mud, and snow, either alternating or combined, beat upon the 332nd's tent city, and the group's collective misery was aggravated by an inexplicable foul-up that had delayed their indispensable overshoes.

By February 8, the three squadrons and the group detachment were reunited at Montecorvino Air Base, ready for action. The 100th Fighter Squadron, having preceded its two sister squadrons, had been on combat duty since February 5.

The three squadrons were gradually broken in to combat in the relatively undemanding roles of convoy escort, harbor protection, scrambles, and point patrolling, extending from Cape Palermo and the Gulf of Policastro to the Ponziane Islands. By the middle of the month the group had settled into permanent quarters, drawn its first pay, and received its first letters.

On February 21 the 100th Fighter Group moved to Capodichino Air Field for a permanent change of station. The 99th at this time was still covering the Anzio-Nettuno beachhead, also from Capodichino, and remained attached to the 79th Fighter Group.

Montecorvino now also enjoyed the benefits of an electrical power generator, the installation of which was celebrated with drinks all around amidst the unaccustomed electric light. More "progress" could be seen in the establishment of an accident board (three pilots had already been killed as a result of mishaps), and a special court-martial board.

Also in that busy month, Mt. Vesuvius's catastrophic eruption coated the Montecorvino Field with ash but caused little damage, in contrast to the havoc wrought upon bases closer to the volcano.

On March 17 the 332nd encountered its first enemy aircraft, a Ju-88 reconnaissance ship, apparently making its daily "milk run" over the Naples area. Lieutenants Laurence D. Wilkins and Weldon K. Groves were able to intercept the enemy and shoot up one wing, but the Luftwaffe machine escaped. Eleven days later another Ju-88 reconnaissance aircraft was intercepted and damaged, but again managed to escape its pursuers. The 332nd was flying the P-39Q Airacobra at this time, and it is indicative of the combat inferiority of the plane that enemy reconnaissance aircraft on two separate occasions could escape. In the words of one of the frustrated pilots, Lt. William R. Melton of the 302nd, "the

Airacobras just didn't have enough to close in, and at that altitude, he just walked away from us."

Even prior to this, Air Force headquarters had intended to re-equip the 332nd with a later model of the P-39, the P-63 Kingcobra, but production and testing delays made the change impossible.

General Ira Eaker, Mediterranean Allied Air Force C.O., urged that the group's P-39s be replaced with a fighter of vastly superior performance, the P-47 Thunderbolt. This fighter, known understandably as the "Jug," was an enormous, radial-engine machine, larger than some prewar single-engine transport aircraft. If issued to the 332nd, the Thunderbolt would, in General Eaker's words, "take a lot of political pressure" off Army Air Forces headquarters to issue the 332nd with first-line equipment. Further, the high-altitude P-47 would be better for the group in that the Anzio beachhead battle had supposedly shown that "the colored combat pilots fly better against the Germans in the air than they do on the ground support mission." Finally, General Eaker repeated the old saw that "colored troops do not normally stand cold weather very well," and that therefore the P-47's cockpit, amply warmed by that giant engine up front, would be even more welcome by the group's pilots. On April 25, the group received its first six, secondhand, P-47Ds, which were evenly distributed among the three squadrons.

On April 15 the 301st and 302nd fighter squadrons had joined the 100th at Capodichino Army Air Field, keeping close to the line of combat as it moved up the Italian "boot." The new base became the focus of enemy attention within nine days of the move. April 24 saw between thirty and forty Ju-88s pound the base. Although damage was surprising slight, foxhole digging, previously considered a chore, became considerably more popular. To keep the men even more on their toes, something called a "Roving Court" made its rounds, assessing on-the-spot penalties upon unwary airmen.

German raids and the Roving Court could not slow the provision of such amenities as a Red Cross station, featuring (at least at its opening) real American ice cream, a PX, the beginnings of base movies, and a group rest camp.

The 332nd's squadrons continued to fly their patrols—strafing, coastal surveillance, and dive-bombing missions in support of Allied ground forces in the Rome area—and incurred their share of casualties.

It must have been with something akin to despair that the men of the 332nd learned that they were to be uprooted once again, to leave some other outfit to enjoy their painstaking improvements, and to relocate at Ramitelli Air Field, near Ancona, on the east coast of Italy. The group had to begin again the wearying cycle of beginning with pup tents, "C" rations, and helmet baths. But the move made sense from a military standpoint, again bringing the group closer to the action. The 332nd was at the same time transferred from the XII Air Force to the XV Air Force. The group now had a new mission, bomber escort, although it could still be utilized in ground support and in attacking targets of opportunity. The 332nd was now also a component of the 306th Fighter Wing.

General Eaker's attitude toward black aviators seems to have been considerably modified by this date, probably as a result of the 99th's creditable record. The day after the 332nd was transferred, with their "Razorback" P-47s to the XV Air Force, General Eaker noted,

These colored pilots have very high morale and are eager to get started on their new strategic task accompanying long range heavy bombers. I talked with General Strothers [sic], their Wing Commander, today. He has watched them closely in their indoctrination phase and he feels, as I do, that they will give a good account of themselves.

General Eaker's confidence was not misplaced. On June 9, on only the third mission of the group from Ramitelli, 332nd pilots shot down five enemy Bf 109s in the Udine area. Thirty-nine Thunderbolts had taken off from Ramitelli at 0700 (with only three aborts), and rendezvoused with the bombers they were to escort as top cover. As the combined formation reached Udine, four Bf 109s made a diving attack from 5 o'clock high on a formation of B-24 Liberators, then made a left turn. In the words of Lt. Wendell Pruitt:

As the Jerries passed under me I rolled over, shoved everything forward, dove and closed in on one Me-109f at 475 miles per hour. I gave him a short burst of machine gun fire, found I was giving him too much lead so I waited as he shallowed out of a turn. Then I gave two long two second bursts. I saw his left wing burst into flame. The plane exploded and went straight into the ground, but the pilot bailed out safely.

The group lost one pilot and plane, but five enemy kills was sweet revenge.

The group continued successful, uneventful bomber-escort missions, but on June 22 it suffered a heavy blow. On that date the commanding officer of the 100th Fighter Squadron, Capt. Robert B. Tresville, and two other 100th pilots were lost. Captain Tresville planned to fly low over the Tyrrhenian Sea to Corsica to evade enemy coastal radar. But the flight met disaster as Lt. C. B. Johnson, then lieutenants Earle Sherard and Samuel Jefferson hit the water. Only Lieutenant Sherard survived. Captain Tresville, apparently unaware of the disaster and disoriented, was seen glancing at his knee map when his Thunderbolt plunged into the sea. So great was the plane's momentum that it continued *under water* for about fifty feet. In his death agony Tresville must have pulled back on the stick, for his fighter actually reemerged, skipped over a wing man, and finally fell back into the water to find its permanent resting place. Lieutenant Woodrow Crockett, deputy flight commander, attempted to complete the mission but was unable to find a break in the low, solid cloud cover. That cloud cover was probably the cause of the disaster, for long-distance flying over water beneath a cloud cover can lead to pilot disorientation, and an inability to distinguish between cloud and water. At the subsequent squadron debriefing the surviving pilots of the mission blamed the crashes on flying too low and for too long over water.

The 100th Squadron still had much to learn; one of the pilots lost due to the cloud cover, for example, apparently had survived the crash after making a perfect belly landing, but had neglected to open his canopy first, and went down with his plane. And, as noted, Captain Tresville had become confused with his direction as well as his altitude. These were common enough mistakes for a new squadron flying long-range combat missions for less than a month. But the lessons had to be paid for in lives.

All of the 332nd's squadrons were out on the flight line the next day for an uneventful bomber-escort mission to the Sofia, Bulgaria, area. But mission number 11 on June 25 proved to be something unique, a maritime strafing escapade that netted the 332nd a destroyer.

All three squadrons were dispatched to strafe enemy troops in Yugoslavia, Albania, and northern Italy. Finding none, they ranged down the Italian coastline to the Pola-Isola-Trieste area where they spotted a German destroyer off Pisaro. The Thunderbolts dived in for the attack, scored hits, and watched the enemy warship explode and sink. The formation hardly paused before attacking radar or radio stations in the wharf area and enemy vehicles. A sailboat that had the temerity to open fire on the Thunderbolts was summarily dispatched. For all this destruction, the 332nd flight suffered only one slightly damaged aircraft. Both Capt. Wendell Pruitt and Lt. Gwynne Pierson were later awarded the Distinguished Flying Cross (DFC) for the destruction of the destroyer.

Missions for the rest of June 1944 were "uneventful" in that no enemy opposition was encountered on any mission, although men of the 332nd still died in aircraft mishaps. Particularly depressing was the death of Lt. Othell Dickson, a young cadet who had come to Tuskegee covered with honors: top aerial gunner of EFTC and third best nationwide. He arrived with a "hot pilot" reputation that he maintained by stunt flying; a slow roll over Ramitelli ended in death for Dickson and a loss for the 332nd. Those who were convinced that Colonel Davis was a martinet who didn't appreciate youthful high spirits could ponder Lieutenant Dickson's fate—which was not uncommon.

Late in June the first of the P-51 Mustang fighters began to arrive at Ramitelli. These were the early B and C "Razorback" models, which lacked the bubble canopy. While the comparative merits of both fighters are still debated, most of the pilots of the 332nd, from their C.O. down, seemed to have preferred the Mustang for its handling. These sentiments may not be entirely fair, as the 332nd had flown its P-47s for only one month before their introduction to the P-51, B and C models. But the 99th and the 332nd could certainly claim that their opinions were not parochial; by the summer of 1944 they had flown secondhand P-39s, P-40s, P-47s, and P-51s in combat, and no other Army Air Forces squadron or group could make that claim.

The Allies by this time had secured domination of the Italian skies, and the USAAF scrubbed its olive-drab and light gray paint scheme to reduce maintenance. From the summer of 1944 until the end of the war, USAAF aircraft retained their pristine aluminum finish. The pilots of the 332nd were usually identified by their 51s' all-red tail surfaces, hence the name "The Red Tails" for the group. Further, aircraft of the component squadrons could be distinguished by the color painted on the trim tabs; the 99th, white; the 100th, black; the 301st, blue; and the 302nd, yellow. Just aft of the propeller were more prominent distinguishing markings; the 99th sported a dark blue and white checkerboard; the 100th a solid red panel; the 301st was believed to be blue and red; and the 302nd carried alternate red and yellow horizontal stripes. The pioneer 99th alone carried proudly an *A* in conjunction with the aircraft number.

Finally, all fighters of the group sported red spinners and red wing bands. Again the 99th was somewhat different; its bands did not extend to the wing tips as did those of the other three squadrons.

Unofficial aircraft markings of the Second World War evolved into something of a folk art form throughout the USAAF. Pilots and ground crew devised slogans, messages, puns, designs, nudes, or combinations therefore unequaled before or since. Female anatomical charms and tints were carefully rendered, usually in conjunction with a punning motto (for example, "Bottoms Up!"). More chaste inscriptions or humor were not unusual, however. Some reflected black American life of the 1940s: "High Yellow," "Fatha," "A Train," "Good Wiggle," and "Harlem Speaks."

The month of July 1944 opened with the transfer of the 99th Fighter Squadron to the 332nd Fighter Group, making the 332nd unique in yet another way, as the only fighter group to comprise four squadrons. Spectacular sixty-eight-plane takeoffs from Ramitelli were now not uncommon.

This transfer represented the fifth change of parent for both the 99th and the 332nd. (The 99th was twice attached to two groups, the 33rd and the 324th, so the transfer to the 332nd was the sixth move.) This move was none too popular with the men of the 99th. They had established an excellent rapport with the 79th, as noted, and looked upon the 332nd as an amateur outfit. But, more significantly, the feeling was common among the 99th that removal from the white 79th and attachment to the black 332nd was a step backward toward total segregation. Lieutenant Colonel George S. Roberts, the 99th's C.O., found such an attitude reprehensible, and had harsh words for the men of his unit; according to Colonel Roberts, a harmonious relationship did not emerge until about three months after the units were officially joined.

While the 99th had been assigned a few P-47s for transitional training before its final transfer (and soon had them taken away), for the most part the squadron had been flying the old P-40 Warhawk. A transfer to the 332nd meant transition to the far superior P-51 Mustang. Yet that transition took a heavy toll. Captain Mac Ross, former group operations officer and former C.O. of the 100th Squadron, the first black member of the Caterpillar Club, and a member of the original Tuskegee Class (42-C), was killed in a Mustang, as was Capt. Leon Roberts, operations officer of the 99th, on the following day. At the time of his death, Captain Roberts had accumulated 116 combat sorties.

These mishaps suffered by experienced combat pilots were probably indicative of the low morale suffered by the 99th at the time of transfer to the 332nd. The squadron was also in poor physical condition. According to the group surgeon, nearly 50 percent of this veteran squadron's pilots had to be grounded, and many of the remainder were in no state to continue combat without a rest. To aggravate matters, apparently the 99th had no squadron medical officer. But most of the men were returned to duty fairly quickly. Under Capt. Vance Marchbanks's regimen, treatment included Saturday night sessions in the group surgeon's tent, in which pilots were invited to discuss personal or professional matters with other flight surgeons. Here was an opportunity to discover incipient psychological problems before they grew beyond the capacity of the group to deal with them. As a result, according to Captain Marchbanks, only one 332nd pilot had to be removed for serious neurosis.

One problem remained beyond the reach of the group surgeon or any other medical facilities—the high number of missions that had to be flown by the 99th and the 332nd. General Eaker explained the problem accurately to Gen. Barney Giles of the Air Staff: "In the recent past, it has been necessary to require the colored pilots to fly more missions prior to retirement from combat than the white pilots in corresponding fighter units in order to retain the 332nd at the same effective fighter strength."

General Eaker noted that fifty missions was the normal cutoff point for pilots (at which stage in his career a pilot could pound the unofficial and glamorous "fifty-mission crush" into his garrison cap). But the 332nd could not move its veteran pilots laterally to other units for noncombat assignments so easily; they could only go to other black (nonflying) units, which were relatively few in number and often overstaffed with officers. In the words of General Giles, "We are dealing with a relatively small, and therefore inflexible program." Giles went on to note that the output at Tuskegee barely met the need for replacements, but concluded that "these Negro units must be given a thoroughly square deal." The men of the 332nd were caught again in the system of military racial segregation. It should have been simple enough to rotate fifty-mission veterans back to Tuskegee as instructors, as was the case with white pilots. But this move would have upset the fixed Tuskegee pattern of white instructors teaching black students, and was apparently never seriously considered.

As for the shortage of black pilots, one solution might have been to open another black flying school, but this would have proved prohibitively expensive. Yet Tuskegee itself was filled to capacity, and could not have been significantly expanded further without becoming impossibly unwieldy. The only other solution would have been to train black pilots at the established Army Air Forces's flying schools, such as Randolph or Kelly Field, but this would have been a breach of the Army Air Forces's committed policy of racial segregation and thus was also not seriously considered, so far as is known. Instead, commanders contemplated expedients such as the disbanding of one of the 332nd's squadrons (politically impossible, of course) or, as suggested by General Arnold in all apparent seriousness, to order an individual veteran pilot home forthwith, and if even this proved impossible the pilot's mother should be so informed. These were no solutions, and to the end of the war, pilots of the 332nd could total up to 125 missions on tours of duty.

At least there were no more moves. Ramitelli Field remained the home of the 332nd to V-E Day. The base was large and relatively well appointed, and only the tricky takeoff pattern, usually over the Adriatic, posed any problem. The runway was constructed of perforated steel mat, not as good as concrete, but still one of the great unsung achievements of World War II. Finally, Ramitelli's close proximity to the bomb line made for relatively quick rendezvous with the bombers that the 332nd pilots were to shepherd. The transfer of the 99th to the 332nd was part of an Allied strategy to cut rail lines in the Po River valley. The tactical air power would pound the rail communications to the German front while the strategic bombers would penetrate far beyond that front and hit transportation facilities, particularly railway yards, that were beyond the reach of the tactical fighters.

The expanded 332nd lost no time in carrying out its part of the Allied interdiction strategy. On July 12, the day after the loss of Roberts, the group escorted B-17s of the 5th Bombardment Wing on a mission against railway yards in southern France. Captain Joseph D. Elsberry, assigned to lead the flight (which on this mission did not include the 99th), ordered the 100th and 302nd to climb above the overcast. This deployment lessened the chances of midair collisions amid the overcast, but it also resulted in a formation that covered about forty miles of sky. The flight reached the bomber rendezvous two minutes late, but the bombers proved to be five minutes behind schedule. The flight fell in over the bombers and commenced to fly a protective "weave" pattern over their charges. About ten minutes after crossing the French coast they sighted a group of aircraft at 10 o'clock high, which bored in on the bombers in a trail formation. Recognizing the enemy, Elsberry ordered his men to drop their belly tanks and prepare for the attack. The Luftwaffe fighters turned away from the bombers as they saw the Americans drop their tanks. But this turn away gave Elsberry his opportunity, and with a 30-degree deflection shot hit an FW 190 and caused him to fall away—a probable. Another FW turned in front of Elsberry. Diving into the enemy, he opened fire and peppered the German, who did a split-S and augured into the ground—a confirmed. About one minute later another FW found himself facing death by pulling in front of the fatally accurate Elsberry, who poured a two-second burst into the enemy from a lead shot; two members of Elsberry's flight witnessed the enemy fighter hit the ground and explode. Another and final victim hurtled past Elsberry in a 45-degree dive. Firing only from his left wing guns, the flight leader kicked right rudder to keep his sights on the enemy, observed hits on the left wing as the FW vainly attempted to pull out of his death dive—a third confirmed. Captain Elsberry is also credited in some records with a Bf 109, but details are sketchy, as are the circumstances under which a Lieutenant Sawyer was credited with an FW 190 and a Bf 109.

The tactics of the enemy fighters seemed inept and unaggressive, particularly since these were excellent aircraft piloted by what were supposed to be veterans. One explanation may be that the fighters were attempting to lure the escort away from the bombers. If so, the ploy failed miserably. A dodge of the Luftwaffe fighters was to make lightning attacks on bomber formations from below in two strings, then to split-S and head for the deck. This tactic was countered successfully by USAAF escorts as they gained experience.

July 15 saw the 99th join the group for its first combined combat mission. The group raided the railway yards at the medieval papal seat of Avignon in occupied southern France and shot down two enemy fighters.

The following day the 332nd bagged two uncommon enemies. Returning from a fighter sweep in the Vienna area, group pilots spotted an Italian Macchi 205 approaching a straggling B-24 for an easy kill. Although the nimble Italian fighter outdived the American flight leader, his wingman turned inside the Macchi and, firing almost continuously, followed him downward until the doomed fighter's left wing hit a mountainside and the plane burst into flames. The flight leader, not to be cheated again of a kill that day, spotted another Macchi approximately 5,000 feet below him. Catching the Italian in a left turn, and firing a 60-degree deflection shot, the American blew off large pieces of the enemy aircraft, which then spun to earth. This action took place well after Italy's surrender, and since the records are remarkably incurious about the identity of the two Macchis, and mention no markings, they can only be assumed to have belonged to the German-dominated Aviazione Nationale Rupubblicana of the Italian Social Republic, Mussolini's rump state in the north of the peninsula.

The enemy put up a scarcely better fight two days later with Bf 109s attempting to break up elements of the 306th Bomb Wing once again attacking targets at Avignon. Nineteen enemy aircraft approached the formation, but only three actually attempted an attack. Even these braver souls broke off their approach, a string attack from astern at 8 o'clock, upon the appearance of the Red Tails. All of the enemy fights were quickly shot down. In the laconic words of the group intelligence officer, "[Enemy] pilots seemed very inexperienced and did not even attempt to fight back."

An even more impressive score was recorded the next day. Sixty-six Mustangs took off from Ramitelli to protect bombers of the 5th Bomb Wing, who were to attack a Luftwaffe base at Memminger, Austria. Approaching the Udine-Traviso area, thirty to thirty-five enemy aircraft approached in units of twos and fives from 3 o'clock high and 5 o'clock low to attack the bombers. But, again, the enemy pilots were neither skillful nor aggressive; nine Bf 109s were shot down on the approach to the target. Over the target area approximately thirty to forty enemy were sighted, a mixed bag of Bf 109s, FW 190s, and Bf 210s. The enemy did not attack the bombers but stayed out of range on the same level as the bombers "as if directing operations." When four FW 190s did dive in for an attack on the bombers at 25,000 feet, two were shot down. The group's total bag for the day: eleven enemy destroyed (nine Bf 109s and two FW 190s). Lieutenant Clarence "Lucky" Lester was the high scorer, with three Bfs to his credit. Losses for the group included three pilots of the group, who were posted missing, although one, Lt. Gene C. Browne, landed safely in enemy territory and was liberated at the end of the war in Europe. After the war, Lieutenant Browne frankly admitted that his overeagerness had earned him a long stay in a German stalag; in his eagerness to down a Bf 109 in his sights he had ignored the warnings of a wingman that another Bf was on his tail. Also on this mission, one B-24 heavy American bomber exploded.

While the inept tactics of the Luftwaffe fighters could be attributed to inexperienced pilots (possibly the Germans were holding back their best for the defense of the Reich itself), group intelligence officers speculated on the odd behavior of those Germans who stayed on the bombers' level. Since the Germans flew in American-style formation, the officers concluded that they were masquerading as USAAF escorts and would attack the bombers at the first opportunity. By the end of the month this theory had been confirmed, but since Colonel Davis's instructions were explicit that his men were never to leave their charges (and these instructions were backed up by penalties for offenders), the 332nd was apparently never caught by this enemy ruse.

An escort mission to Friederichshafen, Germany (through the Brenner Pass and its flak) on the nineteenth netted the 332nd four more enemy, as well as a fourth for Captain Elsberry. The Americans lost three of the escorted B-24s to flak, and only one parachute was sighted coming from the stricken bombers. But the good shepherds of the 332nd also picked up two crippled B-24 bombers in the Udine, Italy, area and carefully escorted them to safety.

Not only were the "heavies" more plodding, even their death agonies seemed on a slower time scale to fighter pilots flying a fine line between the quick and the dead. Some bombers would explode in a dull fireball, and hang, fireball and pieces of plane, for breathless seconds before dropping to oblivion. Others disassembled gradually, wings collapsing, engines tearing off, props inanely whirling. Crewmen attached to shredded or burning parachutes tumbled to earth several miles below. Sometimes the escort fighters would catch a glimpse of the cockpit of a doomed bomber being devoured from the rear by voracious fuel fed flame, pilots rigid in their seats, staring forward, seemingly oblivious to impeding death by fire or explosion.

German fighters proved more aggressive on July 25 during a raid on the Hermann Göring Tank Works at Linz, Austria. One Bf was destroyed, but at the cost of two 332nd pilots. These skillful Germans followed the tactics of massing their entire force on one or two elements of the escort, thus achieving local superiority. "Gremlins" also plagued this mission, as one pilot was unable to drop his wing tanks and another found his guns frozen just as he had an enemy aircraft in his sights—someone had improperly connected his heaters.

The next day's mission—to provide cover for the 47th Bomb Wing attacking Markendorf Air Field, Austria, was considerably more satisfying: five Bfs confirmed and two probables, with no loss to the escorts, although one B-24 heavy bomber (no chutes observed) and one P-38 from another escorting outfit were shot down.

In the good weather of the summer of 1944, the 332nd was well into its stride, battering targets, including the notorious Ploesti complex in Rumania, as well as carrying on its primary mission of bomber escorting. According to General Eaker, the campaign against Ploesti cost 1,500 bombers and 15,000 men, a truly incredible toll. Yet, almost as incredible, the 332nd over Ploesti lost no men or planes and shot down no enemy. But the onslaught against the giant refinery center was no "milk run" for the group. Lieutenant Alexander Jefferson has left an indelible account of that aerial hell:

Grotesque doughnuts of flames [were] thrown by flak. Planes fell in flames, planes fell not in flames. Men fell in flames, men fell safely in their parachutes, some candlesticked. Pieces of men dropped through that hole, pieces of planes. The sight we saw at Ploesti would make an addict's hallucinations look good. Have you any idea what it is like to vomit in an oxygen mask?

The experiences of Capt. James Walker were less horrifying, but equally challenging. Captain Walker was shot down over central Yugoslavia on July 22, after making the mistake of flying over what he presumed was a harmless village. Fortunately, he landed in partisan-controlled territory and was able to join with a crew of nine white airmen in a similar predicament. The ten then began a trek that took them through three hundred miles of some of Europe's most difficult and dangerous terrain and ultimately back to their bases.

On July 27, the 332nd ranged into Hungary to provide cover for the 47th Bomb Wing's raid on the Weiss Armament Works in the Budapest area. Despite aggressive enemy defense of this vital plant, the 332nd shot down four Bfs and four FWs. Two 332nd pilots, forced to bail out, were rescued unhurt later. Another of those mysterious Italian fighters, this time a Reggiane 2001, far from home, was easily destroyed.

By August, the group could mount two missions simultaneously. On August 6, for example, some flights of the 332nd escorted bombers to southern France in support of the impending Franco-American landings in the area, while others shepherded heavies back to Budapest.

Understandably, group morale peaked as the victories mounted. On the base, enterprising enlisted men of each squadron had established their clubs where they could have a few tepid beers and get away from the war and their officers. The "Panther Room" of the 99th is best remembered, probably because that pioneering squadron had more overseas time to learn how to "requisition" materials for their club and to fill it with mementos to remind the men of their accomplishments and of home.

On August 24, the 332nd bagged three more enemy aircraft while providing cover to the 5th Bomb Wing over Pardubice Air Field, Czechoslovakia (two FW 190s, one Bf 109). But American losses were high; although the group was unscathed, four B-24s and one B-17 were lost to flak. Escorts observed parachutes from only the B-17.

Enemy air opposition was fast dwindling, however, and the group could spend more time looking for targets of opportunity on the ground. In two days, August 27 and 30, the 332nd wiped out a total of twenty-two enemy aircraft confirmed, and another eighty-three unconfirmed, all on the ground. Returning from an escort mission with the 5th Bombardment Wing to Blechammer, Germany, after seeing the bombers to safety, fifty-seven Mustangs strafed two different enemy airfields in close proximity in Czechoslovakia. Spotting an observation plane (which was obviously not too observant) taking off from a camouflaged airfield (which was obviously not too well camouflaged), the Mustangs bored in. After working over the field, they claimed twenty-two enemy, which ranged from Ju-87 Stukas (the terror of undefended skies earlier in the war), through Heinkel 111 medium bombers to Junkers 52 transports, plus one locomotive thrown in for good measure.

Three days later the 332nd again surprised negligent Germans on the ground and drew blood on a strafing mission in the Transylvania region of Rumania. Spotting approximately 150 aircraft of all types again ineffectively camouflaged with hay, the four squadron elements made about seven unopposed passes each and left the entire field, aircraft and hay, ablaze. Here the tally was even bigger and more diverse than on the previous run. In addition to the types destroyed three days earlier, the 332nd now added Bf 109s, Dornier 217s, FW 189s, Bf 210s and 110s, a glider, a training monoplane, and four oil-tank cars, for a total of eighty-three confirmed enemy aircraft. (An enemy plane could only be confirmed on the ground if seen to blaze.) The intelligence officer of the 332nd reported soon afterward:

Our pilots strafed the German planes by squadrons. Not a single enemy plane rose to meet them in an effort to stop the destruction, nor was any antiaircraft fire directed toward the vaunted Mustangs as they swept over the field like a cloud of grasshoppers over ripened Western grain. Of the encounter, quiet, unassuming Captain Davis, the Group Deputy C.O., said, "they were parked there like ducks, all we had to do was shoot them. It was a great show." Ex-football star [Alexander] "Bernie" Jefferson said, "No matter how much pressure they are under, no excuse can be made for the Germans leaving so many planes concentrated in such large numbers. They must have lost all discipline."

The Tuskegee Airmen rarely denigrated their enemy, but considering the fact that they had destroyed 105 enemy aircraft on the ground in two days, with no enemy flak or air opposition, and with the loss of only one of their number, the men of the 332nd might be forgiven for a little crowing over an enemy so inept. Although Walter White improbably claimed that "German airmen had become so terrified of the 'black flying devils' that they fled whenever they found their opponents to be members of the 99th," the men of the group knew that the Germans were probably holding back their best, and that in the future they would tangle with that best.

On September 8 the unopposed slaughter continued, when thirty-six assorted Heinkels, Junkers, Dorniers, and FWs were shot up on two fields in Yugoslavia, again at the cost of one pilot and one plane missing. The only complaint of the men of the 332nd was that enemy aircraft destroyed on the ground were not counted for progress toward the coveted "ace" status.

With the close of the month of August, the group could look back upon the completion of another successful month. Segregated and unwieldy as the group might be, it was now well established, aggressive, and successful. Morale continued high. Squadron clubs operated in full swing, with drinks, music, and "spratmo" (gossip). The beach was close at hand, and if it lacked the popcorn and hot dog stands of Atlantic City or Long Beach, the shore was sandy and the water warm. The visit of world heavyweight champion Joe Louis was a highlight of the month, while night movies and USO shows at the base were no longer punctuated by nocturnal Luftwaffe intrusions. Further afield, rest camps had been set up in Rome, Naples, and Montesaro.

In Naples, particularly, the men of the 332nd came to know some of the local *signorini* quite well, perhaps confirming what Shakespeare had noted four centuries earlier in *Two Gentlemen of Verona*, "Black men are as pearls to beauteous women." But twentieth-century racism eventually caught up even to Naples. Something calling itself the "Italian-American Committee for the Preservation of the Italian Race" placarded the port city, solemnly informing the population that "the Negro is a man of the colored races"; "he is an inferior human being"; "the machine gun will cut down the prostitute that sells the honor of her race." It was rumored that white U.S. soldiers were responsible, but the wording seems more Italian in origin and might have been the work of unreconstructed *fascisti*, or possibly disgruntled or jealous Italians of no organized political persuasion.

September 10 was a bright day for the 332nd, as four pilots of the 332nd were presented with the DFC by Gen. Benjamin O. Davis, Sr. Colonel B. O. Davis, Jr., 301st flight leader Capt. Joseph D. Elsberry, assistant group operations officer 1st Lt. Jack D. Hosclaw, and 100th Fighter Squadron pilot 1st Lt. Clarence D. Lester were honored. The ceremony was a welcome break from the all-too-familiar "routine camp duties" that comprised most of the life of the enlisted men of the 332nd. The four officers were led to the runway in an impressive parade. There Colonel Davis was decorated by his father. Father and son were not the type to display emotion, and General Davis expressed his personal feelings with a handshake and a terse "I am very proud of you." He spoke for more than himself. The assembled troops then stepped out on the rousing command "Pass in review!" to marching music by the XV Air Force Band, and review by those honored as well as generals Davis, Ira Eaker, Nathan Twining (commanding officer, XV Air Force), and Dean Strother, who was to succeed General Twining.

One month later, Colonel Davis received the Legion of Merit, an award created by Congress in 1942. The citation read in part: "As Commanding Officer of the 332nd Fighter Group, Colonel Davis demonstrated outstanding leadership and administrative ability in organizing, training, and leading into combat the four squadrons assigned to his Group."

Whatever the personal feelings of the Army Air Forces's hierarchy (and many of these feelings did come out at the end of the war), the stilted official language of the citation did demonstrate an awareness by all that black participation in the USAAF was a fact, at least "for the duration."

General Giles of the Air Staff, no particular friend to the 332nd, noted one month after the award the need for fairness to the group, and, significantly, the necessity to avoid adverse publicity. General Eaker, who as late as 1974 insisted "that all black fighter squadrons were happier, more confident," mandated in 1945 that the group "be given a thoroughly square deal." He asserted to an Royal Air Force pilot that there "is absolutely no discrimination against our colored fighter pilots," and that they "are rendering excellent service."

All of this was consistent with prevailing Army Air Forces attitudes. From 1939 on, practically all top air officers would have preferred that no black Americans apply; a war was on, they had their work and their careers to look to, and they did not see how blacks could help either. But their professionalism enabled them to make the effort to be fair, within the framework of racial segregation, once the decision had been made at higher levels to admit blacks. And as the 99th and the 332nd "proved" themselves, they were perfectly willing to give credit where credit was due. But with the end of the war, most would then argue that the end had also come for the need for black participation, a participation that they felt had been instigated by "politics" in the first place.

September 1944 saw far fewer sorties and missions by the 332nd, the strafing victory of the eighth remaining the high point for the month. News reached the group of the Germans' newest "mystery weapon," the jet fighter. Captain Edward Thomas noted in his diary that "reports say that the new German jet propelled plane can climb vertically and has a level flight speed in excess of 500 M.P.H." Captain Thomas was undoubtedly referring to the Messerschmitt 262, the Luftwaffe's operational twin-jet fighter, and he was not far off in his summary of its capabilities. As early as July 1944, Gen. Carl Spaatz, Eighth Air Force commander, accurately termed the Me 262 the greatest threat to Allied escort fighters in the European Theater of Operations (ETO). Spaatz called on General Arnold to plan for the bombing of German jet factories, to speed the production of improved P-51s, and to send to the ETO, as soon as possible, large numbers of the new American jet fighter, the Lockheed P-80. General Eaker also called for large numbers of USAAF jets, to counter "a considerable jet fighter force" the Luftwaffe could possess by the spring of 1945.

These were not panic reactions; the Me 262A-1 boasted a top speed of more than 100 MPH over that of the latest versions of the P-51. It could not, however, climb vertically. Still, the Red Tails did not even spot the fearsome German jet until the end of the year.

The latter half of September was almost a total loss from a combat point of view. For eight days an unremitting deluge grounded the entire mighty Mediterranean Allied Air Force, but the standdown did give weary pilots and ground crews some rest. The four squadrons at Ramitelli Army Air Field kept busy. Aside from routine camp duties, each squadron organized even more intense off-duty recreation. The 100th Squadron had the Century Art Players, a theatrical group giving one-act plays, and a squadron chorus. Basketball, softball, a ping-pong tournament, and touch football filled the sports picture, and, of course, the Panther Room was well patronized, particularly when squadron veterans of the Salerno campaign met to swap tall tales. The 301st, perhaps the more scholarly squadron, instituted a series of lectures and classes on such subjects as war news, modern languages, and mathematics. All of these activities were needed, as mail deliveries became erratic and the rains continued, and they would become vital during the gloomy Italian winter.

But in early October, the weather broke, and the XV Air Force was thrown into action over Greece to harass and hasten the departure of German garrisons being evacuated in the face of British landings. The German front in the Balkans was breaking up as Russian forces rolled into southeastern Rumania, and a consolidation of German forces became essential.

On October 4, the four squadrons of the 332nd entered the campaign in a strafing mission over airfields at Tatoi, Kalamaki, and Eleusis. A total of nine bombers and transports were destroyed on the ground at the expense of one American lost. Two days later the same airfields (plus Megara) yielded a more disappointing harvest; five enemy bombers and transports burned, but three Americans died. With the German pullout from Greece almost complete, the 332nd was turned against the Balkans. Russian troops from the Baltic to the Balkans were relentlessly pushing the Germans toward the border of the Reich itself. The Germans had already suffered a heavy blow with the loss of Rumania and its oil wealth. By the end of October Bulgaria had broken with its Nazi ally and signed a peace with the Soviet Union. In Yugoslavia the partisans of Tito (Josip Broz) were clearing large areas of their nation from German occupation. These developments, together with the opening of the Second Front in France in June 1944, compelled the Germans to cut their losses in southeastern Europe. They opened escape routes through Yugoslavia in order to redeploy troops to block a Soviet threat to Hungary, Austria, and Czechoslovakia. The 332nd Fighter Group was now thrown into the cutting of these escape routes.

On October 11, 1944, elements of the group pressed a strafing attack from Budapest to Bratislava, Czechoslovakia, a sweep along the Danube of about 150 miles. Encountering cloud cover up to 30,000 feet over the Yugoslavian coast, only twenty Mustangs of the seventy-two that had taken off from Ramitelli could find holes in the cover and press on to the attack. But those twenty were well rewarded: at Estergon, Hungary, they strafed three airfields along the Danube River and river barge traffic, claiming seventeen enemy aircraft on the ground, one oil dump, and two locomotives, at no cost to themselves.

The next day brought even more gratifying results, and aerial victories, for the 332nd. The mission and the target were the same as those of the day before: strafing Danube River traffic. While the 301st strafed oil barges, the 99th, 302nd, and later the 301st, attacked two airfields, and the 100th blasted targets of opportunity. The 302nd was the only squadron of the 332nd that day to encounter enemy aircraft in the air with aggressive intentions. Captain Wendell Pruitt peeled off to attack an He 111 medium bomber. At that point seven Bf 109s and two more He 111s attacked Pruitt's flight from 5 o'clock high. Captain Pruitt's wingman, Lt. Lee Archer, described the battle:

Just after we had destroyed our first plane Pruitt noticed the formation of enemy planes coming directly toward us. Instead of avoiding them, Pruitt flew directly into the formation with his guns blazing. As we passed through the formation the planes scattered. We were now flying side by side with the enemy planes going in the opposite direction. We made a tight turn and fell in behind three enemy aircraft. After getting within shooting distance I fired a couple of short bursts at one of the planes. My fire was accurate and I tore off the wing of the plane. It tumbled down to earth. Then I slid my plane down below Pruitt's plane, which was now on the tail of a second plane. However, before I could fire, Pruitt's shots hit the target. The plane burst into flame. At this time an Me 109 [Bf 109] came in from the left and slid in behind Pruitt, who was now on the tail of a third enemy plane. I immediately pulled up behind him and gave a few short bursts, the plane exploded, throwing the pilot out of the cockpit, and then fell to the ground. Pruitt was still chasing the plane he had lined up. However, on his third burst his guns jammed. As I pulled beside him I could see him fiddling with his controls trying to start his guns. Seeing that Pruitt wasn't getting any results I told him to

Top: Officers of black Aviation Squadron (Separate), date and location unknown. Aviation squadrons (Separate) were catch-all nonflying Army Air Forces units activated for the more-or-less specific purpose of "absorbing" the AAF's "fair share" of blacks under the Selective Service system. *Bottom:* This military police unit, in Columbus, Georgia (April 1942), provided security and control for black troops at Fort Benning, Georgia. Throughout World War II, it was U.S. military policy that no white troops could be under the control of black MPs, although the reverse was deemed perfectly acceptable.

Major personalities in the decision to establish and maintain racially segregated Army Air Corps/Forces units: *(left to right)* Secretary of War Henry Stimson, Assistant Secretary of War John J. McCloy, and Assistant Secretary for Air Robert A. Lovett.

Tuskegee Army Air Field review in early days, before deployment of the pioneer 99th Pursuit into combat. The helmeted officer at the left end of the front rank is probably Lt. Col. Benjamin O. Davis, Jr.

A moment in history. Opening ceremonies at inauguration of black military aviation training, Tuskegee Institute, Alabama. Major General Walter Weaver, C.O. of the Southeastern Army Air Corps Training Center, is third from left on platform. Tuskegee Institute president Dr. Fred Patterson is to his left and Capt. Benjamin O. Davis, Jr., just to the left and behind Dr. Patterson.

Top: The flight line at TAAF. Cadets and their Vultee trainers lined up for inspection, c. 1942. *Bottom:* White USAAF instructor at TAAF with trainees. Benjamin O. Davis, Jr., 99th Pursuit Squadron C.O., is third from left. The relationships between white instructors and black trainees was apparently almost always professional and mutually respectful. The AAC/AAF was determined to give no one the opportunity to charge that it did not make the same facilities and training personnel available for blacks as for whites. If the Tuskegee "experiment" failed, blacks supposedly would then have only themselves to blame.

TAAF ground school cadets study radial aircraft engine under civilian instructor, June 1942.

A lugubrious TAAF armament class studies .30-caliber machine gun, June 1942.

TAAF Message Center, which provided contact with higher AAF headquarters, as well as various installations at TAAF.

The mess hall at TAAF. (Note the coal-burning stove in the back.) TAAF was strictly a utilitarian facility, built quickly, solely "for the duration," and dismantled at war's end.

TAAF's austere cadet barracks, seen here five months before Pearl Harbor, were no more palatial than the mess hall. But no palace was ever scrubbed more thoroughly or more often.

Top: Tuskegee was located deep in the poverty-stricken "Black Belt" of Alabama. For northern blacks, even in the 1940s a trip outside TAAF's gates was like a journey back in time. (*Source:* Charles Price Collection.) *Bottom:* The dream of every World War II GI, black or white—Lena Horne on post! This TAAF visit was in December 1944. (*Source:* Charles Price Collection.)

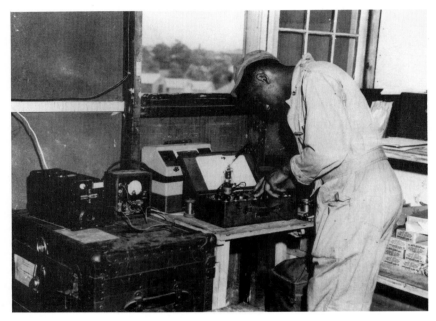

Radio technician testing tubes at TAAF. In that era, before transistors or printed circuits, electronic vacuum tubes were the vital components of any AAF electronic equipment.

TAAF's Link trainer simulated as much as possible on the ground the feel of flying for aspiring military pilots.

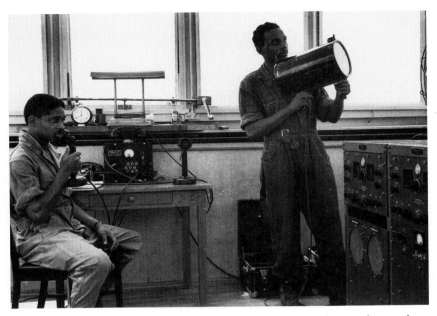

Original USAAF caption: "Colored enlisted men in control tower with microphone and biscuit gun. Photograph taken June 1942." The "biscuit gun" flashed signals to approaching pilots.

Lt. Col. Benjamin O. Davis, Jr. ("The Thin Man"), with his staff, TAAF, c. 1942. To Davis's right is Maj. George S. Roberts, a superb flier and Davis's successor as 99th C.O.

Maintenance training for black USAAF ground crews, Selfridge Field, Michigan.

Navigator training was among the most successful of the nonpilot training given to blacks in the USAAF in World War II and received considerable attention in the media.

Group of 332nd fighter pilots "somewhere in Italy." Lt. Col. Davis is on the far left.

Lt. Gen. Ira Eaker, commanding general, Mediterranean Allied Air Force, and 332nd Group C.O. Lt. Col. Benjamin O. Davis, Jr., during an inspection tour in Italy.

Top: P-40s used for 332nd Fighter Group training at Oscoda Army Air Base, Michigan, May 1943. By this time in the war, the P-40 was obsolete and inferior compared to Luftwaffe fighters, but was still used in combat until more advanced fighters could reach USAAF squadrons.

Bottom: 99th Fighter Squadron P-40 on pierced steel planking (location unknown, c. 1943).

Lt. Gen. Eaker, Maj. Gen. Nathan Twining, Brig. Gen. Benjamin O. Davis, Sr., and Brig. Gen. Dean Strother, a rather heavy collection of "brass" for an inspection of a 332nd base in Italy.

Boxing world heavyweight champ Joe Louis (center) talks to Lt. Joe Lewis (far left) and other ground crewmen. Capt. Lee Rayford, 332nd pilot, is on far right.

Pre-mission briefing, 332nd operations room, in Italy.

332nd armorers work on P-51 wing guns.

Lt. Clarence "Lucky" Lester surveys symbols of his combat success with his crew chief. (Lester was later given credit for only two enemies.) Lester's fighter is an earlier Mustang model without the "bubble" canopy.

Lt. Gen. Eaker at activation ceremonies for the 477th. Brig. Gen. B. O. Davis, Sr., is to
Gen. Eaker's right, flanked by Truman Gibson.

Truman Gibson, Col. Davis, Maj. Gen. James Bevans (deputy commander, Mediterranean Allied Air Force), Col. Campbell, and Maj. George Roberts, 332nd operations room, March 1945, as the air war approached its victorious climax in Europe.

The 447th Bombardment Wing: Loading a B-25 Mitchell bomber with .50-caliber ammunition.

Col. Robert Selway, 477th C.O.

Top: Advance training, TAAF: B-25s in formation. (*Source:* USAF, from Charles Price Collection.) *Bottom:* Ground collision, TAAF, June 6, 1944. Original caption: "Two less AT-6's—two more future footsoldiers." (*Source:* USAF, from Charles Price Collection.)

Top: Tuskegee Army Air Field headquarters, mid- to late 1945. (*Source:* Charles Price Collection.)

Bottom: View of TAAF from the control tower. Within a year after this photo had been taken (toward the end of 1945), this entire facility was torn down, and the area reverted to open fields. (*Source:* Charles Price Collection.)

Col. Benjamin O. Davis, Jr., by then commander of the 477th, with Frank Stanley, president of the Negro Publishing Association, and Truman Gibson during a visit to Godman Field.

move over and let a man shoot who could shoot. He pulled over and I eased my plane into his position. I gave the enemy plane a long burst. Then the Me 109 went into a dive for a runway that I observed below. Seemingly, he had decided to land. I gave him another long burst and he crashed on the runway. The German ground crew opened with all their guns. Lights were blinking at me from all directions. For a few seconds I had to dodge flak and small arms fire that burst all around my ship. But I was lucky and managed to wiggle out.

Lieutenant Archer was top scorer for the day with three Bfs confirmed while Pruitt had downed another Bf and an He 111. Six other pilots each scored one enemy for a total of nine victories in the air. In addition, twenty-six enemy aircraft were destroyed on the ground, plus many ground transport vehicles, ranging from locomotives to motor trucks to river barges. One American was lost to flak. The only untoward note was the intrusion of yellow-tailed P-51s from another group over the Kapsovar Air Field while the 99th and 302nd were about their business. The Red Tails found they had to draw upon all their aerobatic skills to avoid mass midair collision in this friendly "attack" (as the official group historian with some asperity termed the intrusion). Once again enemy tactics ranged from nonexistent to poor to inept.

The last mission in October with significant results took place the day after the group's last Danubian romp. They were to serve as escort for an assault by the 304th Bomb Wing on the Blechammer oil refineries about 125 miles south of Berlin. Seven more enemy were hit on the ground but at the cost of two pilots, including 1st Lt. Walter Westmoreland, a nephew of Walter White.

For the rest of the month the group concentrated on oil installations and targets of opportunity. The men could look back on a month of successes, but also a month with the heaviest losses. The 99th and 100th squadrons were each missing five pilots, the 301st three, and the 302nd three. Fortunately, not all of these losses were permanent, for at least three returned to safety, and hope was always nurtured for those men seen to crash-land and those who had vanished.

The 99th was particularly distressed by the loss of its C.O., Capt. Alfonzo W. Davis. Only 25 at the time of his promotion to squadron commander and at his death, Davis had managed to secure a transfer from the old black 9th Cavalry Regiment to enter aviation cadet training and to graduate with honors from Tuskegee. After commissioning, he had been assigned to the 302nd Squadron, and had worked his way up to the position of flight leader and then operations officer. Two months later Colonel Davis had appointed him group operations officer, later deputy group commander, and finally commanding officer of the 99th Fighter Squadron. But this gifted and popular officer had only six days to lead his men. Captain Davis failed to return from the escorting of a P-38 photo reconnaissance mission to the Munich area. Although he had only one enemy aircraft to his credit, Captain Davis's abilities had already been recognized by the awards of the DFC and the Air Medal with two oak leaf clusters.

October and November saw air activity much reduced due to bad weather. More attention was given to morale, which was characterized as "steady" in October and "improved" in November. Of course, more than the weather was responsible for the state of morale (although it is difficult to imagine anything more dampening to the spirits of pilots and ground crew than tent life during a second November composed mainly of gray, rainy skies, churned mud, and increasing cold). The high hopes of the end of the war by Christmas or there about, heightened by the assassination attempt on Adolf Hitler, faded in the gloom of November, and died in the bitter woods of December's Battle of the Bulge. The Führer had survived to hang his opponents by piano wire from meat hooks, and the war continued. The German army (Wehrmacht) then enjoyed greatly shortened lines of communication, but the Luftwaffe, deprived of the bulk of its oil resources, staged no major comeback, and was particularly scarce over the Italian front.

The only kill registered by the group in November was credited to Capt. Luke J. Weathers, Jr., of the 302nd. Captain Weathers and two other pilots were shepherding a lone heavy bomber home from a mission over the Udine area, when the heavy was attacked by a flight of eight Bf 109s. Captain Weathers peeled off from the bomber's flank and bored in at the enemy in a head-on attack. After a few bursts from the American's guns, one Bf fell away and began to split-S to the earth. Just in time Weathers noticed "little red balls" flying past his canopy, and glancing around realized that another Bf was on his tail and blazing away at him. Captains Melvin Jackson and Louis Purnell had witnessed Weathers's plight and fell in behind his pursuer, but they now found themselves under attack from the rear and had to execute a quick dive. The enemy chose to concentrate on Weathers, who, although out-numbered seven to one, did not panic.

It looked like they had me so I decided to follow the falling plane [his first victim, presumably]. I made a dive, came out of it and looked back. One plane was still on my tail. I was headed back towards Germany, and I didn't want to go that way. I chopped my throttle and dropped my flaps to cut my speed quickly. The fellow overshot me and this left me on his tail. He was in range so I opened fire. A long burst and a few short bursts sent him tumbling to the ground.

While Weathers attributed his maneuver to a desire not to return to the German Reich, it is probably also true that he was being modest, for his was a well-established, if dangerous, technique utilized by experienced combat fliers. The bomber returned safely to base.

Ramitelli Air Field fairly hummed with morale-sustaining and -improving activities. Each squadron in the group boasted a chorus, the 100th began its newspaper and opened an enlisted men's club. Thanksgiving was celebrated with church, turkey dinner, and a movie. Christmas packages began to arrive during the month. The Thanksgiving football "classic" saw the 99th's team win the group championship. The group's basketball team continued its undefeated string and led the league, while Technical Sergeant Burnley (99th Fighter Squadron) won the middleweight boxing championship for the XV Air Force. Leave for Naples and Rome was further liberalized.

The group was particularly fortunate in its medical officers in this trying time. The group surgeon was Maj. Vance H. Marchbanks, Jr. An "Army brat" son of a cavalry warrant officer, Marchbanks turned down an offer of a West Point nomination, graduated from Howard University Medical School in 1937, and was commissioned in the Army Medical Corps Reserve. He entered the Army Medical Corps in 1941 and was rated in aviation medicine as an examiner the following year, was transferred to Tuskegee Army Air Field, and later completed a course in neuropsychiatry at Walter Reed Army Hospital.

When Captain Marchbanks embarked with the 332nd in January 1944, the three squadrons of the group were scattered through three different airfields. The medical section of the group had received no formal training in medical field service, which was precisely what they would be doing. Many medical supplies had to be requisitioned. The sick and injured had to endure long journeys by ambulance to be treated at field and station hospitals. Yet Marchbanks was able to achieve an unusually high state of medical efficiency. The situation eased considerably when the squadrons of the 332nd were finally united at Ramitelli. Major

Marchbanks set up a group aid station that Colonel Davis claimed was one of the first in the Mediterranean Theater. Colonel Davis further credited Major Marchbanks with a "close and constant relationship with almost all the pilots in the Group." Marchbanks also enjoyed a close association with his fellow medical officers (M.O.), and established Saturday night sessions with M.O.'s and pilots. Because almost all had trained at Tuskegee, the M.O.'s and pilots either knew each other or knew of each other.

Major Marchbanks was well aware of the damage that an individual with psychological problems could inflict on so closely knit a group. As Marchbanks outlined his program:

A pilot who began to show tension and anxiety with psychological disturbances and fatigue was placed on a control roster. He was removed from the combat environment by sending him to a rest camp in Naples for five days. Pilots who had flown steadily for a period of a month or longer or who had entailed disturbing experiences, were sent to the rest camp as a prophylaxis against fatigue. Those who had encountered harrowing experiences, such as bailing out, crash landings, without physical trauma, but only mild anxiety, were scheduled for flying immediately for reassurance against their fears, if they were considered a safe risk.

Such generous solicitude could well have provoked the envy of the pilots of the wornout Luftwaffe at this stage of the air war in Europe.

Undoubtedly as a result of Major Marchbanks's work, only one pilot of the original 332nd (not including the 99th) was removed permanently from flying status. A mere six pilots rotated to the Zone of the Interior (USA) for rest and rehabilitation, and all but two of these returned to operational combat flying. A total of 285 pilots were assigned to the 332nd Fighter Group during the period from February 25, 1944, to February 25, 1945. Of that total, seventeen pilots were referred to the group surgeon due to psychological maladies that the squadron surgeons could not handle. Most of these pilots had amassed an average of about two hundred hours of operational flying and were suffering from mild anxiety associated with operational fatigue. Eight of the seventeen were removed from combat flying on medical certificate. The remaining nine returned to duty after treatment, and successfully completed their combat tours of duty. The XII Air Force Medical Disposition Board handled only two psychiatric cases out of a total of twelve various medical problems referred by the 332nd.

A medical analysis of the 332nd Group's ninety-three original pilots shows that 39 percent completed their tours of duty; 5.3 percent were sent to the Zone of the Interior on medical certificates; another 5.3 percent were removed by the Medical Disposition Board and 1 percent by General Hospital (Class "C"); 2.1 percent were removed by the Flying Evaluation Board to the Zone of the Interior after returning from missing in action; 3.2 percent were returned to duty after being posted as missing in action; and 13.9 percent remained on combat duty as of February 1945. Of fatalities or possible fatalities as of that date, 2.1 percent were killed in training, 20.3 percent were missing in action, and 9.6 percent were killed in action. The figures for replacement pilots and the 99th seem to fall within the same range.

By late 1944, escort was the primary mission of the 332nd Group. In this they excelled, even at the cost on occasion of some likely enemy kills. This fidelity to their charges and to Colonel Davis's strict orders apparently made some impression on USAAF bomber crews. In a little café in Naples, a bomber pilot, who was a cousin of a former governor of Mississippi, congratulated Capt. Luke Weathers for saving his life when he was under attack by a Luftwaffe fighter. Later, during the Seventh War Bond Drive, Weathers was awarded the keys to the city of Memphis, while the two leading newspapers of the "Queen City of the South" reported his speech and carried his photo.

But Weather's comrade, Capt. Louis Purnell, remembered a more disconcerting reaction from a white bomber pilot. The pilot had temporarily enjoyed the hospitality of the base, and had expressed his thanks. But Purnell, in the course of his duties as base censor, read one of the pilot's letters home: "Dear Mom, I'm here in a nigger air base in Italy, sleeping in nigger beds, and eating nigger food." Captain Purnell never saw "Mom" 's reply.

As far as the 332nd Group was concerned, the Luftwaffe was rather inconspicuous from December 1944 to February 1945. Although the group flew twenty-three missions in December and eleven in January, they scored no successes against enemy aircraft. Morale remained high, however, at Ramitelli, and December's Christmas packages and mail brightened the winter gloom. Somewhat confusingly, but enthusiastically, the group historian reported that "morale pierced its highest ebb" at the time. The 332nd could look back upon a year in which it had proved itself in the only field that counted—combat. By the end of 1944, the

332nd Fighter Group had destroyed sixty-two enemy aircraft in the air and had pounded airfields, communications, transportation facilities, troop concentrations, and vehicles, ranging through Rumania, Austria, Hungary, Czechoslovakia, Greece, and the crumbling Third Reich itself. And it had shepherded with very small loss the big bombers to targets in all of those countries except Greece.

In December, the Red Tails finally caught their first glimpse of the German jet fighter. The apprehensions of the Army Air Forces brass were now put to the test, for Hitler had finally dropped his ludicrous insistence upon the use of the Me 262 as a bomber and had released the twin jet for fighter-interceptor missions. The Me 262 enjoyed the potential of almost total air superiority over piston fighters, even late-model P-51s. But it was too late for the Luftwaffe. By the time Germany's jets entered squadron service, the destruction of so much of the Reich's oil resources had led to a drastic reduction in supplies of aviation fuel for training. Consequently, pilot skills slipped far below what they had been in the earlier, glorious days. While Allied bombers did not appreciably check production of the jet fighters, the German dispersal of assembly lines to caves and woods did cause problems and delays. Finally, it should be noted that the Allies were not that far behind German aeronautical progress, contrary to popular opinion. While the RAF's Meteor I was inferior in most respects to the Me 262, the Army Air Forces's P-80 Shooting Star would have been more than a match. The Army Air Forces rushed testing and preproduction runs of the new jet fighter, but only two early models found their way to the ETO before the German surrender. Neither saw combat.

The Red Tails' first encounter with the fearsome Me 262 hardly struck numb terror. On December 9, while returning from a bomber-escort mission, a flight of eight group P-51s was attacked by an Me 262 southeast of Regensburg, Germany; the Me 262 made one pass from 9 o'clock high and climbed into cloud cover. A second jet made an ineffective pass at one Mustang east of Munich, from 7 o'clock high, and dived into cloud cover below. In neither encounter did the jet bandits approach closer than 1,000 feet before breaking off. In all, thirteen jet sightings were made by the 332nd on that day. Although the pilots were impressed by the craft's speed, which enabled it to enter and leave combat at will, they were not so impressed with the aggressiveness of the pilots of those jets. The airmen took their measure, and soon enough shot down three of them on one mission.

Although the group did not encounter enemy fighters for the remainder of December or in January, they struck widely and deeply at German targets. Oil refineries were prominent targets for escort missions, but the new jet aircraft factories as well became increasingly important.

Morale remained high despite the lack of aerial kills, for the group was busy and effective. The Ardennes offensive in the west had been thrown back at the Battle of the Bulge, and the Red Army had advanced the phenomenal distance of 275 miles in three weeks, from Warsaw to Frankfurt-am-Oder. The Allies were now deep into Hitler's Third Reich.

The men of the 332nd followed the progress of the Red Army, and the question of "Where are the Russians now?" came up frequently in current affairs classes and discussions. There was nothing particularly ideological in this interest; each area cleared by the Soviets as well as by the western Allies meant that many fewer targets, and the targets that remained would be that much closer.

The Red Tails themselves penetrated ever more deeply into the Nazi heartland with unannounced "visits" to Munich, Stuttgart, Regensburg, Vienna, and Linz (the last once home to the boy Hitler). The month of February 1945 saw the 332nd back in action, with a record total of 141 missions flown. But the Luftwaffe proved even more scarce as the Red Tails raided targets well into Germany.

One such mission, on February 25, sent out forty-five Mustangs from Ramitelli to strafe traffic in the Munich-Linz-Ingolstadt-Salzburg quadrangle. The mission netted ten locomotives and one power station destroyed, and a large number of rail vehicles damaged, as well as two enemy bombers destroyed—again on the ground.

The 477th Bombardment Group—Frustration and Confrontation

6.

While the men of the 332nd were being hardened into an effective fighting unit in the fires of air combat and in the monotonous, exacting duties of field support, the newly formed black 477th Bombardment Group was mired in delay, frustration, and finally, in confrontation with Army Air Forces authority. Not surprisingly, the 477th never entered combat. But its disciplined and nonviolent protest against military racial segregation proved to be a harbinger of the methods utilized by black America in the 1950s and 1960s to end legal racial segregation in the Southern states.

Like the 99th Pursuit Squadron, the 477th Bombardment Group was conceived solely in response to black pressure, rather than to any perception that black Americans in the Army Air Forces could make any great contribution to the war effort. And it remained a paper outfit from its activation in June 1943 until January 1944.

The demand for a black bombardment group grew out of an increasing awareness by black leaders that single-engine pursuit aviation training, while fitting blacks for what was probably the most glamorous job in

World War II, would prove of less value in the postwar "air age" than multi-engine experience. Still, the fact that such experience would come in the context of strict military racial segregation muted any cheers that might have greeted the announcement of the unit's organization. Judge Hastie, the civilian aide on Negro affairs to the secretary of war, wrote publicly that "this may be good news, but those who remember the [premature] 1940 announcement about pilot training will restrain their enthusiasm."

For entirely different reasons, the Army Air Forces's hierarchy was also relatively indifferent to the fledgling black bomber group. The author of "Plans for the Activation of the Colored Bombardment Group (M)" cautioned that "it is common knowledge that the Colored race does not have the technical nor the flying background for the creation of a bombardment type unit." And at the end of the war in Europe, a maverick analyst of the First Air Force concluded that "the First Air Force went into the program believing that Negroes had no character for the work. It came out of the program believing Negroes had no character for the work." It may be somewhat unfair to state that the First Air Force believed that blacks had no "character" for bombardment work; more thoughtful officers believed that blacks lacked the necessary technical education and background, but either way, for whatever reasons, the Army Air Forces expected and got little enough from the group.

The first problem Army Air Forces planners encountered was the lack of any cadre of trained bombardiers and navigators. Black pilot eliminees at Tuskegee were not eligible for the alternative careers open to white eliminees until late in 1942; the pool of black civilians with a technical or aviation background was, of course, very limited. Thus, at its outset, the 477th had 60 pilots and no bombardier-navigators on its rolls. One year and three months later, the group was still short 26 pilots, 43 copilots, 2 bombardier-navigators, and all 288 of its allotted air gunners.

By the middle of 1943, 19,637 blacks were in the Army Air Forces. This number was insufficient to draw upon rapidly for personnel for a four-squadron, multi-engine bombardment group, and to supply replacements for the 332nd Fighter Group as well. The Army Air Forces, which had recently opened the service to black navigator and bombardier training, was forced to lower stanine (qualifying) score requirements for black navigators. While no white applicant was accepted for such training with a stanine below seven, of thirty-two black cadets, only six held stanines of seven or above. The situation eased later with a much higher black stanine becoming more common.

Although instructors at Hondo Field, Texas, where black navigators were trained, believed that the black cadets would perform less efficiently both in school and in the field, no evidence was ever offered as proof. The instruction was accomplished through segregated classes, classrooms, and barracks, although all cadets shared the Cadet Club, the PX, the day room, Officers' Club, and the Bachelor Officers' Mess. In addition, the black cadets flew on extended missions and received the expected services and courtesies at the various bases to which they flew. Although "some grumbling" was noticed at Hondo, in general, "behavior by all post personnel has at all times been 'correct.'" Roughly the same could be said of the bombardier school at Midland, Texas. But a mechanic trainee reported a different reception when his first class reported. No one, from the base C.O. to the black mess orderlies, could believe that the cadets were actually assigned for technical rather than menial work.

The machinery of racially segregated AAF training, however, finally began to turn out the needed support personnel. In fact, a contemporary described how the group's second base, Godman Army Air Field in Kentucky, began to bulge with trainees and came to resemble "life in the Dust Bowl, either drought or flood," something like a miniature Tuskegee Air Field.

However, the 477th was unfortunate from the outset in its commander, Col. Robert Selway. According to Colonel Parrish, Selway was "hostile" to the whole black bombardment program, and the record is clear enough that he had little faith in the ability of blacks to master combat aviation. As one example, Colonel Selway insisted that although blacks could be mechanics, all crew chiefs must be white, thus blocking any incentive for advancement among black mechanics. Colonel Selway's greatest failing, however, lay in his insensitivity toward his men. He further possessed an overly developed sense of caution, aggravated by racial incidents at Selfridge Field, Michigan, and by his ambition to achieve a general's star. Colonel Selway's mentality was obvious in his statement, "The Secretary of War says there is no racial problem and there is no racial problem." Yet Selway had supposedly enjoyed a good record in the command of black airmen, having been the second C.O. of the 332nd Fighter Group in its early days, and in that capacity, in the words of one contemporary source, "changed the attitude from a sullen, lackadaisical, indifferent, careless, irresponsible group, into an alert, more efficient, cooperating, interesting group."

The first of the 477th's many bases was Selfridge Field, a choice about as disastrous as that of its commanding officer. The previous base commanding officer had shot and wounded his black orderly, and in the very month that the men of the 477th had arrived, an unsuccessful attempt had been made by three black officers (not of the 477th) to enter the base Officers' Club. The intruding blacks were personally blocked by the current base C.O., Col. William Boyd. The War Department inspector general's report, completed by General Davis and Col. Harvey Shoemaker, was critical of the C.O. However, two Army Air Forces investigators defended the C.O.'s actions and, since the Officers' Club was now closed, they declared that the racial problem was also closed. The real trouble and the true responsibility, they concluded, lay with "agitators" from Detroit, and "communistic elements [which] are particularly active among Negroes at present." The best solution, therefore, was to remove blacks from Selfridge Field to localities so remote that mail could be censored more easily, thus preventing criticism of the Army Air Forces's racial policies from reaching the general public. General Arnold agreed with this "solution," and helpfully suggested Saint Lucia or Antigua. Although these Caribbean islands were soon found to be impractical, plans went forward to transfer the 477th away from those Detroit "communistic agitators."

In the meantime, further restrictions and humiliations continued. Women's Army Corps personnel and female employees on the base were conspicuously escorted to and from work by military police, and were warned not to socialize with blacks. When the 477th transferred out of Selfridge Field, the escorting stopped. The situation was finally alleviated by the War Department's personnel division, which after studying the Davis-Shoemaker report, agreed that Colonel Boyd had "deliberately and . . . intentionally violated explicit War Department instructions on this subject," and called on the War Department to follow and enforce its own policies.

Selfridge was located in Michigan, a state with a civil rights act; therefore, Colonel Boyd could not plead that he was acting in conformity with local custom and law, a plea that the War Department might have accepted in different circumstances. Consequently, Colonel Boyd was reprimanded, and the construction of a black Officers' Club was halted. A change of station was also authorized for the 477th.

Major General Frank O'D. Hunter, First Air Force commanding officer, who held jurisdiction over both the 477th and Selfridge Field, made no secret of his racial attitudes. He informed a black newspaperman that "Negroes can't expect to obtain equality in 200 years, and probably won't except in some distant future." Further, he attempted to keep Colonel Boyd's reprimand from his personnel file and told General Giles that he himself had ordered the segregation of the Selfridge Officers' Club. Apparently the luckless Colonel Boyd was the scapegoat for attitudes indulged in by a majority of his superiors. General Giles replied that he backed Hunter and Boyd "100 percent in this thing."

In May 1944 the 477th moved to dilapidated Godman Army Air Field, Kentucky, and the 553rd Fighter Squadron (organized to provide replacements for the 477th) to Walterboro Field, Fairfax, South Carolina, disrupting the training schedule further.

The situation was well used by white officers. Another source asserts that "the 477th was used as a promotion mill for white officers," giving the example of a freshly minted captain who, one month after his assignment to the group, was promoted to major. Yet although the average flying time of the black pilots was seven hundred hours, not one held rank above that of major.

Conditions at Walterboro Field were, if anything, worse than at Godman. While morale at the latter base was termed "high, fragile, and sensitive," at Walterboro General Giles found discipline lax, with some personnel displaying arrogance, insolence, and disrespect toward himself, a three-star general. One report noted, with some justification, that the 553rd at Walterboro contained a "troublesome element." Sixteen black officers en route from Walterboro nearly caused a race riot by their reaction to the refusal of service in a Jim Crow restaurant in Fairfax. A pioneer pilot from the 99th engaged in a fistfight with the mayor of Walterboro and had to be spirited from the area. Local authorities fought back. In one instance they arrested a black soldier involved in a disturbance, presented him before the grand jury, and tried and convicted him in one day, without benefit of civil or military counsel.

Much of this racial trouble can be traced to the fact that the men of the 477th had considerably more education than the personnel of comparable white units; 36 percent of the men of the 477th had a professional

background, compared to 24 percent of the men of the 47th Bombardment Group (white). They were better informed as well, mostly from the
North, and aware of their rights. This background, more than "outside
communist agitators," goes far to explain the militancy of the 477th
Bombardment Group.

Finally, by the end of 1944, the group had enough flying crew to
embark upon combat training. But winter weather began to close in and
flying hours were reduced 60 percent due to "low ceiling, icing, and
increased smoke." But the group could look back upon 17,875 flying
hours in one year with only two minor accidents.

By early 1945 the 477th had undergone training not only at Selfridge,
Godman, and Walterboro fields, but had utilized Sturgis and Atterbury
fields as well. Training began to suffer from so many changes of station.

Godman Army Air Field did not escape the troubles that beset Walterboro Army Air Field. Blacks could use all recreational facilities and the
Officers' Club, a situation made possible by the fact that whites could
utilize the segregated facilities at adjoining Fort Knox. Although the War
Department had specified that all recreational facilities be open to all, the
Fort Knox C.O. circumvented the directive by requiring that special
ushers seat personnel entering the base theater in order to avoid "confusion." Not surprisingly, entering personnel were seated by race.

A group of enlisted men from the 477th attempted to sit in the first
empty seats they saw. Their action caused a commotion at both Fort Knox
and Godman, and an NAACP inquiry. The Fort Knox C.O. essayed the
old segregationist defense that blacks were comfortable with segregation.
"Frankly, they haven't any desire to sit scattered around in the audience
any more than other people here," and, also not surprisingly, "what is
creating the problem is a lot of goddam agitators." The C.O. was not an
isolated type at Fort Knox. A Colonel Throckmorton responded to the
First Air Force, regarding a request by Colonel Davis (by then C.O. of the
477th) for quarters on base for some of his officers, "We have four
General officers living here on the post, and, by God, they just don't want
a bunch of coons moving in next door to them." And early in the 477th's
stay at Godman Field, General Hunter declared, in the spirit of Colonel
Selway, that racial problems would not arise, for "there will be no race
problems here for I will not tolerate any mixing of the races and anyone
who protests will be classed as an agitator, sought out, and dealt with
accordingly."

As the 477th continued its lengthy training while white supervisory personnel climbed the ladder of promotion, the "fragile" morale of the group cracked, as documented by General Giles and by Truman Gibson. General Giles noted a lack of respect for Colonel Selway because of his apparent obliviousness to his men. Yet Giles praised Selway and concluded that "there is nothing in the immediate situation to cause alarm." Gibson noted more perceptively that the men of the 477th did not come forward with their complaints in Selway's presence.

In early March 1945, the various units of the group made the last of its no less than thirty-eight moves in a little less than a year, this time to Freeman Field, Indiana. And at Freeman the long smoldering resentment would explode into a widespread "mutiny."

A month before the move from Godman to Freeman Field, Colonel Selway had surveyed the situation at the latter base and had compiled an elaborate scheme of designating each building by race, particularly labeling two structures for racially separate Officers' Clubs. In so doing, Selway had skirted the February 1944 War Department directive that prohibited racial segregation in base facilities while permitting segregation by unit. Selway had simply designated certain buildings for 477th personnel, who just happened to be black, and others for supervisory personnel, who just happened to be white. However, Selway had disregarded Army Regulation (AR) 210-10, which gave the right of membership in base clubs to all base officers. Admittedly, the two directives seem to have been contradictory. General Hunter fully backed the 477th's C.O. by dispatching a secret telegram to Selway giving him full support, and asserting that any "insubordination would be met by arrest of offending personnel, and that continued insubordination would be met by confinement in the guardhouse if necessary." While Colonel Selway and General Hunter maintained that the separate Officers' Clubs had nothing to do with race, Colonel Selway himself gave the game away by referring to the club "that belongs to the white officers."

Further proof that this supposed segregation by unit was simply a ploy for racial segregation was provided by the fact that a number of black officers not assigned to the 477th, such as medical officers, were assigned to the "black" Officers' Club.

The men of the fighting 477th, with their record of prickly assertion of their rights, were not about to endure passively such manipulation. Soon after their arrival, a group of enlisted men and one officer attempted to integrate a café in nearby Seymour, but after some name-calling, the provost marshal quieted the incident. That provost marshal, incidentally, was under two suspended indictments for the killing of two blacks while assigned to the Dayton, Ohio, police force. Back on the base, small groups of officers attempted to use the "white" club, while the officers of the "black" club (which they termed "Uncle Tom's Cabin") defiantly elected an amenable white officer to their club board. On March 15 Colonel Selway assembled all officers of the group to inform them of General Hunter's order of separate facilities.

On April 5, the clash, long anticipated by black and white personnel at Freeman Field, erupted. The day opened with Colonel Selway's ordering of a black press reporter from the base for collecting material for an "unauthorized" story on the 477th.

At 5:00 P.M. Colonel Selway was warned by an anonymous telephone call that a combat-crew training squadron consisting of about one hundred men, which had arrived that afternoon from Godman Field, would attempt to enter the "white" club. Selway immediately posted a provost marshal's guard to the club with orders to arrest any "trainee" (read "black") personnel who attempted to enter, and ordered all but the main entrance locked.

At 8:30 P.M. four black officers presented themselves at the club entrance, were refused admittance, and left without incident. But thirty minutes later a group of nineteen black lieutenants from the Combat Command Training Squadron brushed past the provost's guard and were then ordered back to their quarters under arrest by the club officer. Fourteen more black officers entered without force at 10:20. Fifteen minutes later three black officers forced their way into the now "integrated" club and were arrested, making a total of thirty-three. The next afternoon an additional twenty-four black officers walked in (no provost guard was present) and were again arrested by the club officer. By this time Colonel Selway, who had been on the telephone that morning reporting the incidents to General Hunter, ordered the "white" club closed.

Acting upon advice from First Air Force headquarters, Colonel Selway drew up Base Regulation 85-2, which in essence specifically prohibited "trainee" personnel from using the club reserved for base personnel, and vice versa. General Hunter approved Selway's actions and added that each officer at Freeman Field must sign the regulation. In the meantime, the judge advocate general of the Army Air Forces had advised Selway to release all but the three officers who had used force to enter the "white" club. General Hunter, in turn, received abundant moral support over the telephone indicating general Army Air Forces sentiment. Brigadier General R. L. Owens, deputy chief of the Air Staff, forwarded General Arnold's support, while Gen. William W. Welsh, also of the Air Staff (Training), felt that the real problem was one of reverse discrimination against whites, and warned that "if the thing gets out of hand you may have some of the 'jig-a-boos' up there dropping in on you at Mitchell Field [First Air Force headquarters]." But General Welsh saw an opportunity in the problems at Freeman Field: if they could document that the training of the 477th required extra time and trouble, "maybe we can eliminate the program gradually and accomplish our end."

The following day, General Hunter spoke by telephone to the air judge advocate, who assured him that the black officers' anticipated use of AR 210-10 in their defense was specious. He offered his full support. Hunter ruefully reminded the legal officer that such support had been extended to Colonel Boyd and the result had been a severe personal reprimand and removal. The air judge advocate soon forwarded a written opinion that contained the ingenious argument that while segregation of base buildings by a base commander was "restricted," an individual officer could not make a complaint about the situation. Both the air judge advocate and General Hunter could now argue that the two carefully separated clubs were in reality one, and that simply due to circumstances a perhaps temporary division had been made for "practical, disciplinary, or morale" reasons.

While all of the white officers and a majority of black officers at Freeman signed Colonel Selway's regulation, 101 black officers, deeply suspicious of the document, refused. The recalcitrants were practically all of the 477th Combat Command Training Squadron, plus approximately 20 men of the 619th Bombardment Squadron. Every holdout was then given an individual reading of the 64th Article of War by the base legal officer in the presence of two white and two black officers and a secretary. Each man was then given a direct order to sign and, as each refused, was then placed under arrest.

The following day, the 101 holdouts were transferred by air to Godman Field ("old home" for many) in a flight of C-47 transports. Upon arrival, they were met by troops from Fort Knox in full battle dress, mounted on half-track armored cars.

For all that, the move to Godman Field may have come just in time. Freeman Field had seethed with rumors and racial tension. White troops there were overheard in such comments as "If one of them [blacks] makes a crack at my wife . . . I'll kill him," or "Their club is better than ours. Why don't they stay in their place?" and "I killed two of them in my hometown, and it wouldn't bother me to do it again."

These reactions were in distinct contrast to the demeanor and discipline displayed by black personnel. From the beginning, compared to the spontaneous and rather chaotic protest at Selfridge Field, this was a disciplined and well-organized demonstration. With the sole exception of the three officers who pushed their way into the club, military courtesies were punctiliously observed, and the men were always in proper uniform.

Further, the black officers maintained a strong solidarity. Even those not involved in entering the "white" club were apparently caught up. Colonel Selway, on the night of the incident, drove around the base, encountering on several occasions groups of fifty or more black officers, in correct uniform, who upon being asked what was wrong and who was their spokesman, replied courteously that nothing was wrong and that they had no spokesman.

The men were aware as a group that the real issue at Freeman Field was not segregation, although in the words of one of the 101, "We resented the hell out of segregation." The 101 could not end segregation overnight, but they could bring dramatic attention to the dead-end promotion policies for blacks in the 477th, and perhaps cause some changes in that area. They were also aware that the penalty for willful disobedience of Article 64 in time of war was death.

The considered refusal by a large body of military personnel to obey a direct order by a superior officer in wartime was bound to cause widespread repercussions. Even before the 101 had been flown to Godman Field, Truman Gibson and the Advisory Committee on Negro Troop Policies (the McCloy Committee) had begun inquiries. And, of course, such an affair would arouse political interest. No less than twelve senators and four congressmen, not all of whom were considered to be particularly "progressive," were among those who made inquiries to the War Department about the 101. Faced with such political heavyweights as senators Homer Ferguson, Scott Lucas, Arthur Vandenberg, and Hiram Johnson, and congressmen Emanuel Celler, Michael Curley, and Louis Ludlow, it is not surprising that the War Department Congressional Liaison Office called for particulars of the case. There is also evidence of White House interest.

Even before receipt of the first congressional letters of inquiry, General Marshall had ordered the release of all but the three officers who had used force to enter the "white" club. The astute Marshall undoubtedly had realized the political furor that would erupt were the case fully prosecuted. General Hunter was dismayed by the decision, lamenting that "they cannot do that . . . I cannot command under those circumstances." General Arnold had voiced full support for Hunter, but Arnold was, of course, outranked by Marshall. However, they would have to wait until the full investigation promised by the McCloy Committee had been completed.

The Army Air Forces sent more or less stereotyped replies to the inquiring congressmen, stating that the 101 had refused to obey a legitimate order from their commander regarding base recreational facilities, and had further refused to sign a document stating that they were aware of the order. However, the letters continued, there existed some reasonable doubt "that these officers fully understood the implications of their action." It was therefore determined that the men "should be released from arrest and suitable orders were accordingly issued for their restoration to duty following the administration of an appropriate reprimand." The letter is significant more for what it omitted than for what it included. Congressional inquiries about racial discrimination were met by an account of the refusal to read and sign a base regulation. And the letter gave the definite impression that all of the men were about to be released with no more than a reprimand. But three officers, lieutenants Thompson, Clinton, and Terry, were, in reality, being held for court-martial.

By the time the McCloy Committee began its investigation, in May 1945, the Army Air Forces had dropped the pretense of vocational or unit segregation, noting openly in its summary of the incident that "the Commander issued orders which in effect restricted Negro officers from using the facilities assigned to white officers."

The McCloy Committee issued its report on May 18, 1945, finding that Colonel Selway had acted within regulations by arresting the 101. The committee, however, concluded that Selway's action in segregating Officers' Club facilities was in conflict with army regulations and policies, and recommended that the Army Air Forces's inspector general's report favorable to Colonel Selway be returned "with the request that its nonconformance with Army Regulations and War Department Policies be brought to the attention of the Commanding General, Army Air Forces, for appropriate action." Chairman McCloy was particularly exercised by the Army Air Forces inspector general's conclusion, which seemed to call for the "return to a policy of separate and equal facilities for white and Negro personnel." Adoption of this policy would "be a step backward and would reverse the position taken by the War Department in the Selfridge Field case in which case it was clearly determined that designation of recreational facilities for the use of a particular race or color group would not be permitted." Yet McCloy left the door somewhat ajar for continued confusion by conceding the right of a base commander to allocate recreational facilities by units or by capacity—a position not too far from the justification offered by Colonel Selway.

The AAF was not happy with the McCloy Committee's findings, and General Owens spoke for many officers when he declared that officers' clubs were like home to most officers, and since whites and blacks rarely mixed socially in civilian life "the Army should *follow* the usages and customs of the country," for, after all, the United States was a democracy, and the opinion of the majority should prevail. This, of course, was the standard Army and Army Air Forces boilerplate response to any proposal for even a moderation of military racial segregation.

The Freeman Field 101 case was finally closed in July, when two of the lieutenants held for trial for using force (Thompson and Clinton) were acquitted, and Lieutenant Terry was acquitted of the charge of willful disobedience. But Terry was convicted of the use of force against a provost marshal officer, and sentenced to a modest forfeiture of fifty dollars per paycheck for three months. An even sweeter outcome for the 101 was the relief of Colonel Selway and his replacement by none other than Colonel Davis as commanding officer of the 477th, although this did mean in a sense an even greater degree of segregation.

Here was a major victory for black Americans. One hundred and one military officers had committed a wartime capital offense, and, in the outcome, one officer had received only a trifling punishment. General Hunter, aware of the significance of the whole episode, remained bitter for at least two decades later. He asserted that he could receive no effective support from his superiors because "General Arnold got his orders from General Marshall, and he got his from Secretary of War Stimson, and he got his from Mrs. Roosevelt."

Oddly, although the case of the Freeman Field 101 would appear to have been a major event in U.S. race relations, stirring some 20 percent of the U.S. Senate, for example, to action or inquiry, the mutiny was not extensively reported, even in the black press. And in Italy the men of the 332nd received only the most sketchy of reports. Undoubtedly the death of President Roosevelt, the transition to the Truman administration, and the victorious conclusion to the war in Europe the following month, relegated the Freeman Field 101 to the bottoms of the back pages of the nation's newspapers, if the story was carried at all.

Still, the 477th Medium Bombardment Group (Colored) remained, and the question persisted of what to do with it. The first reaction of the Army Air Forces was to disband the group, but this would have meant the scattering of group personnel, either among white units, which would have violated military segregation policies, or among black units, which might well have spread the 477th's contentious spirit. With the end of the war in Europe the Pacific Theater remained a possibility as the group's first combat arena, well away from civilian America. Tentative plans were drawn up for the commitment of the 477th to the Pacific by October 1945. General MacArthur was apparently willing to accept the 477th. But his Air Forces commander, Lt. Gen. George C. Kenney, was not. General Arnold endorsed Kenney's position, adding opaquely that "it is only from the W.D. [War Department] viewpoint to send them but when Kenney uses them down in Mindanao or Borneo don't be surprised of the criticisms that are raised." Arnold agreed with Kenney that black fliers would "complicate" his war.

The question of the deployment of the 477th was probably academic by then; in the words of one authority, the 477th "had practically collapsed as a unit." A contemporary source recorded that 98 percent of all enlisted men and 75 percent of all officers wished to be separated from the military, sentiments uncharitably attributed to cowardice. This interpretation ignored the traumatic history of the group. In the end, the conclusion of World War II put an end to the question.

The 477th, although lingering on as a unit until 1947, never saw combat. It scored no "kills," blasted no enemy positions, bombed no alien cities. But it had its victories.

Climax and Victory 7.

For the Mediterranean Allied Air Force, March 1945 opened bright and clear, the weather remained fair for much of the month, and the 332nd Fighter Group flew a record of over fifty missions against a crumbling enemy. The high points of the month were the mission to Berlin on March 22, the bagging of three Luftwaffe jets and one possible rocket fighter, and the awarding of a Distinguished Unit Citation, the third for the 99th. Again there was the human cost: the commander of the 301st Fighter Squadron failed to return from that Berlin mission (but survived as a POW), twelve other pilots had to be posted as missing in action, and two were killed in flight-related accidents. Another loss was the rotation of the 302nd Squadron back to the states on March 21.

Truman Gibson, the civilian aide on Negro affairs to the secretary of war, flew into Ramitelli twice in March. His primary mission had been to inspect the all-black 92nd Infantry Division, which had suffered combat reverses and faced the prospect of being pulled out of the line (it was not, but remained at risk for the remainder of the war). Fortunately, by early

1945, the 332nd Fighter Group was not considered a "problem," and Gibson's visits were more in the nature of courtesy calls. The month was made even more memorable by the Red Tails' basketball team winning the XV Air Force championship. (The men were chagrined to lose later in the Adriatic finals to, of all things, an engineer battalion.)

As usual, the missions of the 332nd were primarily escort and ground attack, and they scored heavily in March. Enemy aircraft in the air and on the ground, river traffic, locomotives, and motor traffic were all indiscriminately blasted on an almost industrial scale. And, of course, the group faithfully escorted the "big boys" to and from their targets. But not until March 24 did the group's Mustangs encounter enemy in the air.

On that day, fifty-nine P-51s "broke ground" at Ramitelli on one of the longest missions ever attempted by XV Air Force: target Berlin. While the group was to escort B-17s to the Daimler-Benz tank works in the Nazi capital, it was also their mission to draw off as much as possible of what remained of the German fighters from Allied airborne landings north of the Ruhr. The 332nd was then to be relieved over Berlin. But the relief group failed to rendezvous at the designated time, and the Red Tails were ordered into action over the city.

The pilots were awed by but not particularly sympathetic to the panorama of destruction that stretched beneath them: a roofless, cold, gray, smoky shell of what had been the proudest capital of the old European continent. The only signs of life came from the medieval-appearing giant flak towers, manned by women and boys, spitting out virulently at the air invaders. Yet within what seemed to be the world's largest necropolis, the militaristic heart of the Nazi Reich still beat, perhaps sustaining itself on its own malevolence, with hope gone and faith shattered. Still the Daimler-Benz *werk* continued to mass-produce its panzers in the face of total and obvious defeat. When the fortresses had finished their jobs on Daimler-Benz (and on what was left of the surrounding neighborhoods), more than one escorting Mustang "lowered its nose a bit and let a burst go" to add its personal contribution to the ending of the Reich.

Over the skies of the dying capital, the Mustangs of the 332nd more directly attacked the Reich war machine, downing three of the new Luftwaffe jet fighters. Only one other fighter squadron of XV Air Force had scored against the jets so far. XV Air Force's intelligence debriefing recorded the experiences of lieutenants Robert W. Williams and Samuel Watts, Jr., of the 100th Squadron on that day:

At about 1215 hours, while escorting B-17's of the 5th Bomb Wing, Lieutenant Brown, the flight leader, called in enemy aircraft and had the advantage, so we thought. When I saw the first enemy aircraft, they were somewhat in line abreast formation, making very shallow turns. They must have been cruising at least 450 M.P.H. because we had an indicated 380 M.P.H. after my dive with everything full forward. The jets continued almost straight and in a slight dive, disappearing in the distance. At 1220 hours, my wing man called to me that we were being attacked by two (2) ME-262's from five o'clock high. They came in, in a close formation and fired at my wing man. I was about 500 feet above them, so I rolled over into a steep wing-over and developed a high speed stall from which I recovered, but immediately developed another. When I pulled out, I dropped down almost in the trail of the jet aircraft. I noticed simultaneous trail of propulsion from both aircraft. They continued straight through in a shallow dive for almost a minute after the attack and while still in very close formation they started a shallow left turn. I picked up a 2½ radii lead on the jet on the right and fired a long burst. I fired another burst and held it for about two seconds. I noticed hits on the aircraft and saw him fall out of formation and I believe he went down. I had to break off the attack because my wing man called me for help. In these encounters I observed that the jets stay under the bombers and attack beneath where they cannot be seen by fighters. They fly close formation using jet propulsion intermittently. They were very unaggressive to fighters. Jets take advantage of their speed and make shallow turns in order to not lose speed.

Lieutenant Roscoe C. Browne scored a more confirmed victory. Boring into a group of enemy jets he was amazed to find that they all were gone— except for the one that was now on his tail. Lieutenant Browne utilized his superior flying skill and the maneuverability of his Mustang, feinting and skidding from side to side, and causing his enemy to overshoot him. Now Lieutenant Browne was in the tail position, and firing several well-aimed bursts into the doomed jet. The enemy pilot parachuted, and his aircraft spun into the ground.

Obviously the Luftwaffe machines were better than their pilots in this encounter, but the 332nd did not escape unscathed. Three of their pilots were downed, although one landed in Soviet-occupied territory, and another was shot down and became a POW until the end of the war. The enemy jets unfortunately had also hit the temporary C.O. of the 301st, Capt. Armour McDaniel, who had taken over when Colonel Davis had to turn back with engine trouble short of Berlin; he had to wait out the few remaining months of the war in a German POW camp.

These were the fortunes of war, and within the week the Red Tails again encountered the enemy in the air, scoring victories that were the more prized as the Luftwaffe disputed less and less the skies over their "Thousand-Year Reich."

At the end of March, forty-six P-51s took off from Ramitelli at 1200, for a fighter sweep of the Munich area, with emphasis upon rail targets. The group split into three squadron flights while over Linz, Austria, and were about to begin their strafing runs when five Bf 109s and one FW 190 dove out of a cloudbank at seven Mustangs. The veteran Americans turned into the enemy and promptly shot down all six of the German fighters, who were aptly described as employing "unaggressive" tactics. About five minutes later, the 100th Squadron encountered eight FWs and three Bfs at about 3,000 feet. This enemy formation did engage more aggressively, but lacked any semblance of organized tactics, as each enemy attempted to battle the Mustangs individually. They failed to cover one another, and in consequence lost all but one of their number (and that one a "possible") with no loss to the Americans.

Lieutenant Robert W. Williams gave a vivid description of the fast and fortuitous nature of aerial combat in his report of the encounter:

I dived into a group of enemy aircraft. After getting on the tail of one of the enemy planes I gave him a few short bursts. My fire hit the mark and the enemy plane fell off and tumbled to the ground. On pulling away from my victim I found another enemy plane on my tail. To evade his guns I made a steep turn. Just as I had turned another enemy plane shot across the nose of my plane. Immediately I began firing on him. The [enemy] plane went into a steep dive and later crashed.

The Red Tails had not been deflected from their mission by the German interruption, claiming for that day seven locomotives, and other transportation facilities destroyed or damaged.

Germany's fighters were not significantly inferior to those of the USAAF. The Bf 109 design was probably getting "a bit long in the tooth" (as RAF types might have put it) but the FW 190, as well as its successor, the TA-152, were superior in certain qualities. (The 332nd probably tangled with the TA-152, but incorrectly reported it as an FW since the two bore a close resemblance.) Rather, the Luftwaffe's problem lay in the human element. Having waged war in the air almost full-tilt for over five years, Germany was running out of experienced pilots and the fuel to train their replacements. By the end of the war, a Luftwaffe pilot received less than one-third of the flight training hours of his USAAF or RAF opponent.

In April 1945, the 332nd bettered its March tally of missions, flying fifty-four penetrations from Prague to Verona to Munich. Its assignments ranged from strategic attacks, fighter sweeps, and bomber escorting to tactical armed reconnaissance, and resulted in the shooting down of seventeen enemy aircraft at a cost of five pilots.

The month of April 1945 also witnessed the inauguration of a new American institute of higher education, Naptha University (the origin of the title is obscure), an extension school for the group that, at its beginning, enrolled 15 percent of the 332nd's personnel. Its courses were designed to enable the men to pick up on their interrupted schooling.

On a lighter note, the group's stage review, "Good and Plenty," debuting in April, was judged one of the three best in the XV Air Force area. By winning the competition in the northern area the players were awarded a sixty-day performance tour. On April 16 the men of the 99th Fighter Squadron celebrated in the Panther Room the second anniversary of their overseas service, to the music of the group band.

Mission number 253, April 1, proved perhaps the greatest day of the 332nd's combat history. Forty-five P-51s rendezvoused with B-24 bombers of the 47th Bomb Wing to provide escort for a raid on the St. Polten, Austria, railroad marshaling yards. On the return leg of the mission, near Wels, Austria, eight P-51s spotted four enemy FW 190s below. Diving to the attack the Americans discovered additional Luftwaffe enemy aircraft above them who apparently planned to trap the unwary Mustangs, using the low-flying aircraft as bait. This enemy was skilled and aggressive. Individual dogfights erupted, ranging from 5,000 feet to the deck. The enemy succeeded in leading the Americans over flak positions, but when the melee had ended twelve German aircraft were scattered over the ground around Wels, as well as three Mustangs (one pilot returned).

For F.O. James H. Fischer the day was not yet over. Fischer had just shot down an enemy FW when a flak battery hit him, damaging his rudder and canopy. He headed for Soviet-occupied territory. Passing over Vienna he started climbing for altitude to cross the Alps for a landing in Yugoslavia. As he crossed over a small factory town, the slow-moving, crippled P-51 was hit again by ground fire. Fortunately, a British commando radio unit who had heard his call for "Big Friend" (assistance) had steered him to partisan-occupied Zagreb. Just as he crossed the Yugoslavian coast he ran out of fuel, but could see the Zagreb field in the distance. While gliding toward the field, Fischer, deciding that it would be too risky to land his shot-up aircraft, rolled over and bailed out. Fate dealt him one final blow in passing, as the tail of his fighter hit him as he fell. His parachute did open but he found himself floating upside down toward the ground. His luck now turned. As he landed safely among friendly Yugoslavs, he was spotted by an Allied L-5 observation plane. Soon after, a jeep and an ambulance arrived to take Fischer to the Zagreb airfield. There a C-47 transport returned him to Ramitelli in time for his supper—the same day.

On April 15, a Bf 109 was encountered by two Red Tail Mustangs while strafing rail targets. The pilots experienced little difficulty in raking the Bf with deflection shots from the rear. The enemy burst into flame and crashed into the ground. The encounter is noteworthy only because the hostile aircraft lacked distinctive markings and was painted a dark blue. Here was perhaps a last effort of the fascist Italian Social Republic's air arm. Also on that mission the 332nd destroyed seventeen steam locomotives (sixteen damaged) as the noose tightened on Nazi transportation arteries.

Also on April 15 Colonel Davis led his group on a difficult strafing mission over Austria. Expert navigation by Davis guided his pilots through low clouds and haze to targets he knew would be alerted, due to previous raids earlier in the day. Davis pressed hard the attacks on rail targets for more than one hour, quitting the assault only when no further targets could be found. Although only one enemy aircraft was shot down, Davis's mission accounted for an astonishing thirty-five locomotives, fifty-two rail vehicles, four barges, and four motor vehicles. The last major combat missions of the 332nd Fighter Group were flown on April 23: escort for B-24 bombers of the 55th and 304th bomb wings over northern Italy.

Some accounts of this time credit the group with a probable Me 163. This was the Luftwaffe's rocket interceptor, an amazing machine unparalleled, then or later, in any other air force, for which any fighter pilot should be grateful. These rocket-propelled aircraft were used to protect top-priority targets, such as the synthetic oil plants and Berlin itself. But the record of the Me 163 may have served as a deterrent to all other air services. Its fuels were both highly corrosive and extremely explosive. Pilots who survived landings without spinal injuries inflicted by the landing skid that took the place of conventional gear still ran the risk of having their skin eaten away by the potent propulsion mixture spraying from tanks ruptured from the hard landing, or of perishing in a sudden eruption of that fuel. On occasion, all of these calamities occurred *seriatum.* Finally, the Me 163 had an extremely short range, and its very speed worked against its effectiveness in combat against lumbering allied bombers. Still, it was disconcerting for Allied airmen, engaged in more or less horizontal combat, to encounter this bat-like little horror rocketing up at them almost vertically from nowhere.

The end was now palpably near, and the 332nd was running out of targets they could hit on the ground without endangering friendly troops. Thus the last combat mission of the group was flown a full two weeks before the surrender of Germany. This final mission was the escorting of a P-38 photo reconnaissance aircraft to Prague (still German-occupied). Just before reaching Prague, three of the Mustang escorts investigated a suspicious aircraft and encountered five Bf 109s. The enemy seemed bent only on escape, even rocking wings to appear friendly, but the hardened veterans coldly sent four of the Luftwaffe fighters plowing into the ground at no loss to themselves; they had lost too many good men to the enemy. But the killing would soon cease.

May 8 was V-E Day. The men of the 332nd massed for the awarding of medals and recognition. In a final salute, they passed in review. Their war was over—at least until they were shipped to the Pacific. More formal recognition came on May 11 in a ceremony in which Gen. Nathan F. Twining, XV Air Force C.O., presented more awards against the gleaming aluminum backdrop of spotless Mustangs in formal array.

The men were very much aware that this was not the end of fighting, however. Over everything loomed the prospect of war to the death against the determined Empire of Japan.

Early in May the group had made its final move of its war, transferring from Ramitelli to Cattolica Air Field, a move that brought the men to "spotless white buildings" that were considerably superior even to the accumulated facilities and amenities built up over the months at their old base. But Cattolica was little more than a staging area for redeployment to the Pacific. The favorite topic of conversation now focused on "points," those credits earned by service and combat time, missions, dependents, and age, to determine whether a serviceman would be shipped to action in the Pacific. The fortunate "high-point man" could look for a stateside assignment. The waiting stretched interminably, but the men of the

332nd kept their skills honed by proficiency flying and a training program that stressed classes in Japanese aircraft and warship recognition, Pacific orientation, weather and topography of the Far East, and tropical medicine. In addition, Naptha University broadened its course offerings, while the more cosmopolitan enrolled in courses at the University of Florence.

Another way of putting in the time until rotation, and of particular interest for any of the men who needed a morale boost, were the guided tours to XV Air Force targets in Austria and southern Germany, where men of the 332nd could witness the grim results of the work of the "heavies" they had guarded so faithfully.

On June 8, Colonel Davis was awarded the Silver Star. The group C.O. received the award specifically in recognition of the April 15 raid, but his men felt that it was due as much to his leadership, proven through two years of intense air combat. Colonel Davis could claim no enemy aircraft to his personal credit, but he had amassed sixty missions and was responsible in so many ways for the success of the group, from the tenuous beginnings of the 99th Pursuit Squadron to the glory of 1945. He had held his men fully to his own exacting standards, and although they would never love "The Thin Man," they would respect him and follow him anywhere. Fifteenth Air Force General Dean Strother, no friend whatsoever of black military aviation, nonetheless remarked to a black war correspondent on the occasion, "[Davis] is a fine soldier and has done wonders with the 332nd. I am positive that no other man in our Air Corps could have handled this job in the manner he has."

A few hours after the presentation of awards, Colonel Davis and a cadre of forty officers and airmen boarded B-17s for the drafty, cramped, interminable flight back to the United States and the command of the disintegrating 477th Composite Group (Colored).

Aftermath 8.

Redeployment of the 332nd Fighter Group began in July 1945, with the return to the United States of the pioneer 99th Fighter Squadron and its assignment to the 477th Composite Group, so called because it now comprised a fighter as well as a bomber squadron. The remaining squadrons of the 332nd Group, now commanded by Lt. Col. George S. Roberts, arrived at the New York Port of Embarkation on October 17, 1945, aboard the transport *Levi Woodbury,* to an enthusiastic welcome. The group was immediately forwarded to Camp Kilmer, New Jersey, where most of the enlisted personnel were separated from the service as the group was inactivated. A month prior, the war against Japan had unexpectedly terminated.

Despite the hearty and genuine welcome staged for the Red Tails in New York, the further south the surviving officers proceeded on their ways to Tuskegee or Godman air bases, the more mixed their reception and their feelings in the land for which they had fought. These were not the imaginings of shell-shocked veterans. In June 1945, the Army Air Forces's assistant chief of staff (G-1) had submitted to General Arnold a map of the continental United States which was literally color-coded. The map featured those areas, colored green, which could be presumed not hostile to the postwar deployment of black Army Air Forces personnel. There were not many green areas. Some communities had already threatened to boycott any black units stationed among them.

Those personnel arriving at Tuskegee Army Air Field, where it had all started, found themselves assigned to little more than a catchment area where they put in time. They were given demeaning assignments or none at all. The most outrageous example must have been the assignment of Colonel Roberts, former C.O. of both the 99th and the 332nd, to the post of Bachelor Officer Quarters Officer, a duty always given to a very junior officer. The situation became so debilitating that Pres. Fred Patterson of Tuskegee Institute, who had been so active in the location of aviation at his school, sent a telegram to the War Department, reversing his earlier stand. "I do not believe that the best interest of the Negro in the Army Air Force[s] will be served if the Group were stationed in the community with the personnel of the said group displeased with the location." The Army Air Forces acquiesced and, since it was rapidly contracting anyway, began to phase out TAAF. The pioneer home of the black military aviation closed down in early 1946, to the end commanded by a white officer and with whites in most leadership positions.

The group was moved to Godman Army Air Field where Colonel Davis replaced the infamous Colonel Selway as C.O. of the 477th. Colonel Davis had built up a nucleus of black command officers, thus removing the major source of discontent.

The 477th had excelled almost from the beginning in its flight, navigation, and bombing proficiency. With Colonel Davis in command, the artificial and debilitating distinction between trainee (black) and base (white) personnel was put to rest. The 477th was soon considered something of an elite outfit.

Having left the war-weary P-51s in Italy, the 99th found itself back in P-47 Thunderbolts (models D and N), while the 617th and 618th bombardment squadrons continued to train in B-25 Mitchell medium bombers (models H and J).

Yet the primary mission of the 477th and the 332nd, like that of other USAAF units in those demobilization months, was more the discharge of personnel who had not reenlisted than flying and training. The entire U.S. military was experiencing drastic reductions. By the middle of February

1946, the 477th was down to sixteen B-25s and twelve P-47s. (About 111 to 126 aircraft and 994 personnel were normal for a fighter group during the war.) But in those difficult times Colonel Davis preserved morale and flying proficiency, although losses mounted from the failure of aging aircraft pressed beyond the best efforts of maintenance crews. Godman Army Air Field itself, a wartime temporary facility, was rapidly deteriorating.

So it was that the 477th endured its next and final move to Lockbourne Army Air Field near Columbus, Ohio, in March 1946. In light of the "welcome" extended to the 477th in Ohio, Colonel Davis might have been excused for believing that his group was returning to Tuskegee in the Deep South, or even back into a combat zone. The editor of the Columbus *Citizen,* maintaining that "this is still a white man's country," objected to "servants" doing America's future fighting. When the Lockbourne site was settled upon, an all-weather Army Air Forces unit decamped immediately and unceremoniously. Apparently some such reception had been expected, for the 332nd had reconnoitered the base from an altitude of 18,000 to 20,000 feet, and had "infiltrated" the area on the ground in groups of no more than four, in order not to alarm the natives. For all that, the men of the 477th and the 332nd experienced slights, with some restaurants, for example, refusing to serve them even in uniform. But Lockbourne was a vast physical improvement on Godman, and the two units settled in on their final base.

While most of the problems faced by the 477th and the 332nd were common to all Army Air Forces units during that period of pell-mell demobilization, the policies of racial segregation, still adhered to by all of the U.S. armed services, aggravated an already difficult situation. Because there were few slots for them elsewhere, blacks with low AGCT scores were sent to Lockbourne in large numbers, lowering morale and efficiency. At the same time, Lockbourne was "raided" by higher authorities for skilled black personnel who were in short supply because of their high scores in technical fields. But these losses could not be made up; skilled black technicians were in extremely short supply, but no white Army Air Forces technician could be sent to Lockbourne, there to be commanded by a black.

Officers of the group could not advance in grade because they could not be promoted beyond the limited slots in the 477th or the even more limited places outside the group. Thus the shortage of black pilots and officer technicians presented no real opportunity for advancement. Colonel Davis was past due for assignment to a senior Army Air Forces school, a precondition for further personal advancement. But the Pentagon temporized, realizing that Colonel Davis and his staff would have to be replaced by white officers, and that this replacement, even if temporary, would result in protests from the black community.

The 477th and the Army Air Forces in general, however, suffered from no general shortage of black personnel, for the military offered a relief from civilian social and economic pressures. In fact, the Army Air Forces suspended black enlistments entirely in mid-1946 because of an extraordinary rise in the numbers of entering blacks.

On July 1, 1947, the 477th was deactivated and immediately redesignated the 332nd Group. Also in that month the Army Air Forces became an independent service, the United States Air Force (USAF). One month later, in yet another change of designation, the 332nd Group was transformed into the 332nd Fighter Wing. The title "Wing" was misleading, however, for the 332nd was really of group size, and remained perpetually short of skilled technicians, such as weather, navigation, and intelligence officers. In June 1948, the wing lacked twenty-eight pilots as well. The 332nd and the newly minted USAF were both clearly marking time.

But black Americans were not. Without a break, they continued the wartime momentum of their demands for change into the postwar era. This time there would be no repetition of the post-1918 years when modest wartime gains were wiped out. Of course, many white Americans still defended the old customs and laws. Black veterans found that the American Legion, the Veterans of Foreign Wars, and the Disabled Veterans of America maintained their Jim Crow policies. Blacks did not participate in the generous state and federal veteran job training and education benefits in anything like their proportion to the general World War II veteran population. The National Urban League estimated that of 102,200 Southern veterans receiving such training, only 7,700 were blacks, even though blacks comprised an astounding one-third of all Southern vets. Racial murders and "incidents" also continued as before the war. But there were differences now, aside from postwar black determination to put an end to such things; at least the more gruesome received negative national publicity.

Many black veterans had seen something of the outside world while in the military, and few could have been unaffected by the lofty rhetoric of

Allied war aims: a better world based on justice, equality, and freedom. Many "voted with their feet" against the old ways; according to one source, only 67 percent expected to return to their old homes after the war, as opposed to 87 percent of whites, and no less than two-thirds of blacks polled did not plan to go back to the same line of work they were in before Pearl Harbor. In the eloquent words of one perceptive study made toward the end of the war:

A million Negroes—practically all the young men of the group between eighteen and thirty—have been given an education far beyond any school or college. They have been well housed and well fed. Their health has been safeguarded and their strength built up. They have been trained and disciplined—for the most part in wholesome fashion. They have seen other parts of the country and of the world. Along with slights, most [black] soldiers have sensed wide horizons and have had some warming experiences of respect and admiration as they moved over America, through the Pacific, and in Europe. Coming back from such experience, the whole young male population of the race will never again fit into the serfdom of southern feudalism or into second class status in northern industrial cities. It is too late ever again to keep Negroes "in their place."

The U.S. military hierarchy could not remain insulated from the tide of world events that had affected American blacks during the late war; neither could they adamantly resist black aspirations. As early as the spring of 1945, John J. McCloy had directed his Advisory Committee on Special (formerly Negro) Troop Policies to work out proposals for the utilization of blacks based upon wartime experience in the postwar military establishment.

Consequently, the Army and the Army Air Forces in May 1945 began collecting data on the employment of blacks in the war in Europe. The various AAF reports are of particular significance. While their content varied considerably, each confused "intelligence" with "education." While all but one recognized the black American's historic lack of opportunity, each ascribed the documented evidence that blacks performed their military duties at a lower level than whites in most skills to "lower intelligence," as well as to lack of initiative and judgment. At times the reports spoke of a lack of education, of opportunity, and of intelligence in almost the same breath, leading the unwary reader to no other logical conclusion than that even increasing education and opportunity for blacks could not really help the situation.

Not surprisingly, the most pejorative report was submitted by First Air Force. With a startling lack of judgment, First Air Force headquarters assigned their report to none other than Colonel Selway of Freeman Field notoriety. Colonel Selway was careful to label his findings a "documented historical report." General Hunter, First Air Force C.O., who had supported Colonel Selway to the fullest against the 477th's recalcitrant 101, insisted that "the Report is an honest and trustworthy document." Colonel Selway undoubtedly considered this a heaven-sent opportunity to "set the record straight" on the black troops who had given him so much grief; his went further than any other report in damning blacks. He attributed what he termed their "lack of qualifications or failure in performance" not to low intelligence or lack of education. The fault lay rather in their lack of initiative, even of character, as demonstrated by their fear of combat, by their high venereal disease rate, malingering, psychological problems, and lack of commitment, discipline, curiosity, and respect for property. Selway ended what was basically a tirade by recommending strongly "that there be no Negro flying with the postwar Army Air Forces," although he did concede that a few small cadres of black enlisted men could serve on selected bases. Apparently Colonel Selway's postwar Air Force would have no need for black officers in any capacity.

The most extensive Army Air Forces Command studies on the employment of blacks in the postwar Air Force were brought together in a lengthy memorandum by Lt. Col. Louis Nippert for General Arnold. The memorandum, "Participation of Negro Troops in the Postwar Military Establishment" (September 17, 1945) summarized the findings of the Command studies and made recommendations. It is also a mine of information today for the study of the black military experience in the Second World War.

This memorandum followed closely the contradictory and largely negative studies upon which it was based, calling for the continuance of almost total racial segregation in the postwar AAF. In fact, in one important aspect, the memorandum called for increased racial segregation when it recommended that the degree of racial separation in messing, socializing, and recreation be based on the prevailing customs of the surrounding civilian communities. Yet, as noted, AR 210-10 had opened membership in officers' clubs to all base commissioned personnel, and the general movement of War Department directives, although often ambiguous, was toward a lowering or blurring of military racial barriers.

The study called for the continuance of black pilot training (despite Colonel Selway) and technical specialties, but not above the level of manning for a group, that blacks should command only blacks, that nontechnical service black units be no larger than a battalion, and that there be equality of treatment and standards in training and discipline and overseas assignments. Blacks should be sent only to those U.S. locations favorable to their welfare (where that was was anyone's guess). Black officers and NCOs must be carefully selected and trained for their assignment to black units, and the Army Air Forces should absorb a proportion of blacks based upon the relative sizes of the three major armed forces, not to exceed 10 percent of total Army Air Forces strength—and all within the framework of racial segregation. For all intents and purposes it was back to 1941 as far as the Army Air Forces hierarchy was concerned. Apparently very little had been learned from wartime experience, except for the need for black units to be kept small and treated fairly, unexceptionable enough conclusions for the time.

The only high-ranking AAF officer to call for even a beginning to integration was the commanding officer of Tuskegee Army Air Field, Col. Noel Parrish. Colonel Parrish's report carried the authority of having been written by the white officer who had successfully commanded what was by far the largest concentration of AAF blacks in the United States. Colonel Parrish boldly condemned military racial segregation as unworkable and self-defeating, a handy excuse by whites and blacks for poor performance. He called for the assignment and treatment of blacks in the AAF as individuals, a position probably drawn from his experiences in flight instruction, a process he always believed called for individual attention. Parrish flatly asserted that "Negro officers should either be assigned according to qualifications or dismissed," and that the present "defensive, bewildered, evasion" of assignments by race instead of by qualification should cease, at least for officers. Certainly the record of the 99th, the 332nd, and the 477th should have vividly demonstrated to the Army Air Forces the crippling complications, as well as maldistribution and waste of resources that resulted from the requirement to assign black personnel by race as well as by qualification and need. And, as Colonel Parrish concluded, "There can be no *consistent* segregation policy because segregation is itself inconsistent and contradictory."

But Colonel Parrish's voice was a lonely one. His memorandum represented what might be considered a "radical" shade of the Army Air

Forces's spectrum of opinion on racial matters. Major General M. F. Harmon, chief of the Air Staff, represented mainstream AAF views when he told Colonel Parrish at the time that military racial integration is "inevitable, it will not come in your lifetime or in mine, or maybe in the lifetime of anyone living today, but some day this is bound to come about. But the country, the world, and even the blacks are not ready for it now, and we've just got to kind of go along with this thing during the war and keep from making an issue of it." Brigadier General E. Barber expressed similar sentiments in his "Recommendations for Organization, Command, and Utilization of Negro Soldiers in a Future Emergency": "Amalgamation is inevitable, but . . . it will take many years before it can be accomplished." And "amalgamation" of the races would not come "until the Negro race as a whole is raised completely up to the standards of the white race in intelligence, education," but a start could be made with a "super elite" all-black combat unit. Lieutenant General Hoyt S. Vandenberg, assistant chief of the Air Staff, and later chief of staff of the U.S. Air Force, seemed to speak for his colleagues when he declared that "segregation is essential" because of the "lower average intelligence of the Negro," and a lack of leadership and ability. General Vandenberg even felt that the 332nd's record was poor and that this record bolstered his arguments. At any rate he believed that the results were not worth the extra effort. General Vandenberg did not call for the elimination of blacks from the AAF, as did Colonel Selway, but his clear implication was that only political pressure kept them in the service where they had made no real contribution.

Meanwhile the board of officers organized in response to the McCloy Committee's directive for the study of postwar utilization of black troops was assembling personnel and evidence. From the start the War Department had proved itself somewhat more open than the Army Air Forces to moderation of racial segregation in the Army. The civilian aide on Negro affairs to the secretary of war, Truman Gibson, and the Advisory Committee on Negro Troop Policies had acted as limited forces for change. The Army's attitude toward black combat troops was affected not only by the poor combat record of the all-black 92nd Infantry Division but also by the excellent performance of the integrated combat riflemen platoons melded into white battalions late in the European war for which numerous black service NCOs took reductions in rank to enter. General Marshall was so impressed by the reports from the European Theater on these integrated black infantrymen that he boldly wrote to John McCloy, "I agree that the practicability of integrating Negro elements into white units should be followed up." Apparently McCloy had already brought up the possibility.

Truman Gibson, mindful of the highly unscientific Army studies of the interwar period, urged that "the current study avoid an unquestioning acceptance of the premises on which past policy was based and recognize that the nature of the racial problem before the Army has materially changed since 1940," and particularly, the study should "inquire into the present policy of segregation." Gibson had already succeeded in persuading the Army to utilize the historical division to evaluate the flood of material arriving on the subject of black troops in the war. Even at this early date (Spring 1945), War Department policy can be discerned as far in advance of that of the Army Air Forces on the question of racial segregation. Writing to McCloy, Gibson recommended "that the basic Army policy be changed to call for eventual non-segregation and assignment of Negro troops solely on the basis of ability and that the designated officer [General Gillem] be directed to plan on this basis" (no commas in original). Gibson's memo was probably in response to General Marshall's recommendation.

The impetus for change must have had its effect upon the Gillem Board (named for its chairman, Lt. Gen. Alva C. Gillem, Jr.), as seen in both the recommendations of that board and in the witnesses it called. Major black witnesses were Walter White, General Davis, Colonel Davis, Truman Gibson, Pres. Fred Patterson of Tuskegee Institute, and Judge Hastie. White witnesses of "progressive" hue were Colonel Parrish and Dr. William Alexander of the Rosenwald Fund. Against this impressive array, calling for the ending of military racial segregation, was set a cadre of military witnesses overwhelmingly advocating just the opposite.

The recommendations of the board were not startlingly innovative. In fact, the board's report is less impressive for what it said than for how it was said. In sum, the report called for a continuation of the more progressive attitudes and trends discernible within the War Department since 1943. Absolute equality of treatment in the utilization of personnel formed the foundation of the report's recommendations. Thus the report called for better training, planning for, and recruitment of blacks, including black women. Recognizing wartime gains in education and in white acceptance, it called for the improved utilization of this pool of trained manpower. The success of the integrated black infantry platoons in Europe encouraged the board to call for the continuation of such small "experimental" units in the postwar Army, and the utilization of blacks with special skills in Army overhead or service units "as individuals." Here was the only true break with segregation that the board recommended.

While Colonel Parrish later labeled these recommendations as "conservative," Truman Gibson, more privy to War Department and Army attitudes, confided in a memo to the new secretary of war, Robert P. Patterson, that the Gillem Report "means, of course, a completely integrated Army," and called for the publicizing of the report and a policy statement that would clearly set forth the goal of the eventual ending of military racial segregation. John McCloy indeed interpreted the Gillem Report to mean "for officers, complete equality without regard to race, and abandonment of all forms of segregation." McCloy and Gibson probably felt that any board of military officers that paid more attention to the testimony of the executive secretary of the NAACP or to the former and current black aides to the secretary of war was clearly something out of the ordinary and likely to lead to change.

But the immediate impact of the Gillem Report was practically nil. One reason was that the report was not issued as an order, but simply as a War Department circular. The very title of the report was transformed between the board and the printer by the addition of the word "policy" to the end of the title, a subtle change understood by those who could interpret Pentagon-ese: the report of the Gillem Board was just another study, not orders. Two years after the issuance of the report, Colonel Parrish warned that "the all Negro Air Corps is becoming an accepted institution . . . There is danger of assuming that 'the problem' is solved."

The only action by the War Department through 1949 that might be considered to have been in keeping with the Gillem Board's recommendations was the publication of "Army Talk, 170," an educational pamphlet dealing with the Army's black personnel. The goal of this effort was to increase the efficiency of personnel, and to that end the pamphlet stated flatly that "the Army's ultimate aim is to be able to use and assign all personnel in the event of another major war, without regard to race." But would it take "another major war" to bring about military racial integration?

The Army, however, faced a more practical and immediate personnel problem. For the next two years it had to fight the "Battle of the Numbers," caught between trying to attract new recruits, which were increasingly difficult to come by with the lapse of Selective Service calls after November 1946, and accelerating civilian prosperity. At the same time it attempted to curtail a flood of black enlistments and to discharge low-scoring soldiers in an Army that in some respects seemed to be falling apart.

To keep down the influx of black enlistees and, after 1948, draftees as well, the Army resorted to different standards for black and white entrants. From April 1948 to January 1950, it actually suspended all black enlistments. These were startlingly backward steps that somehow sparked surprisingly little protest from blacks. Military matters simply were not on the minds of most Americans in those postwar years.

The Army, indeed, had legitimate problems with its black troops, but those problems were primarily the result of its racial segregation policies. At their hub was the persistent fact that whereas low-scoring white recruits could be "diluted" throughout the military, blacks of whatever ability had to be concentrated in a strictly limited number of separate units.

But among higher civilian authorities the climate was definitely turning toward military racial integration. The first secretary of the newly created Department of Defense, James Forrestal, had set the Navy on the path of racial integration from 1944 on, when he had succeeded the obstructionist Frank Knox as secretary of the navy. And, of course, Pres. Harry Truman, at least since the publication of the President's Commission on Civil Rights' pamphlet, "To Secure These Rights" (1947) was known to favor military racial integration to some degree. Truman was the first president to address the NAACP, in 1947, and to visit Harlem. He established the Fair Employment Board in the Civil Service, an area in which he could exercise direct authority. In fact, President Truman was the first U.S. chief executive to deal publicly with race relations and to demand civil rights legislation.

The President's Committee on Civil Rights had called for legislation and action immediately to end military racial segregation. It furthermore broke with the unexamined tradition that "the military is not a sociological laboratory" and asserted that the armed services should protect the full civil rights of its members.

President Truman by 1948 was facing the political fight of his life, with both the leftist and the conservative Southern elements of the Democratic

Party not only defecting from his candidacy, but forming their own political parties. And when the Republican Party adopted a progressive platform calling for the end to military segregation, many of Truman's advisors saw the black vote as essential to any hopes for victory.

Having lost the Southern conservative Democrats, Truman felt free to woo the black vote. On July 26 he issued Executive Order No. 9981, recording his determination to see "equality of treatment and opportunity" for all in the armed forces of the United States, and creating the President's Committee on Equality of Treatment and Opportunity in the Armed Forces. Truman was also reacting to pressure from black leaders who feared that the forthcoming military draft bill would continue segregation. While Executive Order No. 9981 is considered by many to have been revolutionary, it did little more than codify trends already predominate in the military establishment, or at least in its higher echelons. No mention was made of segregation or integration. Yet the president within a few days of his issuance of the order succinctly clarified that order to mean integration of the military, and began to implement its mandate. The Committee on Equality of Treatment and Opportunity in the Armed Forces (known as the Fahy Committee after its chairman, Charles Fahy) began to meet in October 1948. There is no doubt that President Truman set as the goal of that committee full and immediate equality of treatment, if not actual racial integration, of the armed services.

Even earlier, a major change of attitude could be discerned among higher commanding officers. During the immediate postwar years, these officers, citing the record of blacks during the war and their own persistent fears of "disturbances," were almost uniformly opposed to racial integration. But by 1948, they or their successors generally greeted racial integration with something akin to relief. A major worry had been taken out of their hands. If it worked, fine; if not, it would not be their fault. By June 1950 (coincidentally the month of the start of the Korean War), the acting deputy chief of staff of the Army reported that racial integration had proceeded "rapidly, smoothly, and virtually without incident." By that date the Army and the Air Force were retaining racially segregated units primarily for personnel who were not eligible for specialist training yet could not be discharged at the moment. However, the Army would pay a heavy price for failure to tie up these loose ends sooner; the all-black 24th Infantry Regiment turned in a distinctly spotty combat record in the early months of the Korean War (along with plenty of white units), until its breakup in November 1950.

By the spring of 1947 the Army Air Forces, still fighting the "Battle of the Numbers," was coming to the realization that in a time of dramatically reduced funding, racial segregation was intolerably inefficient. According to several authorities, the first secretary of the fledgling Air Force, Stuart Symington, had, like Forrestal, been a believer in military racial integration since at least 1944.

To begin the implementation of this new Air Force commitment, Gen. Idwal Edwards, Air Force deputy chief of staff for personnel and a former member of the McCloy Committee, instituted in the spring of 1948 a study of Air Force racial segregation. (One might be forgiven for presuming that with all of the material gathered for the McCloy Committee and the Gillem Board, plus Colonel Parrish's definitive 1947 Air Command and Staff School Study, "The Segregation of Negroes in the Army Air Forces," and the Nippert and Gillem reports, General Edwards would have had at hand all the data on the subject he could have needed.)

The study, carried out by Lt. Col. Jack Marr, apparently concluded (the actual study has seemingly been lost) that "sound management" dictated that USAF personnel assignments be given solely on considerations of merit. Lieutenant Colonel Marr further concluded that due to racial quotas and segregation that the 332nd Fighter Wing was now not a particularly efficient unit, was "incapable of expansion," and therefore provided no mobilization potential. If committed to combat, it was "virtually certain that qualified replacements could not be provided to maintain it." The latter point was one that had plagued the 332nd Group throughout its wartime service, resulting in the men having to fly mission totals far in excess of those of pilots in "white" squadrons. In fact, Colonel Marr did not think that the group was a very good combat outfit, either, for that reason. Obviously "corrective action" was imperative, although Colonel Marr did not spell out what this might be.

Much of the continuing pressure in the postwar years upon the USAF to change its racial policies came apparently from Truman Gibson's assistant, J. C. Evans, already noted for his efforts in opening the CPTP to blacks back in 1939. Evans's pressure was subtle and is difficult to document, but he had been on the scene since before the war, enjoyed excellent personal relations with Air Force Secretary Symington, and his recollections comport basically with the documentary record. And in

1947 Evans succeeded Truman Gibson as civilian aide on Negro affairs to the secretary of war.

When the USAF did decide to integrate, the process was not a drawn-out affair like the Army's. Even General Vandenberg, the new Air Force chief of staff, was now positively anxious to integrate. Secretary Symington told President Truman in early 1949 that "our plan is to completely eliminate segregation in the Air Force. For example, we have a fine bunch of colored boys [the 332nd]—our plan is to take these boys, break up that fine group, and put them with other units and go right down the line 100 percent."

Symington was as good as his word. The 332nd would be the first target of USAF racial integration. All officers had to face a screening board—Colonel Davis presiding. Enlisted personnel, including Women's Air Force, took a written test and were screened by personnel counselors. The fate of each enlisted person was determined by a balance of test scores, past performance, specialty qualifications, and career choice. All faced four possibilities: retention in their present military occupational specialty (MOS), assignment to a different MOS, scheduling for additional or more advanced training, or separation from the Air Force. Marginal or extraordinary cases were also referred to Colonel Davis's board. Similar procedures were utilized for other all-black USAF units.

Interestingly, some opposition to Air Force racial integration came from black officers themselves, mistrustful of the service that had clung so tenaciously to racial segregation throughout the war years, and that had, in fact, actually instituted segregation less than a decade previously. The officers of the 332nd were particularly apprehensive of the screening board, even if presided over by Colonel Davis. Colonel Spann Watson, a charter member and combat veteran of the 99th, for example, felt "degraded" by having to appear before such a tribunal to determine his fitness. In the words of a letter of protest by two anonymous officers of the 332nd:

Now take an ordinary captain assigned to the 301st Fighter squadron, 332nd Group who must get by a "screening board" which is some additional machinery he must get by because he is a Negro officer, in spite of the fact that he was graduated from a flying school staffed and operated by Regular Air Force Personnel (white), sent to Italy . . . flew fifty . . . missions, returned to the states . . . and has been flying by Air Force standards since, acquired 1500 to 2000 hours. This captain now must be rechecked after five or six years in the Air

Force, and [*sic*] to determine whether he is "temperamentally unsuited."

Undoubtedly some officers feared competition within a racially mixed unit, or the loss of a relatively secure and undemanding position among a band of brothers. But, of course, it could also be argued that no white officer had to face a screening board to determine whether he was fit to work within a racially mixed unit. In the end, 23 percent of Lockbourne's personnel were separated from the service. On July 1, 1949, the 332nd Fighter Wing and segregated black flying in the United States Air Force had come to an end.

By this time the U.S. Air Force had moved so quickly along the road to racial integration under Secretary Symington that the Fahy Committee had merely to certify that the USAF meant to carry out fully the president's mandate. By the end of 1949, 1,253 racially integrated units had been established in the USAF, compared to only 167 in June of that same year. By May 1950 a mere twenty-four units were segregated by race. In fact, in that first year of racial integration, Colonel Parrish reported that there seemed to be more cases of whites going out of their way to hasten integration or to mitigate the effects of lingering segregation than there were of negative racial incidents.

Racial integration did not necessarily end racial prejudice, however, and the Air Force, which had integrated the most quickly and with the best will of the three armed services, fell behind in the 1960s in its commitment to equality of opportunity, and experienced serious racial trouble, sparked by off-base conditions and cases of individual discrimination.

But a good start had been made in the pre–Korean War years, and in the joyous words of J. C. Evans:

Observing ancient customs and creeds banished almost by the stroke of a pen— and with no untoward incidents of record—this record almost speaks for itself in saying with respect to other outmoded practices and procedures in the affairs of man, "Here in brief outline is a plan for progress with power and precision. Prepared, planned, projected, and proven all within a year, this shows what can be done despite all fearful foreboding to the contrary."

Summary and Retrospect 9.

Much of the racial progress in the U.S. Air Force in the post–World War II years can be traced to the pioneer 99th Pursuit Squadron and the 332nd Fighter Group. In 1940, before the establishment of the 99th, there were no blacks in the Army Air Corps. By 1948, 26,000 blacks were in the U.S. Air Force, including 249 black officers. (Comparable white figures were 294,000 airmen and 46,000 officers.) These figures were still far below the 10 percent goal set for black armed services participation in both pre- and postwar studies, but nonetheless they represented enormous progress. By 1971 U.S. Air Force black strength had surpassed 10 percent with 78,000 out of a total of 624,595 airmen. But in that year black officers still represented only 1.7 percent of a total of 125,214 USAF officers. In fact, the numbers of black officers in the USAF have never approached 10 percent.

It would be difficult to imagine any progress taking place at that time without the pioneering Tuskegee aviation organizations. The question had often been posed, "How do Negroes fight?" and later, "How do Negroes fly?" The 99th and the 332nd were thus subjected to intense and often hostile scrutiny, as was the black 92nd Infantry Division. No one had inquired about the fighting ability of the 331st Fighter Group or the 91st Division, and certainly no questions were raised about the general fighting ability of white men. Yet an analysis of the 99th compiled by the Statistical Control Division of the USAAF's Office of Management Control after the 99th's first six months in combat, when it would have been at its most inexperienced, showed "no significant general difference between this squadron and the balance of the P-40 squadrons in the MTO." The analysis revealed that "from October forward . . . the 99th destroyed 12 E/A [enemy aircraft] while losing 2; the other squadrons destroyed 3 E/A while losing 0.3 on the average." But the 99th, presumably because of maintenance deficiencies, reported slightly more aircraft noneffective, and dispatched only 79 percent as many sorties as the control squadrons. Since the Statistical Control Division had not been involved in the struggle for black participation in the USAAF, and presumably had no ax to grind, its figures are all the more significant.

Like the 99th, the 332nd appears to have been a good average fighter group. Consistently assigned fewer missions than comparable "white" groups in its peak period of aerial combat during the period of August 1944 to April 1945, the four-squadron 332nd encountered far fewer enemy aircraft than three squadron "white" groups. Yet in 141 encounters, it destroyed 532 enemy aircraft, while in 1,252 encounters the three "white" control groups shot down a combined total of 334 of the enemy. In fact, when the percentage of enemy aircraft shot down is expressed as a percentage of enemy aircraft encountered, the 332nd was the high scorer. Of course, this is a crude comparison, for it compares encounters, which can include any number of enemy aircraft, to the exact numbers of enemy aircraft destroyed. (Even that number must be handled with care; it is based on fast-moving, confused combat situations.) And the factor of luck was always present. For example, in the month of January 1945, only one group (not the 332nd) encountered any enemy aircraft, but it did so on an impressive 46 occasions. Yet two months earlier the same group had encountered nothing.

In losses during the same period, the 332nd suffered one-third of the losses to enemy aircraft of the four groups compared. But on a squadron-to-squadron basis the losses of the four-squadron 332nd are proportionate.

These figures, compiled by XV Air Force itself, hardly bear out its contention to the Gillem Board that "the Negro pilots never became engaged in a so-called 'knock down and drag out fight.'" In the column of losses not attributed to enemy action, the Army Air Forces was unanimous that the 332nd was inferior to comparable fighter groups, and even Colonel Parrish conceded that maintenance in the 332nd was "not quite as good as most white squadrons [sic, "groups"]." The 332nd averaged more noneffective aircraft, but the margin was close and in some months the 332nd actually had fewer noneffectives. Its percentage of aircraft airborne differed from the control groups so little as probably to be statistically insignificant. The three control groups averaged 88.6 percent aircraft airborne, the 332nd 85 percent. Startlingly, it seems that the 332nd actually suffered from less mechanical trouble to its aircraft than the control XV Air Force groups, if the difference in size is taken into account. This conclusion is the more impressive in view of the far fewer numbers of black Americans with experience in mechanical or technical trades. Even those accepted for aircrew training had only a little over half as much mechanical experience as white trainees. At times, in fact, stanine scores had to be lowered for black pilot, navigator, and bombardier trainees in order to fill quotas. As noted earlier, black participation in prewar civil aviation was minuscule, and in the prewar aircraft industry practically nonexistent. Finally, the total exclusion of blacks from the Air Corps before 1940 deprived the 332nd of any cadre of experienced ground crew, not to mention pilots.

World War II had presented an opportunity that many blacks had seized and retained throughout that conflict and into the postwar years. Despite stubborn resistance to any consideration of racial integration by the Army Air Forces, the segregated men of the 332nd proved that blacks could fly and fight—if any such proof were needed. But more important, the experiences and the accomplishments of the Tuskegee Airmen served as a focus of pride and encouragement in the decades to come and ensured that, eventually, in war or in peace, there would be no more segregated skies.

USAF HISTORICAL STUDY NO. 85
USAF Credits for the Destruction of Enemy Aircraft World War II

Name	Rank	Date	Credit

99th Fighter Squadron

Name	Rank	Date	Credit
Allen, Clarence W.	2nd Lt.	1/17/44	0.50
Ashley, Willie, Jr.	1st Lt.	1/27/44	1.00
Bailey, Charles P.	2nd Lt.	1/27/44	1.00
Baugh, Howard L.	1st Lt.	1/27/44	1.00
Braswell, Thomas P.	2nd Lt.	3/31/45	1.00
Campbell, William A.	Maj.	3/31/45	1.00
Custis, Lemuel R.	Capt.	1/27/44	1.00
Davis, John W.	2nd Lt.	3/31/45	1.00
Diez, Robert W.	1st Lt.	1/27/44	2.00
Driver, Elwood T.	1st Lt.	2/5/44	1.00
Eagleson, Wilson V.	2nd Lt.	1/27/44	1.00
		2/7/44	1.00
Hall, Charles B.	1st Lt.	7/2/43	1.00
	Capt.	1/28/44	2.00
Hall, James L.	2nd Lt.	3/31/45	1.00
Jackson, Leonard M.	1st Lt.	7/26/44	1.00
		7/27/44	1.00
	2nd Lt.	2/7/44	1.00
Mills, Clinton B.	1st Lt.	2/7/44	1.00
Rich, Daniel L.	1st Lt.	3/31/45	1.00
Roberts, Leon C.	1st Lt.	1/27/44	1.00
Smith, Lewis C.	2nd Lt.	1/27/44	1.00
Toppins, Edward L.	1st Lt.	1/27/44	1.00
	Capt.	7/18/44	2.00
		7/26/44	1.00
White, Hugh J.	2nd Lt.	3/31/45	1.00

Totals
  Number of Credits = 28.50
  Personnel Count = 20
  Number of Credit Entries = 30

100th Fighter Squadron

Name	Rank	Date	Credit
Bell, Raul W.	2nd Lt.	3/31/45	1.00
Brantley, Charles V.	2nd Lt.	3/24/45	1.00
Briggs, John F.	1st Lt.	8/24/44	1.00

Browne, Roscoe C.	1st Lt.	3/24/45	1.00
		3/31/45	1.00
Hall, Richard W.	2nd Lt.	7/27/44	1.00
Hosclaw, Jack D.	1st Lt.	7/18/44	2.00
Johnson, Carl E.	2nd Lt.	7/3/44	1.00
Johnson, Langdon E.	1st Lt.	7/20/44	1.00
Lane, Earl R.	1st Lt.	3/24/45	1.00
		3/31/45	1.00
Lester, Clarence D.	2nd Lt.	7/18/44	2.00
Lyle, John H.	F.O.	3/31/45	1.00
Palmer, Walter J. A.	2nd Lt.	7/18/44	1.00
Rhodes, George M., Jr.	2nd Lt.	8/14/44	1.00
Simons, Richard A.	2nd Lt.	4/26/45	1.00
Williams, Robert W.	1st Lt.	3/31/45	2.00
Wilson, Bertram W., Jr.	2nd Lt.	3/31/45	1.00

Totals

Number of Credits = 21.00

Personnel Count = 16

Number of Credit Entries = 22

301st Fighter Squadron

Carey, Carl E.	2nd Lt.	4/1/45	2.00
Edwards, John E.	2nd Lt.	4/1/45	2.00
Elsberry, Joseph D.	Capt.	7/20/44	1.00
Fischer, James H.	F.O.	4/1/45	1.00
Funderburg, Frederick D.	2nd Lt.	6/9/44	2.00
Gorham, Alfred M.	2nd Lt.	7/27/44	2.00
Govan, Claude	Capt.	7/27/44	1.00
Jefferson, Thomas W.	2nd Lt.	4/26/45	2.00
Lanham, Jimmy	1st Lt.	4/15/45	1.00
		4/26/45	1.00
McDaniel, Armour G.	Capt.	7/20/44	1.00
Manning, Walter P.	2nd Lt.	4/1/45	1.00
Morris, Harold M.	2nd Lt.	4/1/45	1.00
Price, William S., III	1st Lt.	4/16/45	1.00
Sawyer, Harold E.	1st Lt.	7/12/44	1.00
Stewart, Harry T.	1st Lt.	4/1/45	2.00
White, Charles L.	1st Lt.	4/1/45	2.00

Totals

Number of Credits = 24.00

Personnel Count = 16

Number of Credit Entries = 29

302nd Fighter Squadron

Archer, Lee A.	2nd Lt.	7/18/44	1.00
	1st Lt.	10/12/44	3.00
Brooks, Milton P.	Capt.	10/12/44	1.00
Bussey, Charles W.	1st Lt.	6/9/44	1.00
Gleed, Edward C.	1st Lt.	7/27/44	2.00
Green, William W., Jr.	2nd Lt.	7/16/44	1.00
	1st Lt.	10/12/44	1.00
Groves, Weldon K.	1st Lt.	7/18/44	1.00
Hill, William L.	F.O.	8/23/44	1.00
Hutchins, Freddie F.	1st Lt.	7/26/44	1.00
Jackson, Melvin T.	1st Lt.	6/9/44	1.00
Kirkpatrick, Felix J.	1st Lt.	7/27/44	1.00
McGee, Charles E.	1st Lt.	8/24/44	1.00
Pruitt, Wendell O.	1st Lt.	6/9/44	1.00
	Capt.	10/12/44	2.00
Romine, Roger	1st Lt.	10/12/44	1.00
	2nd Lt.	7/18/44	1.00
		7/26/44	1.00
Smith, Luther H., Jr.	1st Lt.	7/17/44	1.00
		10/12/44	1.00
Smith, Robert H.	2nd Lt.	7/17/44	1.00
Thomas, William H.	1st Lt.	8/24/44	1.00
Warner, Hugh S.	2nd Lt.	7/18/44	1.00
Weathers, Luke J., Jr.	Capt.	11/16/44	2.00
Wilkins, Laurence D.	1st Lt.	7/17/44	1.00

Totals

Number of Credits = 30.00

Personnel Count = 19

Number of Credit Entries = 28

Note: All hits occurred in the Mediterranean Theater of Operations.
Source: Air University, Office of Air Force History, 1978

Notes

Notes are identified by page number. Sources abbreviated at first appearance can be found in full in Bibliography.

Abbreviations

ACS   Air Command and Staff
AMHI   U.S. Army Military History Institute, Carlisle Barracks, Carlisle, Pa.
FAA   Federal Aviation Administration
HRC   U.S. Air Force Historical Research Collection, Maxwell Air Force Base, Montgomery, Ala.
LC   Library of Congress, Washington, D.C.
MAFB Maxwell Air Force Base, Montgomery, Ala.
NA   National Archives, Washington, D.C.
OAFH Office of Air Force History, Washington, D.C.
RG   Record Group
RS   Record Service

Chapter 1. Beginnings

1 ROBINSON'S FLIGHT: "Milestones"; information supplied by N. Komans, FAA, in a telephone interview, September 8, 1978. Interview with Janet Bragg, Philadelphia, July 12, 1983; Ms. Bragg was an associate of Mr. Robinson.

ROBINSON, BULLARD, OR PECK: Mizrahi, "A Volunteer in Spain"; Peck, *Armies with Wings*. For Bullard, see Carisella and Ryan, *Black Swallow*, which, however, is uncritical. Another black aviator of World War I is the now-forgotten Sosthene Mortenol, a native of Guadeloupe and a Polytechnique graduate, who from July 1915 to the end of the war was commander of the air defenses of Paris. Information supplied by Air Attaché, Embassy of France, Washington, D.C., November 6, 1978.

2 "CHIEF" ANDERSON: Powell, *Black Wings*. Powell, a black civil aviator, made an impassioned plea here for black self-help to break into the aviation industry and flying. Also Chicago *Tribune*, March 24, 1935, and Civil Aviation Administration, "Domestic Air News." For early black flights see also Rose, *Lonely Eagles;* Rose is uncritical. See also Smithsonian Institution, *Black Wings*.

3 AIR LINE PILOTS' ASSOCIATION: Leggett, "Racism in Commercial Aviation," 3–4; Strickland, *The Putt-Putt Air Force*, 1, 39; Rose, *Lonely Eagles*, 14; Washington, "Training of Negroes at Tuskegee," 1; Department of the Census, "Negro Aviators"; Northrup, *The Negro in the Air Transport Industry*, 28; Wynne, *Afro-Americans and the Second World War*, 28.

JAMES PECK: Caidin, *The Ragged, Rugged Warriors*, 28.

BLACK REGIMENTS: Woodward, "The Negro in the Military Service of the United States"; Quarles, *The Negro in the Civil War;* Aptheker, "Negro Casualties in the Civil War"; Foner, *Blacks and the Military*, 32–71; Leckie, *The Buffalo Soldiers;* P. Foner, *The United States Soldier between Two Wars: Army Life and Reforms, 1865–1898* (New York, 1970), chap. 7; A. L. Fowler, *The Black Military Experience in the American West* (New York, 1971); Fowler, *Black Infantry in the West;* Utley, *Frontier Regulars;* Fletcher, *The Black Soldier and Officer.* For a contemporary's account, see Nankivell, *History of the 25th Regiment.*

4 "ONLY THREE SURVIVED 'THE POINT' ": James C. Evans, "Counselor to SECDEF [Secretary of Defense]" (Washington, D.C., 1970), 154; *Survey Graphic*, April 1942, 194. Lt. Henry Flipper (Class of 1877) was dismissed for supposed financial irregularities, while Lt. J. H. Alexander (Class of 1887) died on duty in 1894. Foner, *Blacks and the Military*, 64; Gatewood, "John Hanks Alexander"; Chew, *A Biography;* Green, "Colonel Charles Young"; "The Negro as a Soldier and Officer."

DAVIS, SR.: Gatewood, *"Smoked Yankees,"* 6–7; Foner, *Blacks and the Military*, 93–94; Fletcher, *The Black Soldier and Officer;* MacGregor and Nalty, eds., *Blacks in the United States Armed Forces*, vol. 3; Steele, "The 'Color Line' in the Army"; Villard, "Negroes as Soldiers"; Villard, "The Negro in the Regular Army"; Villard, *The Story of the Negro* (see esp. chap. 15); H. Head, "The Negro as an American Soldier."

BROWNSVILLE AFFAIR: See Weaver, *The Brownsville Raid;* Lane, *The Brownsville Affair;* Cook, "The Brownsville Affray of 1906"; Tinsley, "The Brownsville Affray"; Thornborough, "The Brownsville Episode."

5 COMMISSIONED BLACKS: Foner, *Blacks and the Military*, 52, 103–6; Nelson, "Integration of the Negro in the U.S. Navy"; Nelson, *Integration of the Negro into the United States Navy*. In the U.S. Coast Guard, blacks could aspire only to kitchen duties (Finkle, *Forum of Protest*, 157).

"THE FACT IS": Lane, *The Brownsville Affair,* 14; Barbeau and Henri, *The Unknown Soldiers,* 67. Barbeau and Henri are also uncritical.

COLONEL YOUNG: Barbeau and Henri, *The Unknown Soldiers;* Heinl, "Col. Charles Young"; Chew, *A Biography.*

6 THE 92ND AND 93RD INFANTRY DIVISIONS: Foner, *Blacks and the Military,* 109–26; Barbeau and Henri, *The Unknown Soldiers;* Lee, *The Employment of Negro Troops,* 4–20; Flemming, "American Negro Combat Soldiers"; Pearson (War Department), *The Development of National Policy;* War Department, "Colored Soldiers in the U.S. Army." General Robert Lee Bullard, Second Army C.O., later claimed that "my memories of the 92nd Negro Division are a nightmare," and believed black American soldiers to be cowardly, depraved, and "sensual" (*Personalities and Reminiscences,* 292–94, 297). General Bullard must have believed himself particularly unlucky in this matter: he had also commanded black troops in the Spanish-American War (Bullard, "The Negro Volunteer"). A. F. Millett is superficial on Bullard's racial attitudes; see his *General Robert L. Bullard and Officership in the United States Army, 1881–1925* (Westport, Conn., 1975). The chief of staff of the 92nd was violently anti-black: see Greer, "Extract from Reports of Officers." Greer's attitudes are confirmed in his letter to an unnamed U.S. senator (Davis and Hill, *Blacks in the American Armed Forces,* 178–79; see also Coffman, *The War to End All Wars,* 314–17). Contemporary black views of black participation in the war are found in Scott, *The American Negro in the World War,* and Miller, *Kelly Miller's Authentic History.* Both are uncritical and fairly typical of the genre. More interpretative and critical is Du Bois, "The Black Man and the Wounded World."

PLANTATION SONGS: Barbeau and Henri, *The Unknown Soldiers,* 68–69; Patton, *War and Race,* 14–103.

"STILL A NEGRO": AWC, "The Use of Negro Manpower in War"; sub-study, "The Negro Officer," U.S. Army War College, Carlisle Barracks, Pa., 1925.

7 24TH INFANTRY: Haynes, *A Night of Violence;* Schuler, "The Houston Race Riot, 1917"; Park, "The Twenty-fourth Infantry Regiment"; Adams, "The Houston Riot of 1917." Rumors of secret executions of black servicemen persisted at the time, resulting in a Congressional investigation. It concluded that no one had been illegally put to death by the Army. But of the eleven soldiers known to have been executed in France, ten were black. U.S. Senate, 67th Cong., *Hearings Before a Special Committee.* U.S. Army Center of Military History, *Order of Battle of the United States* 3, pt. 1, p. 240, gives a total of ten executions in France, but does not break them down by race.

"CONFINED TO THE MESS BRANCH": Nelson, *Integration of the Negro into the United States Navy,* 9; Foner, *Blacks and the Military,* 103–6.

BULLARD: Bullard returned to the United States in 1940, a step ahead of the Germans. He secured a job as an elevator operator and was never used in World War II in any professional capacity (Carisella and Ryan, *Black Swallow,* 89). A few blacks found their way into Air Service Construction companies (Lee, *The Employment of Negro Troops,* 55), and four were actually sent to flying school at Ft. Sill, Oklahoma. There, treated with "extreme discourtesy," three requested transfer and the hardy fourth was washed out two days before graduation (Barbeau and Henri, *The Unknown Soldiers*, 63).

SCOTT'S APPOINTMENT: Dr. Du Bois's position during World War I is analyzed in Moon, *The Emerging Thought of W.E.B. Du Bois;* Patton, *War and Race,* 85–86. Finkle claims that the "Close Ranks" editorial put Du Bois "on the defensive for the rest of the war . . . and would return to plague him in World War II" (*Forum of Protest,* 49). The editorial was carried in the July 1918 issue. See also Moton, "American Negroes."

THE 369TH: Lee, *The Employment of Negro Troops,* 7–8; Guzman, *Negro Yearbook;* Foner, *Blacks and the Military,* 125–28.

"ONLY IN FRANCE": Foner, *Blacks and the Military,* 125–27; "The Lynching Record for 1918"; Guzman, *Negro Yearbook,* 18; NAACP, *Burnings at the Stake.*

8 "ALMOST SERVANT": Lee, *The Employment of Negro Troops,* 108; Wynne, *Afro-Americans and the Second World War,* 31; "Historical Evaluation of the Negro's Military Service," from "Colored Soldiers in the U.S.," which was used as a working paper for the War Department's "Report of Board of Officers on Utilization of Negro Manpower in the Post-War Army," 4; Patton, *War and Race,* 159–61.

"THEY WERE BUT SKELETONS": Hastie, "The Negro in the Army Today," 223; Foner, *Blacks and the Military,* 131. See also Hastie, "Negro Officers in Two World Wars."

POTENTIAL ENLISTEES: Memo to Chief of Staff, U.S. Army, October 26, 1947, 4; filed under Gillem Papers.

RESERVES: Lee, *The Employment of Negro Troops,* 28; memo, Civilian Aide to Secretary of War, to Assistant Secretary of War for Air, July 4, 1942, NA RG 107, Box 177, Entry 9. For black reserves, see "Colored Soldiers in the U.S."

UTILIZATION OF BLACKS IN WAR: AWC, "The Use of Negro Manpower in War." A guide to the postwar racial studies of successive classes at the AWC may be found in the War Department's *Special Bibliographic Series, Number 2,* 12–13. The original studies are on file at the AMHI, Files 127-5, 127-6, 127-23. Ref. C of the 1925 study deals with the black officer. The Pershing quote is from Lee, *The Employment of Negro Troops,* 32–33; the assistant chief of staff quote is in Morris J. MacGregor, *Integration of the Armed Forces, 1940–1965* (Washington, D.C.: Center of Military History, 1984), 11–12. See also the 1936 AWC study, "The Use of Negro Manpower in Time of Emergency." Also noteworthy is the General Staff College, Washington Course, "Organization and Training of Negroes," of April 21, 1920, as well as an untitled 1923–24 course (File 127-23), and the 1925 AWC course, "The Use of Negro Manpower in War." These studies are also analyzed in Patton, *War and Race,* 122–27.

9 CPTP: Strickland, *The Putt-Putt Air Force;* G. L. Washington, "History of Military and Civilian Pilot Training of Negroes at Tuskegee," 1–5; Patton, *War and Race,* 166–67; White, *A Man Called White,* 186.

10 AIR CORPS REFUSAL FOR ENLISTMENT: Evans, "Counselor to SECDEF," 140, 144; J. C. Evans, interview, Washington, D.C., September 7, 1977; Paszek, "Negroes and the Air Force," 1–9; Strickland, *The Putt-Putt Air Force,* 44–45.

"THERE MUST BE SOME EMOTIONAL REASON": J. C. Evans, interview, August 22, 1977; Nichols, *Breakthrough on the Color Front*, 46. For a considerably more positive recollection of Lovett, see Hasdorff, "Reflections on the Tuskegee Experiment," 176.

"THE TRAINING OF BLACK PILOTS": England and Sanders, "Legislation Relating to the AAF Training Program"; Lee (*The Employment of Negro Troops*, 54–65) goes into the background of Public Law 18 in almost excruciating detail, but also notes the heavy white pressure brought to bear to include blacks in the program.

11 "WE ARE HAVING DIFFICULTY": Memo, Chief of Air Corps (Gen. H. H. Arnold) to Chief of Staff of Air Corps, May 25, 1940, 353.9-4-A, OAFH.

"THEREFORE, THE LAW IS COMPLIED WITH": Memo, Chief, Air Plans Division, USAAC, to Gen. H. H. Arnold, April 8, 1938, 353.9-4-A, OAFH.

"THE ADAPTABILITY OF THE NEGRO": Osur, *Blacks in the Army Air Forces*, 23 (Osur is a basic source).

CONTRACT FOR MILITARY PILOT TRAINING: Evans, "MS. A Compilation," 138; Rose, *Lonely Eagles*, 11; Strickland, *The Putt-Putt Air Force*, 39–40; Washington, "History of Military and Civilian Pilot Training of Negroes at Tuskegee," 58–81.

13 "THE TUSKEGEE CPTP WAS WELL UNDERWAY": The early months of Tuskegee's CPTP are authoritatively outlined in Washington, "History of Military and Civilian Pilot Training of Negroes at Tuskegee," 1–101, 118–24. See also Strickland, *The Putt-Putt Air Force*, 41–42; "The Negro Is Flying," *Flying and Popular Aviation*, March 1941; and former Tuskegee president, Dr. Fred Patterson, interview, August 8, 1976.

WAR DEPARTMENT ANNOUNCEMENT: Lee, *The Employment of Negro Troops*, 75–76; MacGregor and Nalty, eds., *Blacks in the United States Armed Forces*, 30, 32.

"NEGRO PILOTS CANNOT BE USED": Memo, Arnold to AAC Assistant Chief of Staff, May 31, 1940, 145.85, OAFH.

1938 AIR CORPS STUDY: Memo, Chief of AAC Plans, to General Arnold, April 7, 1939, 7 353.9-4-A, OAFH.

14 HASTIE'S APPOINTMENT: Lee, *The Employment of Negro Troops*, 78–79; Foner, *Blacks and the Military*, 136–40. The importance of the black vote at this time is analyzed in Dalfiume, *Desegregation of the U.S. Armed Forces*, 28–29, and Finkle, *Forum of Protest*, 134–35. See also Weiss, *Farewell to the Party of Lincoln*, 272–77. Willkie spoke out publicly against military Jim Crow, and one authority claims that the GOP's platform was "much stronger" in its appeal to black voters (Finkle, *Forum of Protest*, 134–35, 151, 155). The Democratic Party National Headquarters wrote the president, calling General Davis's promotion a "master stroke" (Roosevelt Papers, October 30, 1940). Three years earlier, Pres. R. R. Moton of Tuskegee Institute had written to FDR suggesting that Davis be awarded his star, then retired: "He is not in command of his regiment, as you know, because of his race, and I have never heard him make a complaint or even mention the matter." Moton was turned down. Possibly his was the logic of despair, although Colonel Davis was by then sixty years old (Moton to FDR, June 14, 1937; Adm. Watson to Moton, July 12, 1937: Roosevelt Papers, OF 2369). Strong rumors circulated at the time that

Colonel Davis would resign his commission if not promoted to brigadier general, an embarrassing possibility for the administration (McGuire, *Taps for a Jim Crow Army*, xxv). See also "Brigadier General Benjamin O. Davis," and Richard Dalfiume, "Military Segregation and the 1940 Presidential Election," *Phylon* (Spring 1969); and Davis entry in *Dictionary of American Military Biography*, ed. R. Spiller (Westport, Conn., 1984). Stimson remarked mildly in his diary that Judge Hastie "seems like a rather decent negro" (quoted in McGuire, *He, Too, Spoke for Democracy*, 13).

"NEGROES ARE BEING GIVEN": Lee, *The Employment of Negro Troops*, 55. Text in NA RG 70, 291.21, Assistant Secretary of War to President, October 8, 1940.

NO BLACKS IN TRAINING: Peck, "When Do *We* Fly?"

RANDOLPH ASKS FOR PROOF OF TRAINING: Ibid. See also White, "It's Our Country Too." The NAACP organ, *The Crisis*, was not particularly impressed by the administration's maneuvers, as witness the lead article in its September 1940 issue, "White House Blesses Jim Crow," as well as "Too Dark for Army Air Corps" in the December issue. See *Crisis* articles along the same line in the December 1940 and February and April 1941 issues.

MEETING WITH ROOSEVELT: MacGregor and Nalty, eds., *Blacks in the United States Armed Forces*, 26–27; Lee, *The Employment of Negro Troops*, 74–75; White, *How Far the Promised Land?*, 186–89. The actual voices of the participants in this conference were actually preserved on a primitive sound-on-film device (Butow, "The FDR Tapes").

16 RIOT AT MACDILL: Lee, *The Employment of Negro Troops*, 114; Hastie, "On Clipped Wings," 5. These squadrons, plus the odd lot arms and services of the AAC (on loan from other arms and services), air base defense units (underworked units, if there ever were any), quartermaster battalions, ordnance companies, and transportation companies, all overrepresented by blacks, and most smacking of make-work, are treated in Osur, *Blacks in the Army Air Forces*, 25–27; Lee, *The Employment of Negro Troops, passim*. See also Guzman, *Negro Yearbook*, 66–71. The chief of the Air Staff agreed that Judge Hastie's charge was "bluntly true" (Dalfiume, *Desegregation of the U.S. Armed Forces*, 86). The air base "defense" units could not even mount guard duty, as General Arnold carefully pointed out to the governor of Arkansas (Arnold to Gov. Homer Adkins, May 2, 1942, Arnold Papers, 320.2, Box 85). The following year, General Arnold wrote of "colorizing" these units to absorb the Air Corps total of 10 percent blacks (May 10, 1943). See also Memo, Hastie to Arnold, 145-81-91 (NC), July 3, 1942, in Arnold Papers.

STIMSON: Minutes of Board of Directors, NAACP, September 9, 1940, Spingarn Papers, Box 37; Gropman, *The Air Force Integrates*, 6 (Gropman is another basic source); Morison, *Turmoil and Tradition*, 554–55. According to the late Brig. Gen. Noel F. Parrish, USAF (Ret.), former commanding officer of Tuskegee Army Air Field, Stimson's racial thinking was molded in large measure by his experience in the Philippines, where he served as governor over what he termed his "little brown brothers" (interview with General Parrish, Philadelphia, August 21, 1976). In fairness to Stimson, it should be pointed out that the authoritative J. C. Evans claims that Stimson personally desegregated the Pentagon early in the war, at the prompting of Judge Hastie, Hastie's successor, Truman Gibson, and Mary Bethune, and forbad racial epithets in the War Department in 1942 (Evans interview, September 7, 1977; McGuire, *He, Too, Spoke for Democracy,* 57).

"THE EXISTING POLICY": Marshall to Sen. Henry Cabot Lodge, Jr., September 27, 1940, 145.81 (NC), OAFH.

17 "LACK OF EDUCATIONAL OPPORTUNITIES": Marshall to Stimson, December 1, 1940, OAFH.

GENERAL ARNOLD: Gen. Noel F. Parrish, interview with James Hasdorff, OAFH, March 30, 1973, 4. Parrish noted that General Arnold never visited Tuskegee Army Air Field (pp. 16, 17).

"APPARENT LACK OF INHERENT NATURAL MECHANICAL ADAPTABILITY": Operations Division, "Colored Troop Problem."

"MISERY LOVES COMPANY": Dalfiume, *Desegregation of the U.S. Armed Forces,* 78; War Department Research Bureau, "Attitudes of Enlisted Men toward Negroes"; Wynne, *Afro-Americans and the Second World War,* 27, 36–37; MacGregor and Nalty, eds., *Blacks in the United States Armed Forces,* 5:216.

18 U.S. CITIZENS' ATTITUDES: MacGregor and Nalty, eds., *Blacks in the United States Armed Forces,* 187; Dalfiume, *Desegregation of the U.S. Armed Forces,* 127.

ANY DEFICIENCIES IN BLACK ACCOMPLISHMENT: MacGregor and Nalty, eds., *Blacks in the United States Armed Forces,* 5:200.

ONLY EXCEPTIONS: Walter White, *A Rising Wind* (New York, 1945), 74. See also War Department policy statement of December 15, 1941, in Arnold Papers, 291.2, Box 72; Wynne, *Afro-Americans and the Second World War,* 27; Evans, "MS. A Compilation," 76.

"FOR THE MOMENT": Maj. Gen. D. Noce, Acting Chief of Staff, Army Service Forces, comments on Gillem Board, Assistant Secretary of War, NA RG 107, 291.2, December 28, 1945.

"SOCIOLOGICAL LABORATORY": As MacGregor and Nalty put it, the armed services "have never mirrored American society, as some leaders have claimed." In fact, the services have sought in many different ways to modify and control the behavior of its members, if not of their attitudes (MacGregor and Nalty, eds., *Blacks in the United States Armed Forces,* introduction).

19 FIRST BLACK COMBAT UNIT: [Paszek,] "Negro Airmen of the A.A.F."; Murray, *Negro Handbook,* 1.

"A SERIOUS MISTAKE": Hastie to Lovett, May 2, 1941, NA RG 107, Assistant Secretary of War, Box 177, Entry 91. Judge Hastie told a biographer that he had objected to the Tuskegee segregation plan to Stimson and had gotten nowhere. In his diary for October 19, 1942, he noted awkwardly that this matter "took a great deal of drain out of me" (McGuire, *He, Too, Spoke for Democracy,* 43–44).

"AT SOME PLACE": Hastie to Secretary of Army General Staff, 145.81-91 (NC), July 1, 1942, OAFH. See also MacGregor and Nalty, eds., *Blacks in the United States Armed Forces,* 46–48.

"IN THE AIR CORPS": News release of NAACP, January 18, 1941, NA RG 107, ASW, Box 178, Entry 91.

"A STEP IN THE RIGHT DIRECTION": White, "Air Pilots, But Segregated."

TUSKEGEE OFFICIALS: Parrish, "The Segregation of Negroes in the Army Air Forces," 89.

20 BLACKS FLYING PURSUIT: Hastie, "On Clipped Wings"; Ware, *William Hastie*, 106, 126–27.

"SECOND BEST": See Arnold memo, July 22, 1942, Arnold Papers, 320.2, Box 85. As late as spring 1943, Gen. Barney Giles, soon to become chief of the Air Staff, wrote to his assistant of the "present and extreme difficulty" in obtaining technically qualified black personnel (Arnold Papers, April 26, 1943).

21 COFFEY SCHOOL: Memo, Chief of Air Staff, May 25, 1940, 353-9-4-A, OAFH.

BREACH OF SEGREGATION: Lee, *The Employment of Negro Troops*, 60, 64–65; MacGregor and Nalty, eds., *Blacks in the United States Armed Forces*, 49. General Arnold also pointed out the "difficult" matter of the training of black navigators and gunners on already "overtaxed facilities" (Arnold Papers, July 22, 1942, 320.2, Box 85).

"TRIPARTITE CULTURE": Evans interviews, September 7, 1977, and by telephone, August 24, 1978. Gibson to Colonel Gerhardt, September 11, 1942, NA RG 107, Subject File, Civilian Aide to Secretary of War, 1940–47.

"FURNISHED MANY PRECEPTS": Adjutant General files, letter, November 8, 1940. Copy in OAFH, 289.28-1.01, 10.

COVER ILLUSTRATION: *Service*, September 1936.

PATTERSON: Guzman, *Negro Yearbook*, 334. G. L. Washington later elaborated Dr. Patterson's rationale: the Air Corps, dominated as it was by Southern-born officers, was not about to tolerate any racial integration in the foreseeable future. Even if a small amount of integrated training was permitted, it would prove little—combat would be the proof. Tuskegee, by cooperating with the War Department, would be able to ensure fair treatment of aviation cadets, and would be willing to invest more time and effort in their training than possibly hostile or indifferent white instructors and ground crew. Dr. Patterson had already drawn upon his influence to secure a black C.O. for the fledgling black squadron, something the Air Corps would have been unlikely to have done on its own. Finally, black cadets would have been easily absorbed in existing facilities with but little increase in numbers of instructors and ground crew specialists. At Tuskegee these would have to be supplied from scratch—and they would be black (Washington, "History of Military and Civilian Pilot Training of Negroes at Tuskegee," 39–42). Dr. Patterson, in his interview with author, August 8, 1976, confirmed this interpretation. See comments of Noel F. Parrish during an editorial conference, in Ulysses Lee file. "[Dr. Patterson] made the most effective of all protests against segregation on the field itself" (NA, April 2, 1948, 7), and his comments on Lee MS, Ulysses Lee file, February 13, 1952, Office of Chief of Military History, NA, Box 512. (The Ulysses Lee file is not to be confused with the Lee file, also in the National Archives.) See also Parrish, "The Segregation of Negroes in the Army Air Forces," 38.

22 KIMBLE: History of SEAAC/AFTC, 220.1, vol. 2, microframe 405, OAFH; Dalfiume, *Desegregation of the U.S. Armed Forces*, 125; Patterson interview; Ware, *William Hastie*, 126–27.

"MONEY-SPINNING POTENTIAL": Parrish, "The Segregation of Negroes in the Army Air Forces," 92; see also "History of 66th AAF Flying Training Detachment"; Patterson interview.

"EVERYTHING WAS DONE TO AVOID RACIAL STRIFE": History of SEAAC/AFTC, 220.2, microframe 423, OAFH

QUOTAS: Ibid., 220.2, vol. 2, microframe 405, OAFH.

23 FINANCIAL PROBLEMS: History of SEAAC/AFTC, December 10, 1940, 220.765-2, microframe 981, OAFH; Paszek, "Brief History of the 99th Fighter Squadron," 6–8; "History of Tuskegee Army Air Field"; G. L. Washington, interview, August 21, 1976.

ROSENWALD FUND: Washington, "History of Military and Civilian Pilot Training of Negroes at Tuskegee," 169–87; "History of 66th AAF Flying Training Detachment," 27–30; Tuskegee *News*, February 10, 1972; Patterson interview; "Milestones"; Montgomery *Advertiser*, April 7, 1941; Roosevelt, "My Day."

ANNUAL OUTPUT: "Milestones"; Lee, *The Employment of Negro Troops*, 119; A vivid but somewhat uncritical source for the earliest days of black flying training is Rose, *Lonely Eagles*, 11–26.

Chapter 2. Training

25 CAPTAIN MADDUX: Lee, *The Employment of Negro Troops*, 119; Osur, *Blacks in the Army Air Forces*, 25; Paszek, "Negroes and the Air Force," 9; "Historical Record of the 99th Fighter Squadron," 1–2, OAFH; "Milestones," July 18, 1941. For contemporary black reactions, see White, "Air Pilots, But Segregated," as well as his earlier "A Negro Enlisted Man: Jim Crow in the Army [Air] Corps" and "Too Dark for Army Air Corps" (December 1940). For more positive reactions, black and white, see Carter, "A Negro Pursuit Squadron"; Montgomery *Advertiser*, April 7, 1941; Birmingham *News*, December 10 and September 15, 1941; "Ninety-Ninth Squadron"; "99th Pursuit Squadron, All Negro"; "Negro Pilots Got Wings."

26 MOTON FIELD: Lee, *The Employment of Negro Troops*, 119; Osur, *Blacks in the Army Air Forces*, 25. Unless otherwise indicated, material on the 99th Pursuit Squadron is based upon squadron records, U.S. Air Force records, USAF HRC (microfilm copies in OAFH); "Milestones," July 18, 1941.

DAVIS, JR.: Information on Gen. Benjamin O. Davis, Jr., drawn from interview with author in Alexandria, Va., February 18, 1977. Davis refused to deal with his West Point experiences in this interview, but confirmed his "silent treatment" during an interview with National Public Radio, February 24, 1991, and in his autobiography, *Benjamin O. Davis, Jr.: American* (Washington, D.C.: Smithsonian Institution Press, 1991), 21–50, in a chapter titled, "Silence." Additional information on General Davis was obtained from oral interviews with Tuskegee veterans R. W. Diez (August 21, 1976), H. Johnson (March 17, 1977), Louis Purnell (August 9 and 18,

1978), J. C. Evans, Dr. Fred Patterson, and Noel Parrish. Also testimony before Gillem Board, October 15, 1945, Gillem Papers, Box 7, Tab H. Lee, "He Thinks Air Force," 6–8; Strother, "The Cadet Who Refused to Quit"; *Survey Graphic,* April 1942, 194; Col. Vance Marchbanks, Jr., USAF, MC (Ret.), "Extracts from the Life of a Service Brat," unpublished memoir, n.d. (c. 1964), 9–10; "First Negro Commissioned in U.S. Air Corps."

DAVIS'S FLIGHT TRAINING: Charles Alfred "Chief" Anderson, interview, July 27, 1976; Evans, telephone interview, August 21, 1978; Purnell interview, August 18, 1978. Washington, "History of Military and Civilian Pilot Training of Negroes at Tuskegee," 374. Nonetheless, General Davis has recorded that for him flying "was a complete, unadulterated joy" (Davis, *Benjamin O. Davis, Jr.,* 84).

27   BASE THEATER DESEGREGATION: Marchbanks, "Extracts from the Life of a Service Brat," 9–10.

"SEGREGATION IS INEFFICIENT": Pittsburgh *Courier,* December 15, 1945.

"THE COLORED MAN IN UNIFORM": Guzman, *Negro Yearbook;* Foner, *Blacks and the Military,* 159. See also Fletcher, *America's First Black General.* When General Davis, Sr., would arrive in Washington, D.C., he could be served a first-class meal only at Union Station. Oral history interview, Lt. Gen J. H. Edwards, USAF (Ret.), September 2, 1973, USAF Oral History Program. For the view that General Davis, Sr., was more the "accommodationist" to military Jim Crow, see Finkle, *Forum of Protest,* 156; McGuire, *He, Too, Spoke for Democracy,* 66–67. In the socially punctilious prewar Army, Davis would be careful to leave his calling card when he knew the (always white) recipients would be out—hardly the routine of a racial radical (Parrish interview).

TAAF: History of SEAAC/AFTC, 289.28, vol. 1, and 222.01, microframe 850-4, OAFH. The early and subsequent history of Moton Field (contract Public Law 18 flying training) and Tuskegee Army Air Field may be found in "History of Tuskegee Army Air Field"; "History of Southeastern Army Air Force[s] Training Detachment, Moton Field, Tuskegee Institute, Alabama," and G. L. Washington, "The History of Military and Civilian Pilot Training of Negroes at Tuskegee, Alabama, 1939–1945"; Lee, *The Employment of Negro Troops,* 116.

"NUMBER 1 PRIORITY": "History of Tuskegee Army Air Field," August 16, 1941, 289.28-1.9.

"FULLY EQUIVALENT": History of SEAAC/AFTC, December 10, 1940, 222.765-2, vol. 1.

28   "NO ONE AT MAXWELL FIELD": Ibid., 222.01, microframe 850.

"SOURCE OF EMBARRASSMENT": "History of Tuskegee Army Air Field," 289.28-2, IDEA OF BLACK PARTICIPATION: Parrish oral history, 14. See also Parrish, "The Segregation of Negroes in the Army Air Forces." Parrish would later claim that high authority in Washington wanted the entire program killed, but named no names. Parrish oral history, Oral History Program, OAFH, 8 (much OAFH material is duplicated from the various Air University depositories of MAFB); and Hasdorff, "Reflections on the Tuskegee Experiment" (based on OAFH oral history).

"JUST KEEP 'EM HAPPY": Osur, *Blacks in the Army Air Forces,* 163 n. 5.

"WORLD WAR": Parrish oral history, 19–20.

ARMY AIR CORPS PLAN: History of SEAAC/AFTC, December 10, 1940, 220,765-2.

PARRISH: Material on Parrish here based in part on Davis interview, February 18, 1977, and interviews with Tuskegee veterans Purnell and Elwood Driver (February 4, 1977), Emory H. Smith (1977), Ira O'Neal (August 17, 1978), and Dr. Patterson; also Parrish, "The Segregation of Negroes in the Army Air Forces"; "History of Tuskegee Army Air Field," 289.28-2, esp. 37; Hasdorff, interview with Parrish, and "Reflections on the Tuskegee Experiment"; Nichols, *Breakthrough on the Color Front*, 47–49. Washington takes a more reserved view of Parrish and blames him for the eventual postwar closure of Tuskegee Army Air Field ("Training of Negroes at Tuskegee," 396). But General Davis is unstinting in his praise of Parrish (Davis, *Benjamin O. Davis, Jr.*, 76, and Mrs. Agatha Davis's poem on p. 79: "he will talk to you as man to man . . . / He has a fine set of values no one can ever change, / And so some white men think of him as being very strange").

29 "HOW DO NEGROES FLY?": Parrish, "The Segregation of Negroes in the Army Air Forces," 22; Nichols, *Breakthrough on the Color Front*, 49. According to one knowledgeable source, many Southern whites actually believed that it was good luck to take a black aloft on a flight (Motley, ed., *The Invisible Soldiers*, 255).

"A SEGREGATED UNIT": Parrish, "The Segregation of Negroes in the Army Air Forces," 12, 64, 65.

NIGHTTIME AIR CRASH: Parrish interview; Driver interview.

30 ENTERTAINMENT: The situation in the Tuskegee area is documented in the "History of Tuskegee Army Air Field," 289.28-5, microframe 211; Parrish, "The Segregation of Negroes in the Army Air Forces," 17, 60, and *passim;* Hasdorff, "Reflections on the Tuskegee Experiment," 177–78; "History of 66th Flying Training Detachment"; Washington, "History of Military and Civilian Pilot Training of Negroes at Tuskegee," 218–365; O'Neal interview. Mrs. Agatha Davis summarized her reaction to Tuskegee in an "epic poem," "Dear Mom, This Is a Hell of a Hole" (Davis, *Benjamin O. Davis, Jr.*, 77–84).

"TUSKEGEE AIR FIELD": Parrish, "The Segregation of Negroes in the Army Air Forces," 26.

CLASSES OF THE 66TH: Washington, "History of Military and Civilian Pilot Training of Negroes at Tuskegee," 11–12; Paszek, "Brief History," 10. The classes 1943-A through 1944-C had a more encouraging elimination rate of about 36 percent, compared to 28 percent for white classes in SEAACTC ("History of Tuskegee Army Air Field," 289.28-2, 83; "History of 66th AAF Flying Training Detachment," 6).

31 "OF THE LAST CLASS OF TEN TO REPORT": Paszek, "Brief History," 11.

GRADUATES OF THE CPT SECONDARY: Osur, *Blacks in the Army Air Forces*, 52.

INITIAL GROUND CREW FOR 99TH: Lee, *The Employment of Negro Troops*, 117.

BASE INTELLIGENCE OFFICER: "History of Tuskegee Army Air Field," 289.28-1.01, 33, 40.

COLONEL KIMBLE: Parrish oral history.

"THESE NEGROES ARE WONDERFULLY EDUCATED": "History of Tuskegee Army Air Field," 289.28-101, 51.

32 MAJOR ELLISON: Ibid., appendix I, 5. Davis speaks well of Ellison (Davis, *Benjamin O. Davis, Jr.*, 75).
"WHY DO THEY ALL COME TO TUSKEGEE?": Osur, *Blacks in the Army Air Forces*, 42. "SANDMEN": "History of Tuskegee Army Air Field," 289.28-2; Motley, ed., *The Invisible Soldiers*, 197, 243–46, gives some vivid accounts of "sanding," but should be read cautiously: for example, she accepts uncritically an account by a Tuskegee veteran that has Montgomery "ninety miles" from Tuskegee, about ten times the actual distance. Davis never mentioned "sanding" or the equivalent in his autobiography or interviews.

33 EQUAL FACILITIES: Arnold Papers, April 26, 1943, 291.2, Box 72. "History of Tuskegee Army Air Field," 289.28-101, appendix I, 5. Judge Hastie praised the white TAAF instructors as "thoroughly competent" ("On Clipped Wings," 7). The black journal *Survey Graphic* praised the instructors as "militantly proud of their charges" (April 1942). The existence of any type of quota is denied pointblank by three who should know: Davis interview; General Parrish, letter to author, September 13, 1976; and G. L. Washington, telephone interviews with author, August 27 and September 13, 1976, and August 5, 1978. Truman Gibson, Hastie's successor, wrote to the assistant secretary of war for air, Robert Lovett, that Tuskegee's "training had been conducted in a fair and impartial manner" (Gibson to Lovett, May 1, 1943, NA RG 107, Secretary of War, Box 96). In fact, the assistant chief of the Air Staff wrote to the chief of the Air Staff later in the war claiming of Tuskegee "stanine standards substantially lower than those required for white applicants" (memo, December 8, 1944, NA RG 18, 291.2E, Box 104). Gen. Ira Eaker, commanding general of the Mediterranean Air Force (under which the Tuskegee pilots would do most of their combat flying) asserted that stanine scores for black cadets had to be dropped to II in order to have scores of VII (Eaker to Chief of Staff, War Department, n.d., NA RG 107, Assistant Secretary of War, 291.2, Box 40). See also Osur, *Blacks in the Army Air Forces*, 30. By now, this contention should be laid to rest.
"DISCOURAGEMENT, DESPAIR, AND CYNICISM": Judge Hastie, memo, September 22, 1941, in MacGregor and Nalty, eds., *Blacks in the United States Armed Forces*, 94. Wilkins's comments appear in a memo to Stimson, August 13, 1942, NA RG 107, Secretary of War, Box 17, Entry 91.

34 ELLISON: Parrish interview; "History of 66th AAF Flying Training Detachment," 15; Washington, "History of Military and Civilian Pilot Training of Negroes at Tuskegee," 317-A; Rose, *Lonely Eagles*, 19.
KIMBLE: Alabama Archives and History, Drawer 176, May 13, 1942; Rose, *Lonely Eagles*, 23; History of SEAAC/AFTC, 222.01, vol. 2, microframe 1168; Parrish oral history, 7; Parrish interview; Civilian Aide to Secretary of War, December 21, 1942, Box 252, Entry 91; Washington, "History of Military and Civilian Pilot Training of Negroes at Tuskegee," 18. The black Pittsburgh *Courier* summarized black reaction to the situation in its headline, "Hate Rules at Tuskegee Base Charged to Colonel Frederick Kimble." Davis, 75–77.
"GREAT WHITE FATHER": Parrish oral history, 7.

35 "COLORED WATER": T. L. Washington, interview, August 21, 1978 (T. L. Washington was director of maintenance at Tuskegee Army Air Field, and subsequently for the

99th Fighter Squadron); Dalfiume, *Desegregation of the U.S. Armed Forces,* 84; Air Adjutant General to Commanding General, Flying Training Command, June 3, 1942, Arnold Papers, 291.2, Box 72. Judge Hastie quickly protested Kimble's policies to the Army General Staff, to no avail (Hastie to Secretary of the General Staff, July 1, 1942, NA RG 107, Civilian Aide to the Secretary of War, Box 178, Entry 91). Hastie's recipient replied with the usual Army headquarters' boilerplate: "For the War Department to attempt the solution by regulation or fiat of a complicated social problem which has perplexed this country for a number of years is bound to produce diversions that may go so far as to affect the full effectiveness of our war effort" (ibid., July 14, 1942). Note the amount of time elapsed between Hastie's letter and the response.

SUMMER OF 1943: Air Adjutant General to C.O., AAF Flying Training Command, March 3, 1942, Arnold Papers, 291.2, Box 72.

"RATHER TRAIN IN 40 DEGREE BELOW ZERO": Minutes of meeting, Advisory Committee on Negro Troop Policies, October 13, 1943, NA RG 107, 291.2, Assistant Secretary of War.

"ONE OF THE GREATEST MISTAKES": George C. Marshall to Dr. Forrest Pogue, interview, Lexington, Va., February 14, 1957, Pogue MSS, Eisenhower Institute, Smithsonian Institution, Washington, D.C. See also Nichols, *Breakthrough on the Color Front,* 43.

INDOCTRINATION CLASSES: "History of Tuskegee Army Air Field," 289.28-2, 116.

HAZING: History of SEAAC/AFTC, 322.01, vol. 3, microframe 334.

36 "DUE TO YOUR . . . STAND": Letter, R. H. Powell to Gov. James Dixon, November 30, 1942, Alabama Archives and History, Drawer 176. In his letter, Powell thanked the governor for his efforts "to protect our white citizens from the determined encroachment of our colored population" (note the difference between "citizens" and "population"). Maj. Gen. J. P. Smith to Gov. James Dixon, February 26, 1942, Alabama Archives and History. Two years later Governor Dixon, protesting the 1944 War Department order prohibiting racial segregation in recreation facilities, but permitting it by unit, warned President Roosevelt that "we of the south will find it difficult to hold the south within its traditional Democratic allegiance in the years to come" (Governor Dixon to FDR, August 29, 1944, FDR OF 93–B, FDR Presidential Library). Davis writes of similar correspondence with Alabama senators John Bankhead and Lister Hill (Davis, *Benjamin O., Davis, Jr.,* 73).

GRADUATION: Washington, "History of Military and Civilian Pilot Training of Negroes at Tuskegee," 33; "History of 66th AAF Flying Training Detachment," 11–12.

37 AVIATION CADETS DESPERATELY NEEDED: Washington, "History of Military and Civilian Pilot Training of Negroes at Tuskegee," 351–64; Strickland, *The Putt-Putt Air Force,* 42.

LAWSON: Rose, *Lonely Eagles,* 22. Yet there seems to be no discernible pattern in Air Corps/Forces orders to report for training. In approximately twenty-five interviews and responses to author's questionnaire, the time from acceptance to orders ranges from a little over one year to two months. But the problem was real, and

Judge Hastie was concerned that some accepted cadets would find themselves over-age (past 26) before receiving their orders to report to TAAF (Osur, *Blacks in the Army Air Forces*, 29). The chief of the Air Staff thought that the problem might be alleviated by opening the Enlisted Reserves to such blacks, but had the gall to add that such action might enable blacks to "enjoy" four years of draft exemption (Chief of Air Staff to Assistant Chief of Air Staff, June 9, 1942, Arnold Papers, 320.2, Box 85).

ROSS: *Flying*, June 1942. Purnell interview; DeBow, "I Got Wings," 29.

38 MOVE TO OSCODA: "History of 332nd Fighter Group."

TRAINING: History of SEAAC/AFTC, 220.01, vol. 2, Installment History, micro-frame 1072. See also comments of Gen. George Stratemeyer, chief of the Air Staff, to the director of military requirements, January 11, 1943, NA RG 18, 291.2-AAF. T. L. Washington claims that maintenance at the time was so efficient that all crashes at TAAF were due to pilot error (T. L. Washington interview).

"HURRY-UP-AND-WAIT": "History of Tuskegee Army Air Field," 289.28-2, 69.

39 PARRISH REPORT: History of SEAAC/AFTC, 222.01, vol. 2; Parrish interview; Parrish oral history.

DAVIS PROMOTION: Parrish to C.O., SEAAFTC, February 10, 1943; copy in Arnold Papers, 291.2, Box 72; T. L. Washington interview.

"CONFUSION REIGNED SUPREME": "History of the 99th Fighter Squadron," 1; Paszek, "Brief History," 13–14.

40 CROWDING AT TAAF: "History of Tuskegee Army Air Field," 289.2, 111.

PRECISION FLYING: Ibid., 44, 82, 126–27; Rose, *Lonely Eagles*, 23; Osur, *Blacks in the Army Air Forces*, 41–43; History of SEAAC/AFTC, 222.01, vol. 2; "History of Tuskegee Army Air Field," 289.28-2, 44. Parrish "The Segregation of Negroes in the Army Air Forces," 13; Washington, "History of Military and Civilian Pilot Training of Negroes at Tuskegee," 416; Lee, *The Employment of Negro Troops*, 451–53; Gropman, *The Air Force Integrates*, 12. Maintenance was rated as "very satisfactory," and technical inspection as "excellent" by an AAF inspector early in 1943. General Stratemeyer reported that the results of the training of enlisted technicians were "excellent, the men did well" (memo, General Stratemeyer to Director of Military Requirements, January 11, 1943, NA RG 18, 291.2). A statistic that should have impressed the AAF was the sharp decrease in the venereal disease rate during this period (History of SEAAC/AFTC, 222.01, vol. 2, microframe 293; "History of Tuskegee Army Air Field," 289.28-2, 46–47).

"PERMANENT DRILL TEAM": History of SEAAC/AFTC, 69. Over three decades later, Lt. Gen. B. O. Davis, Jr., asserted that because of the incomplete training of many of the 99th's pilots even at that late date, the delays were "a damn good thing" (Davis interview).

41 "DOES THIS MEAN . . . ": Eleanor Roosevelt to Assistant Chief of the Air Staff for Training, March 30, 1943, NA RG 107, 291.2, Box 177. See also Mrs. Roosevelt's secretary to Truman Gibson, March 3 and 13, 1943, NA RG 18, 291.2, Box 529.

LIBERIAN TASK FORCE: Memo, Gen. Dwight D. Eisenhower for Chief of Army Staff, March 25, 1942, Arnold Papers, 291.2, Box 75.

"AFRICAN BACKWATER": Paszek, "Brief History," 15; Washington, "History of Military and Civilian Pilot Training of Negroes at Tuskegee," 427.

"OUTSTANDING BY ANY STANDARD": Parrish interview.

Chapter 3. Testing and Proving

43 LOADING UP: History of the 99th, 4–5; Parrish interview; Francis, *The Tuskegee Airmen*, 27–28.

44 OUEDN'JA: Francis, *The Tuskegee Airmen*, 28; NA RG 107, 291.2, Assistant Secretary of War, October 28, 1943.

"LIKED THE P-40": For the P-40, see Taylor, "Flying the Curtiss P-40"; and Wagner, *American Combat Planes*, 252–59. All sources seem to agree that the P-40 in all its permutations was a well-built, mediocre military aircraft.

"TERRY AND THE PIRATES": Francis, *The Tuskegee Airmen*, 29.

46 "WHEN THE SCREAMING P-40 WARHAWKS": Birmingham *News*, July 18, 1943. The *News*'s attitude was not unique. The Atlanta *Journal*, six months later, reporting on the 99th's combat over the Anzio-Nettuno beachhead, wrote that their success "will be gratifying to all Americans, whatever their race or position."

47 "HAD SEEN LITTLE ACTION": "Experiment Proved?" Truman Gibson, Judge Hastie's aide at the time, wrote to Davis that the article "was slightly on the snotty side," adding that "I think this inference [*sic*] is inexcusable" (Gibson to Davis, September 21, 1943, NA RG 107, Civilian Aide, "Selfridge File," Subject File, 1940–47). See also "Capital Stuff," New York *Daily News*, September 30, 1943.

49 "THE NEGRO TYPE": Copies of General House's critique of the 99th can be found in NA RG 18, AAF, 291.2-C, September 16, 1943; Paszek ("Brief History") points out that the Momyer-House critique must have been based upon a mere three weeks of combat, and the squadron's first three weeks at that (23). See also Lee, *The Employment of Negro Troops*, 452–60; Osur, *Blacks in the Army Air Forces*, 47–52.

GENERAL SPAATZ: Spaatz to Arnold, September 19, 1943, 141.281-22, OAFH. The Momyer-House critiques can also be found in this source.

"WE HAVE RECEIVED": Arnold to Spaatz, September 10, 1943, Spaatz Papers, Box 12.

TRAINING TIME: General R. W. Harper to Assistant Chief of Air Staff, Plans, September 28, 1943, NA RG 18, AAF, 291.2-C.

STRAFING MISSIONS: Paszek, "Brief History," 20.

50 "OPERATED IN A VACUUM": Davis interview.

"THERE IS NO HOPE": NA RG 107, Assistant Secretary of War, October 13, 1943, Box 40; ibid., Assistant Secretary of War, October 28, 1943, 291.2, for minutes of Special Committee.

"IT IS MY CONSIDERED OPINION": Arnold to FDR, n.d., Arnold Papers, 320.2, Boxes 25, 85; also found in War Department, "Report of Board of Officers on Utilization of Negro Manpower in the Post-War Army," Box 40.

O'DONNELL: War Department, "Report of Board of Officers on Utilization of Negro Manpower in the Post-War Army," Box 40 (italics in original).

51 STATISTICAL CONTROL DIVISION REPORT: Paszek, "Brief History," 23. According to
official records of the 79th Fighter Group, the 99th scored second from the bottom
in the four-squadron group, but it was also the squadron with the least service time
(GP 79-HI, Box 64, OAFH).

53 "TOTAL OBLITERATION OF CONSCIOUSNESS": White, *How Far the Promised Land?*,
255; GP 79-HI, OAFH. As early as the spring of 1943, White had urged President
Roosevelt to see to it that the 99th/79th relationship remain, to no avail (White to
FDR, April 22, 1943, FDR Presidential Library, Folder 83, September-December
1942). The unofficial history of the 79th, *The Falcon*, gives relatively little information about the 99th, but what it gives is straightforward.

"WITH THE PANTELLERIAN": History of the 99th, October 1943.

54 "WE ARE UP TO OUR NECKS IN MUD": Ibid., November 1943. For Italian mud, see
Francis, *The Tuskegee Airmen*, 46.

55 "THIS WAS DISHEARTENING": History of the 99th, December 1943.

58 INFERIORITY OF FIGHTERS: Ibid., January 1944; Diez interview.

"SOME LITTLE DIFFICULTY": History of the 99th, February 29, 1944.

59 MISSION ACCOMPLISHED: Ibid., March 19, 1944.

60 SEPARATION FROM THE 79TH: A dinner dance for all four of the 79th squadrons had
just been held to celebrate the first anniversary of the group in combat. Forty percent of the white squadrons were composed of Southerners (Byers, "A Study of the
Negro in Military Service," 27).

EAKER: History of the 99th, April 20, 1944.

"ETERNAL CREDIT IS DUE": Ibid., May 15, 1944. See also Francis, *The Tuskegee Airmen*, 60, for Clark and his praise of the 99th's ground-attack role.

61 MOVE TO RAMITELLI: "Official History of the 79th Fighter Group."

Chapter 4. Home Front / Battle Front

63 "DOUBLE-V": For black military and civilian racial attitudes during the Second
World War on the U.S. home front see Wynne, *Afro-Americans and the Second
World War*; White, *How Far the Promised Land?*; Dalfiume, *Desegregation of the
U.S. Armed Forces*, all *passim*. For examples of contemporary black militancy see
Davis, "Will a Long War Aid the Negro?"; and Bond, "Should the Negro Care Who
Wins the War?" and examples given in this text. The black gadfly conservative
George S. Schuyler gloated that "A Long War Will Aid the Negro."

"CLOSE RANKS" SENTIMENT: "A White Man's War?" *The Crisis*, January 1942, April
1942. The thought was actually expressed almost two years earlier by Morrell in "A
White Man's War," without the question mark. The theme became almost hack-
neyed, being taken up by *Time*, "White Man's War," March 2, 1942; Adam Clayton
Powell, Jr., "Is This a White Man's War?" in *Common Sense*; Roi Ottley, "A White
Folks' War," in *Common Ground*; Eliot Janeway, "Fighting a White Man's War,"
Asia; and H. R. Clayton, "Fighting For White Folks?" *The Nation*.

"NOW IS THE TIME": Quoted in Wynne, *Afro-Americans and the Second World War*,
20.

64 "HERE LIES A BLACK MAN": Evans, "MS. A Compilation," 109.

"I HOPE HITLER WINS!": White, "What the Negro Thinks of the Army," 67.

"BY AND LARGE": Wynne, *Afro-Americans and the Second World War,* 106.

DISSATISFACTION AMONG BLACKS: Office of War Information, *The Negro's Role in the War;* "Attitudes of the Negro Soldier," draft, July 26, 1943, in Lee File, draft, July 26, 1943, NA RG 107, Secretary of War, Box 182, Entry 91; War Department, *Attitudes of White Enlisted Men toward Negroes for Air Force Duty,* November 30, 1943, and "What the Soldier Thinks," August 2, 1943; "The Adjustment of the Negro Soldier to the Army." See also Stouffer et al., *The American Soldier,* 506; Wynne, *Afro-Americans and the Second World War,* 28.

"THE NEGRO HOPES": Clark, "Morale among Negroes"; Goodwin Watson, ed., *Second Yearbook of the Society for the Psychological Study of the Social Sciences* (New York, 1942), 246–47.

ROOSEVELT ADMINISTRATION: In addition to Wynne *(Afro-Americans and the Second World War),* Finkle *(Forum of Protest),* and Dalfiume *(Desegregation of the U.S. Armed Forces),* see Clark, "Morale among Negroes." Wynne points out that over two hundred national, regional, state, and local organizations, official and unofficial, were established or were in existence at the time to combat racial discrimination (Wynne, "Impact of the Second World War on the American Negro"). But note the tart assessment of FDR by J. M. Blum: "Roosevelt did condemn mob violence in any form, but, he ducked the racial issue as he did generally during the war" (Blum, "United Against," 584).

65 "SOCIAL EXPERIMENTATION": "It's Our Country Too"; "White Man's War." See also "Negroes at War"; High, "How the Negro Fights for Freedom."

THE BLACK PRESS: NA RG 107, Assistant Secretary of War, 291.2, Boxes 10 and 40. The Army compiled a weekly summary of the black press from at least April 1944 to June 1945 (Lee File, NA RG, Box 512). Finkle gives figures for black press readership and circulation *(Forum of Protest,* 51–52). See also NA RG 341, Assistant Secretary of War, 291.2, Box 272; Gillem Report typescript, unpaged, Box 40; and Jones, "The Editorial Policy of Negro Newspapers." See also Wolseley, *The Black Press and the U.S.A.;* and Washburn, *The Federal Government Investigation of the Black Press during World War II.*

66 ARMY STUDY: NA RG 107, Assistant Secretary of War, 291.2, Box 40.

RED CROSS: Copy of ARC statement of January 21, 1942, in NA RG 107, Assistant Secretary of War, 291.2, Box 40. According to MacGregor and Nalty *(Blacks in the United States Armed Forces,* 137–40), the ARC actually opposed racially segregated blood banks because of the administrative burden they would impose. See also Lee, *The Employment of Negro Troops,* 331–32; and Ware, *William Hastie,* 107–9; Kendrick, *The Blood Program in World War II;* and McGuire, *He, Too, Spoke for Democracy,* 73–77; McGuire, "Judge Hastie, World War II, and the Army's Fear of Black Blood"; McGuire, "Military Hemophilia."

SELECTIVE SERVICE: Selective Service System, *Special Groups,* 51, 56, 190. See also Murray, "Blacks and the Draft." Foner, *Blacks and the Military,* 698–99; Hershey, "They're in the Army"; Lee, "The Draft and the Negro." Flynn, "Selective

Service and American Blacks during World War II." Stimson moaned that "the Army had adopted rigid requirements mainly to keep down the number of colored troops and this is reacting badly in preventing us from getting some very good but illiterate [white] recruits from the southern mountain states" (McGuire, *He, Too, Spoke for Democracy,* 38).

67 ARMY COUNTERINTELLIGENCE REPORT: Dalfiume, *Desegregation of the U.S. Armed Forces,* 153; excerpt from correspondence, "Summary of the Racial Situation," for the Chief of Counter-Intelligence, Hdq., USAAF, NA RG 18, 291.2-A, Box 103, November 29, 1943. For documented accounts of such segregation, see Foner, *Blacks and the Military,* 153–54. Other incidents are found in Byers, "A Study of the Negro in Military Service," 51–88, but Byers is not always reliable.

"HARVEST OF DISORDER": Lee, *The Employment of Negro Troops,* 348–79.

INCOME AND UNION MEMBERSHIP: Wynne, *Afro-Americans and the Second World War,* 57–59; Fair Employment Practices Committee, *First Report;* Merrill, *Social Problems on the Home Front,* 9, 24; Finkle, *Forum of Protest,* 213.

68 "DOES THE YOUNG NEGRO AMERICAN": Clark, "Morale among Negroes," 246–47.

GOEBBELS: A contemporary account is provided by Johnson, *To Stem This Tide;* Merrill goes so far as to assert that homefront casualties were comparable to those in battle, surely before D-day (98).

69 "ALL OF THE REPORTED RACIAL DISTURBANCES": Memo, Chief of Army Staff to all Commanding Generals, July 13, 1943, NA RG 18, AAF 291.2-C; MacGregor, *Integration of the Armed Forces,* 267–69. Dr. Fred Patterson, president of Tuskegee Institute during World War II, met with General Marshall on several occasions during the war and found him helpful and courteous, but "not without prejudice" (Patterson interview). Marshall's biographer, Dr. Forrest Pogue, formerly director of the George C. Marshall Research Institute/Library Foundation, confirms this opinion. Dr. Pogue, interview, Washington, D.C., July 15, 1977.

RACIAL INCIDENTS: Lee, *The Employment of Negro Troops,* 349–52.

INCIDENTS GROW MORE SAVAGE: Ibid., 356, 375. Racial incidents are also described in NA RG 107, Assistant Secretary of War, Decimal File, 291.97, 1940–45, 346–79; also NA RG 107, Adjutant General, 291.2, October 2, 1942; ibid., April 14–June 3, 1941; and NA RG 107, 333.9 and 322.97, August 7, 1941; Byers, "A Study of the Negro in Military Service," 81.

70 ARKANSAS INCIDENT: Byers, "A Study of the Negro in Military Service," 352–55; New York *Times,* Chicago *Tribune,* August 15–20, 1941; Judge Hastie did acknowledge that the troops around Gurdon had been disorderly (Ware, *William Hastie,* 114). It is worth noting that reporters for black newspapers toured many military camps in 1941 and predicted trouble (Finkle, *Forum of Protest,* 164). At the time Judge Hastie warned, somewhat circularly, that "this continuing wave of violence may lead to rioting at any time" (Ware, *William Hastie,* 116).

"THE LACK OF ANY SERIOUS TROUBLE": McCloy, letter to the editor, Washington *Post,* quoted in Dalfiume, *Desegregation of the U.S. Armed Forces,* 119–22.

"BIRACIAL INCIDENTS": Memo, Col. E. D. Cooke to Inspector General, June 25, 1942, 145.81-91 (NC), HRC. See also analysis prepared for General Marshall, describing the "three-way friction" in the South between whites, Southern blacks, and Northern blacks (microfilm 145.81 [NC], microframe 0714, OAFH).

BLAMING "AGITATORS": Stimson and Bundy, *On Active Service in Peace and War,* 464. McCloy quote in Osur, *Blacks in the Army Air Forces,* 183. The Army Intelligence Service apparently saw things differently, terming the U.S. black press "ardently democratic" (Ware, *William Hastie,* 122). See also Dalfiume, *Desegregation of the U.S. Armed Forces,* 86–87.

71 "THEY CHERISH A DEEP RESENTMENT": "The Fort Dix Straw."

TOWN-BASE CLASHES: AAC/AAF/SEAACTC, "Clashes between Civil and Military Police in Tuskegee, Alabama"; Nichols, *Breakthrough on the Color Front,* 51. The C.O. of TAAF, Colonel Parrish, later stated that local whites were armed and ready to move on the base (Parrish interview). The black journal, *California Eagle,* screamed in huge headlines, "Tuskegee Riot, Mob Attacks Negro Flying Field," September 4, 1942 (which provided some justification for McCloy's and Stimson's exasperation with the black press). See also Lee, *The Employment of Negro Troops,* 356, and report of Truman Gibson, Judge Hastie's assistant, n.d., Adjutant General Files, USAAF, 220.765-3, OAFH. TAAF continued to suffer unrest. Later in the war a black nurse stationed at the base, anxious to return to her post in time, was badly beaten by police for refusing to leave a bus (Byers, "A Study of the Negro in Military Service," 199). In March 1944, twelve black officers attempted to "integrate" the white dining hall. Although the officers were served without incident, a "decided tenseness" prevailed for months afterward. Colonel Parrish had to assure local whites that such race-mixing applied only on base ("History of Tuskegee Army Air Field," 289.28-5, frame 64; "History of Eastern Flying Training Command," vol. 3, microfilm 322.01, frame 331; Osur, *Blacks in the Army Air Forces,* 94–95). Perhaps not coincidentally, elimination and accident rates supposedly increased and morale lowered at TAAF after the cafeteria incident ("History of Tuskegee Army Air Field," microfilm 289.28-5, frame 65). These allegations, however, were denied after the war by Colonel Parrish (comments on Lee MS, February 13, 1952, NA RG, Lee File).

72 THE 364TH INFANTRY: Lee, *The Employment of Negro Troops,* 367–73; NA RG 319, Military Intelligence Division, Cross-Reference Sheet 000.2412, 9th Service Command, November 26–27 and December 21, 1942; "Rioting Folder," NA RG 319, Military Intelligence Division, Cross-Reference Sheet 000.51, July 19, 1943.

RANDOM, INDIVIDUAL VIOLENCE: Lee, *The Employment of Negro Troops,* 375–76. See also Army Special Forces, "Racial Situation in the United States." In the midst of the "Red Summer" of 1943, the Army inspector general went so far as to claim that "in my opinion the toughest problem confronting service commanders today is the one of preventing disturbances involving colored troops" (Lee, *The Employment of Negro Troops,* 377–78).

73 "A MULATTO SOLDIER": NA RG 407, 291.2, Adjutant General Central File, August 14–24, 1944; Seattle *Times,* August 18, 1944; Seattle *Post-Intelligencer,* August 19, 1944. In addition to the one fatality, twenty-six Italians required hospitalization, as well as three black and three white soldiers.

No fear of military police: All of the above incidents, plus the shooting of black soldiers by white civilians, are found in NA RG 319, 291.2, Army Intelligence Decimal File, 1941–48, April 7, May 4–5, November 7, and December 20, 1944. In some instances, military intelligence seemed absorbed in trivia: a letter from a black woman complaining of jostling and offensive remarks from airmen on a Washington, D.C., bus led to correspondence among Judge Hastie, Truman Gibson, Assistant Secretary of War for Air Robert Lovett, and the Army Air Forces inspector general. The conclusion was that nothing more was involved than loose talk by some loud-mouthed enlisted personnel (Arnold Papers, 320.2, Box 85, November 10, 1943). And Army Intelligence solemnly reported that a white man who sang "Old Black Joe" on a bus was beaten by a black man, and that "a white soldier was found in bed with two Negro women" (ibid., February 25 and 27, 1945).

Hastie's resignation: Osur, *Blacks in the Army Air Forces*, 70.

74 "The Air Forces are deliberately rejecting": Hastie to Secretary of War, January 5, 1943, NA RG 18, Assistant Secretary of War for Air, 291.2, AAF (Hastie resignation letter).

75 "We Negroes are often forced": Judge Hastie's resignation is covered extensively in a series of articles by McGuire. See also McGuire, "Black Civilian Aides"; Ware, *William Hastie*, 31–34; Lee, *The Employment of Negro Troops*, 166–72. Hastie singled out the AAF for biting criticism in his pamphlet "On Clipped Wings," and told the Pittsburgh *Courier* that "Air Force policy forced me to resign" (June 2, 1943). The venerable W.E.B. Du Bois hailed Hastie's action, as did the entire black press (Ware, *William Hastie*, 131; Finkle, *Forum of Protest*, 156, Lee, *The Employment of Negro Troops*, 161–62). The only black criticism came years later from Gibson's successor, J. C. Evans, who characterized Hastie as a "hit-and-run-type man who wanted to make some gains and leave in triumph," and added, somewhat ambiguously, that "his outstanding accomplishment was his resignation and delineation of the problems that led to it" (Evans's oral interview transcript, with Lee Nichols. n.d. [c. 1953], Office of Chief of Military History, 2; also Evans interview with author).

"The rubber stamp Uncle Tom": Reddick, "The Negro Policy of the American Army since World War II," 201–2; New York *Age*, July 3, 1943. Chicago *Defender*, January 23 and 30, 1943. Finkle notes that Gibson had a bad press (*Forum of Protest*, 185), and his later statement that elements of the all-black 92nd Infantry Division had "melted away" on occasion in Italy brought down on his head even harsher criticism from the black press. Two such papers called him various forms of an "Uncle Tom" in an impressive display of journalistic originality (Chicago *Defender*, March 24, 1945; George Schuyler in the Pittsburgh *Courier*, March 31, 1945). Other black journals were more temperate. Gibson replied logically that "it is hard for me to see how some people can, on the one hand, argue that segregation is wrong, and on the other hand, blindly defend the product of that segregation" (*Afro-American*, April 15, 1945). Lee, *The Employment of Negro Troops*, 577–79. Osur claims that Gibson had "excellent" contacts with the black press, for whatever good it did him (*Blacks in the Army Air Forces*, 180). Gibson was also a good friend of Benjamin O. Davis, Jr., going back to their student days at the University of Chicago (Davis, telephone conversation with author, August 4, 1978).

GIBSON AND STIMSON: White, *How Far the Promised Land?* Hastie, of course, can be found in the Stimson diaries, Yale University; see, e.g., entries for March 5 and October 19, 1942.

GIBSON'S VISIT TO TUSKEGEE: Adjutant General Files, 220.765-3, April 4, 1942, OAFH; Osur, *Blacks in the Army Air Forces*, 174; Parrish interview, August 15, 1976.

76 "SINCE IT WAS WELL AWARE": Osur, *Blacks in the Army Air Forces*, 71–72. Another authority claimed that "a close examination of the personal and public records will demonstrate . . . that most of Hastie's recommendations pertaining to the fair treatment and effective utilization of black manpower were either accepted by the War Department or put into effect after his resignation" (P. McGuire, review of Osur book, *Journal of American History* [January 1979]: 182–83). See also McGuire, *He, Too, Spoke for Democracy*, 65–66.

BLACKS NOW ELIGIBLE FOR SERVICE PILOT: Arnold Papers, 291.2, Box 72, January 9, 1943. See also Lee, *The Employment of Negro Troops*, 172; and NA RG 18 AAF, 291.2A, January 9, 1943; Osur, *Blacks in the Army Air Forces*, 71–72; Hinkson, "The Role of the Negro Physician in the Military Services."

"COMMINGLING OF WHITE AND COLORED RACES": Alabama Archives and History, Drawer 176, May 20, 1942.

CHANGE IN NOMENCLATURE: General George Stratemeyer to Assistant Chief of Air Staff, January 9, 1943, NA RG 18, AAF, 291.2-A; letter, Eastern Flying Training Command to all commands, May 15, 1945, 222.01, vol. 3, OAFH.

McCLOY NAMED CHAIRMAN: Osur, *Blacks in the Army Air Forces*, 73; NA RG 107, Secretary of War, 291.2, Box 40, September 23, 1943; Lee, *The Employment of Negro Troops*, 157.

77 INACTION OF WAR DEPARTMENT: Lee, *The Employment of Negro Troops;* Assistant Secretary of War for Air, 291.2, November 4, 1942.

MIAMI BEACH: Evans interview, August 23, 1978; Grant, "The Development and Function of AAF OCS and OTS"; Osur, *Blacks in the Army Air Forces*, 35–37, 160; Lee, *The Employment of Negro Troops*, 169. The Miami Beach OCS C.O. was reported to have addressed his charges thusly: "Saturday nights is [*sic*] cut-up for black troops, and you will be called upon at times to assist in the patch-up work" (Motley, ed., *The Invisible Soldiers*, 246); Hon. Charles Diggs, U.S. Congress, interview, August 17, 1978; Gen. L. Theus, interviews with OAFH, December 27, 1973, and with author, February 12, 1977; Foner's account (*Blacks and the Military*, 150) is misleading.

78 STARING AT BLACK OFFICERS: Marchbanks, "Extracts from the Life of a Service Brat," 9–12.

TRAINING OF BLACK CADETS: Lee, *The Employment of Negro Troops*, 463–65; Osur, *Blacks in the Army Air Forces*, 53.

KEESLER FIELD AS HELL ON EARTH: Osur, *Blacks in the Army Air Forces*, 53–54. This is the unanimous opinion of Tuskegee veterans interviewed by the author, and

confirmed by McGuire (*He, Too, Spoke for Democracy,* 70–71). The governor of
Mississippi protested to President Roosevelt regarding the use of black instructors at
Keesler AFB and they were withdrawn forthwith (NA RG 18, 291.2, AAF, Febru-
ary 6, 1943). The commanding general of the AAF Technical Training Command
admitted that the issue was "too hot" for his office (Arnold Papers, 291.2, Box 72,
February 26, 1943).

79 "IT IS ESSENTIAL": War Department, "Command of Negro Troops"; War Department, "Leadership and the Negro Soldier"; Lee, *The Employment of Negro Troops,*
389–92. Nichols (*Breakthrough on the Color Front,* 434) claims that the War Department made "efforts to suppress" "Leadership," but there is no corroborating
evidence.
PAMPHLET: Lee, *The Employment of Negro Troops,* 393.
CAPRA'S FILM: Capra, *The Name above the Title,* 358; *The Negro Soldier* (1944).
According to R. D. MacCann (*The Peoples' Films* [New York, 1973]), the film bene-
fited from the advice of Walter White, although White, perhaps understandably,
makes no such claim in his autobiography. But there is no doubt that General Davis,
Sr., pushed the film (MacGregor and Nalty, eds., *Blacks in the United States Armed
Forces,* 463–64), along with Nelson Rockefeller, Fiorello LaGuardia, Cardinal Spell-
man, and Harold Ross (editor of the *New Yorker*). General Marshall, Stimson, and
John J. McCloy reviewed the film, which underwent an extraordinary rigmarole before release to white audiences—who overwhelmingly enjoyed it. The two most influential film critics of the time, however, saw Capra's work for what it was—Bosley
Crowther of the *New York Times* calling it "sugarcoated," and James Agee of the
New Yorker dismissing it as "pitifully, painfully mild." One reason for this untruthful
film's popularity lies simply in the fact that it was the first to deal with the black past
in any terms beyond those of slavery and caricature. Further, the film was technically an entire realm beyond the jackleg "race movies" of the time and was instru-
mental in driving them from the screen (Cripps and Culbert, "The Negro Soldier").
Capra himself may have inadvertently revealed the cause of the film's inadequacies
when he wrote in his autobiography that it would be "done with taste and *repression*" (*Name above the Title,* 387). Sharp-eyed viewers may spot Colonel Parrish in
the second reel.

80 FIVE FILMS: Aside from *The Negro Soldier* and *Wings for This Man,* they are as follows:
Office of War Information, *Negro Colleges in Wartime* (which, of course, includes Tuskegee Institute); Department of Agriculture, *Henry Browne, Farmer* (which deals with a
black Alabama dirt farmer whose son is a Tuskegee cadet, and contains some invalu-
able scenes of the base and downtown Tuskegee); and *Teamwork* (U.S. Army, 1946),
a tough-talking film that admitted the existence of racial prejudice (unlike all of the
above), and featured General Davis, Jr. The War Department's *Westward Is Bataan*
paid some attention to black troops, particularly those in the service branches, while
Welcome to Britain contained a brief treatment of the differences in racial attitudes
(then) between the United States and the United Kingdom. Film documentaries dealing with the 99th and the 332nd can be found in two Paramount newsreels: NA RS
200 contains the first Tuskegee graduating class, while NA RS 208 has clips on the

Ortona strike; and Universal newsreel NA RS 208. Unedited, undated silent films by the USAAF dealing with the subject are NA RS 18, CS, 276; 1059, 2;18 CS, 122. For an authoritative, if somewhat jaundiced, analysis of U.S. film in World War II, see Koppes and Black, *Hollywood Goes to War*.

"I REPORTED TO THE SECRETARY OF WAR": [Lyon,] "Training of Negro Combat Units by the First Air Force," 2:185.

81 GENERAL GLENN'S REACTION: Osur, *Blacks in the Army Air Forces*, 119.

WAR DEPARTMENT POLICY: Letter, General Arnold to USAAF Commanding Generals, May 2, 1944, OAFH, 145.81-90; Arnold Papers, 320.2, Box 85, November 10, 1943.

"IMPLACABLE HATRED": Osur, *Blacks in the Army Air Forces*, 93.

SERIOUS INJURY OR DEATH: But the AAF did experience a potentially disastrous racial riot soon after the war, in October 1946, when large numbers of mutinous black airmen, again at MacDill, refused to obey orders, milled about, and threatened to attack a white housing area. In odd contrast to wartime leniency, heavy prison sentences were meted out on the ringleaders. The trouble was blamed on poor riot control and, without any evidence, the usual "communist agitators" (Gropman, *The Air Force Integrates*, 64–68).

82 FAIRFAX, SOUTH CAROLINA: Osur, *Blacks in the Army Air Forces*, 94.

MACON, GEORGIA: Ibid., 104. The Army inspector general complained of "an unwillingness of commanding officers to bring offenders to trial when the seriousness of the offense manifestly indicated the need thereof (Lee, *The Employment of Negro Troops*, 378).

THEORETICAL RACE MIXING: "History of the Eastern Flying Training Command," July 1–August 31, 1944, 1:35 44, 222.01. Smith interview; "History of Tuskegee Army Air Field," 289.28.5; Osur, *Blacks in the Army Air Forces*, 94–95; Parrish, "The Segregation of Negroes in the Army Air Forces," 67. For War Department position on recreational facilities, see War Department Adjutant General to Commanding Generals, A.G. 353.8, May 3, 1943; War Department, "Command of Negro Troops."

84 AAF "TRADITION": "History of Tuskegee Army Air Field," March 5, 1944; Lee, *The Employment of Negro Troops*, 215–16. For the TAAF scence in 1944 to early 1945, see Osur, *Blacks in the Army Air Forces*, 42–43; USAAF study, "Colored Officers"; "History of Tuskegee Army Air Field," 289.28-101. Higher authorities agreed, however, that morale at TAAF was high at the time. In September 1944, the War Department forwarded to the Advisory Committee on Negro Troop Policies (the McCloy Committee) a memorandum claiming that "the morale of the Negro pilots at Tuskegee Air Base was outstanding . . . This was achieved because of the understanding leadership of the Commanding Officer, Colonel Noel F. Parrish" (NA RS 18, Assistant Secretary of War, 291.2, Box 104). For conditions in early 1945, see "History of Tuskegee Army Air Field," 289.28-5, frame 369. The history of SEAAC/AFTC, while conceding in late 1944 that the high ratio of officers to enlisted men was bad for morale, still reported overall morale as having made "great strides," and efficiency as "excellent" (OAFH, 221.01, vol. 2, frame 1476).

85 NO OPEN SLOTS: Ira O'Neal, C. Diggs, interviews with author; Francis, *The Tuskegee Airmen*, 162–63.

"SCORES OF CROSS COUNTRY FLIGHTS": Parrish, "The Segregation of Negroes in the Army Air Force," 75–77. See also Parrish, interview with Hasdorff.

"RADICAL" OPINION: Alabama Archives and History, drawer 176. Early in the war, the War Department Intelligence Division worried about the possibility of German, Japanese, communist, or liberal press agitation, but concluded that military racial disorders stemmed from lack of discipline, poor police or MP work, or lack of recreational facilities. Yet it called for "all possible steps . . . to reduce and control the publication of inflammatory and vituperative articles in the colored press." Not surprisingly, the commander of Army Ground Forces, Gen. Lesley J. McNair, tartly replied that the study "appears to contribute nothing very tangible" (Lee, *The Employment of Negro Troops*, 361–63). Stimson confided to his diary early in the war that he had direct evidence "that the Japanese and Germans are conducting a systematic campaign among the American Negroes stirring up their demands for equal representation" (entry for May 12, 1941, quoted in Osur, *Blacks in the Army Air Forces*, 173). See also Gill, "Religious, Constitutional, and Racial Objections."

"ENERGETIC SOCIALISTS": History of SEAAC/AFTC, 220.01, vol. 2, frame 420.

"OUR GLORIOUS SOVIET ALLY": Parrish interview. The AAF director of military requirements wrote to General Arnold about "subversive elements" at TAAF. Arnold Papers, 320.2, Box 85, June 1, 1942.

"SERIOUS AND CONCERNED EFFORTS": History of SEAAC/AFTC, 22.01-11, microframe 420, 1163.

86 *INTELLIGENCER:* AAF *Intelligencer,* 256.60, OAFH; Osur, *Blacks in the Army Air Forces,* 65; Finkle, *Forum of Protest,* 149. See also Lee, "Subversive Individuals of Minority Status."

"WE CRITICIZED": Quoted in Record, *Negroes and the Communist Party,* 220. So far was the CPUSA/CPA from serving at the time as the vanguard for the toiling American masses that its secretary, Eugene Dennis, was forwarding names of alleged Axis agents and other subversives to William Donovan, legendary head of the Office of Strategic Services, in the full knowledge that Donovan would turn these names over to J. Edgar Hoover and the FBI (Bradley F. Smith, *The Shadow Warriors: O.S.S. and the Origins of the C.I.A.* [New York, 1983], 98).

DIEZ AT CPA MEETING: Diez interview.

"EFFECTIVE 'SMEAR' CAMPAIGN": Assistant Chief of Staff, U.S. Army, G-2, to AAF Headquarters, n.d. (received June 19, 1942), Arnold Papers, Box 57.

87 "DIRTY DOZEN": NA RG 107, 291.2, Assistant Secretary of War, October 13, 1943.

Chapter 5. The 332nd Fighter Group

89 MOVE TO OSCODA ARMY AIR FIELD: Unless indicated otherwise, references to the 332nd and its components are based on official Group and component squadron records.

90 "THERE WERE MANY OF US": MacGregor and Nalty, eds., *Blacks in the United States Armed Forces,* 124; White, *A Rising Wind,* 89. See also Arnold Papers, 320.2, Box 85, July 31, 1942. The office of the assistant secretary of war for air explained to

Judge Hastie the service rationale for the activation of three more black fighter squadrons: "This action has been taken as the most rapid method of assimilating a large group of Negroes into the Air Force[s] since activating light and medium bombardment squadrons would require training navigators, bombardiers, etc., and existing facilities for this training are now seriously overtaxed" (Memo, Lt. Col. R. T. Coiner, Jr. to Hastie, August 12, 1942, NA RG 107, Assistant Secretary of War, Box 77). By January 1944, General Spaatz was more positive, informing General Arnold that one fighter squadron alone was not sufficient for a thorough test of black fliers' abilities. Of course, by then the three squadrons of the 332nd had been activated and were undergoing their training (Lee, *The Employment of Negro Troops*, 467).

LEFTOVER FLYING TIGERS: Rose, *Lonely Eagles*, 66–67.

AIRACOBRAS: For the Airacobra see *Encyclopedia of the World's Combat Aircraft* (New York, 1976), 60; Wagner, *American Combat Planes*, 266–72; also Lemuel Custis, interview, March 4, 1978.

92 "THERE WERE NO 'OFF TO THE WARS FEELING OF PRIDE' ": Marchbanks, "Extracts from the Life of a Service Brat," 15–16. See also Motley, ed., *The Invisible Soldiers*, 208.

93 MELTON: "History of the Mediterranean Allied Air Force," December 10, 1943, and March 14, 1944.

94 P-47s: Ibid., Eaker to Giles, March 13, 1944; for characteristics of the P-47, see Wagner, *American Combat Planes*, 273–80. A comparison between the P-47 and the P-51 was given by General Davis in a telephone interview, August 18, 1978.

98 UNOFFICIAL AIRCRAFT MARKINGS: The best analysis of the 332nd's artwork is found in Rose, "Art and the Airman." All illustrated histories of the USAAF in World War II amply attest to the artistic imagination and individuality of that service's unsung runway artists.

99 SQUADRON'S PHYSICAL CONDITION: Marchbanks, "Extracts from the Life of a Service Brat," 22; XV Fighter Command (Prov.), "Medical History." For a general contemporary study of military combat fatigue problems, see Ginker and Spiegel, *Men under Stress;* also Link and Coleman, *Medical Support of the Army Air Forces*.
"IN THE RECENT PAST": Eaker to Giles, March 24, 1945, Eaker Papers, Box 22.
"WE ARE DEALING": Giles to Eaker, March 15, 1945, ibid.

100 ORDERING PILOTS HOME: Deputy Chief of Air Staff to Arnold, December 7, 1944, Arnold Papers, Box 20. The pilot had complained to his mother of his having to fly twenty-five or thirty missions. Luftwaffe pilots, stretched to the limit by then would, of course, have hooted at these figures. There is no evidence that General Arnold expended anything like this amount of time on the problems of any disgruntled white pilot.
"THE PILOT'S MOTHER": Arnold to Spaatz, July 21, 1944, Spaatz Papers, Box 15.

102 AIRFIGHT OVER AUSTRIA: Francis, *The Tuskegee Airmen*, 91. Another 332nd POW claimed that the Luftwaffe had compiled a special book on the group, and knew of most of its personnel and activities (ibid., 151). No corroboration has been found for this assertion.

103 DAVIS'S ORDERS: Davis interview. This order of General Davis is confirmed by all Tuskegee Airmen interviewed by author.

104 "Grotesque doughnuts of flame": Motley, ed., *The Invisible Soldiers*, 220. "Remarks of General Eaker at Press Conference, Rome, December 2, 1944." Eaker Papers, Box 27, "Press Conferences" folder.
Walker: Francis, *The Tuskegee Airmen*, 96.

106 "black flying devils": White, *How Far the Promised Land?*, 225.

107 "Italian-American Committee": Byers, "A Study of the Negro in Military Service," 721; Ulysses Lee File, Box 511, NA RS, Technical Intelligence Report, May 26, 1945.
"As Commanding Officer": History of the 332nd, September 20, 1944; Francis, *The Tuskegee Airmen*, 83, 109–11.

108 General Giles: Osur, *Blacks in the Army Air Forces*, 47; Giles to Eaker, October 14, 1944, Eaker Papers, Box 22.
General Eaker: Osur, *Blacks in the Army Air Forces*, 165.
Captain Thomas: Francis, *The Tuskegee Airmen*, 165.
The Lockheed P-80: Spaatz to Arnold, July 22, 1944, NA RS, Spaatz Papers, Box 15.

109 The Red Tails: Eaker to Spaatz, October 4, 1944, NA RS, Eaker Papers, Box 24, "Spaatz" folder. A worried AAF Board, in its report ([T]-7A, 7B), concluded that the best of America's piston-engine fighters "are no match for a good jet fighter" (NA RG, Eaker Papers, Box 22, October 14, 1944).

114 "A pilot who began to show tension": Marchbanks, "Extracts from the Life of a Service Brat," 24–25, 29–32.

115 Replacement pilots: XV Fighter Command (Prov.), "Medical History." See also Link and Coleman, *Medical Support of the Army Air Forces*, 494, 499, 500.
Weathers in Memphis: Francis, *The Tuskegee Airmen*, 128.
Letter to Mom: Purnell interview, February 18, 1978.

Chapter 6. The 477th Bombardment Group

120 "This may be good news": Hastie, "On Clipped Wings," 6; "First Bomber Pilots," *The Crisis*, January 1943; Bombardier, "The Story of the 477th Bombardment Group."
"It is common knowledge": "Plans for the Activation of the Colored Bombardment Group (M)," December 30, 1943, in [Lyon,] "The Training of Negro Combat Units by the First Air Force," 1:192, 420.04C, OAFH.
AAF expectations: Ibid., 231. This study, by Capt. E. D. Lyon, in two volumes, is almost unique in its candor and commitment. Not only does it document racial antagonism at the highest AAF levels, it took on the so-called "Documented Historical Report: Air Force[s] Negro Troops," of the First Air Force, (July 19, 1945), and labeled it for what it was, a clumsy attempt by those officers deeply chagrined at the turn of events at Freeman Field to justify themselves. Captain Lyon characterized the authors of that study as fit for a "fourteenth-century jury." His further career, if any, is now impossible to document. His report was classified at the "Secret" level for almost a third of a century (Gropman, *The Air Force Integrates*, 271; Osur,

Blacks in the Army Air Forces, 197). Unless otherwise indicated, references to the 477th at Selfridge, Godman, Walterboro, and Freeman airfields are taken from Lyon's study.

PERSONNEL SHORTAGE: Osur, *Blacks in the Army Air Forces*, 109.

121 BEHAVIOR: Lee, *The Employment of Negro Troops*, 464–65.

CADETS ASSIGNED TO TECHNICAL WORK: Rose, *Lonely Eagles*, 121–22.

GODMAN ARMY AIR FIELD: Osur, *Blacks in the Army Air Forces*, 110.

SELWAY: Parrish oral history, 13.

"THE SECRETARY OF WAR": [Lyon,] "Training of Negro Combat Units by the First Air Force," 2:26.

"CHANGED THE ATTITUDE": Ibid., 2.

122 WOUNDING OF BLACK ORDERLY: Murray, ed., *The Negro Handbook*, 100–101. Dr. L. Kubie, a psychiatrist consultant for the Air Force, examined the colonel and concluded that the officer's drinking was more to blame than any racial feeling. But Dr. Kubie went on to analyze the psychiatric pathology of military racial segregation. Like Captain Lyon's bold effort, Dr. Kubie's audacious report was buried for almost thirty years (Osur, *Blacks in the Army Air Forces*, 54, 168; NA RG 107, Civilian Aide to the Secretary of War, Selfridge File, 1940–47, "Selfridge Field" folder; memo, Assistant Chief of Staff to G-1, USAAF, March 20, 1944, Arnold Papers, 291.2, Box 93, item 348).

AAF RACIAL POLICIES: "The Composite History of the 477th Composite Group."

CARIBBEAN ISLANDS: [Lyon,] "Training of Negro Combat Units by the First Air Force," 1:150.

ESCORTING: Osur, *Blacks in the Army Air Forces*, 56.

ENFORCEMENT OF POLICIES: MacGregor and Nalty, eds., *Blacks in the United States Armed Forces*, 457.

123 GENERAL GILES: [Lyon,] "Training of Negro Combat Units by the First Air Force," vol. 2, Appendix E. Colonel Boyd's stinging reprimand is in Parrish, "The Segregation of Negroes in the Army Air Forces," 67–68.

AVERAGE FLYING TIME: Byers, "A Study of the Negro in Military Service," 201; Gropman, *The Air Force Integrates*, 20.

"HIGH, FRAGILE, AND SENSITIVE": [Lyon,] "Training of Negro Combat Units by the First Air Force," 1:56–60. Lyon asserted that "the prime purpose at Godman has been to keep the trainee personnel occupied, in order that there would be no dissension on their part which would be brought to the attention of the public through the medium of the press" (p. 57). One might be forgiven for presuming that the "prime purpose" of any USAAF base during the Second World War would have been training for war. See also NA RG 18, 291.2-E, Box 104, memo to Assistant Secretary of War from Secretary of Advisory Committee on Negro Troops, September 18, 1944; Arnold Papers, 291.2, Box 72, July 21, 1944.

JIM CROW RESTAURANT: USAAF *Intelligencer*, September 1944, 10–13. See also reports on conditions at Walterboro AAFB by the acting chief of the Air Staff to the assistant secretary of war for air outlining a "general lack of discipline" (Arnold Papers, 291.2, Box 72, July 21, 1944).

ARREST OF SOLDIER: [Lyon,] "Training of Negro Combat Units by the First Air Force," 2:180; Watson OAFH interview transcript, USAF Oral History Program, April 3, 1973, 7. Watson was the officer involved in the altercation with the mayor. Also Johnson interview, March 17, 1977.

MEN OF THE 477TH: [Lyon,] "Training of Negro Combat Units by the First Air Force," 2:134.

124 FLYING HOURS: "History of the 477th Bombardment Group, July 16–October 15, 1944," 72; also "Negro Units at Godman Field and Walterboro Army Air Base." General Hunter is also reported to have told a black journalist at about this time that "Negroes can't expect to obtain equality in 200 years and probably won't except in some distant future" (Osur, *Blacks in the Army Air Forces*, 57).

"WE HAVE FOUR GENERAL OFFICERS": Osur, *Blacks in the Army Air Forces*, 111–12.

"THERE WILL BE NO RACE PROBLEMS": Ibid., 59.

125 COMPLAINTS ABOUT SELWAY: Memo from Gibson to Lieutenant Colonel Gerhardt, June 7, 1944, NA RG 107, Secretary of War, Box 126.

THIRTY-EIGHT MOVES: [Lyon,] "Training of Negro Combat Units by the First Air Force," 1:136. This was on average one move every ten days.

OFFICERS' CLUBS: Report of Acting Inspector General, USAAF, April 14, 1945. Filed in Chief of Staff of Army, "Participation of Negro Troops in the Post-War Military Establishment"; copies in HRC and Arnold Papers.

TWO DIRECTIVES: Pertinent paragraphs of both directives are reproduced in Chief of Staff of Army, "Participation of Negro Troops in the Post-War Military Establishment."

THE CLUB "THAT BELONGS TO THE WHITE OFFICERS": [Lyon,] "Training of Negro Combat Units by the First Air Force," 1:184–86.

"BLACK" OFFICERS' CLUB: Watson OAFH interview transcript.

126 PROVOST MARSHAL: [Lyon,] "Training of Negro Combat Units by the First Air Force," 1:95.

FREEMAN FIELD: The most detailed account of the events of April 5, 1945, are found in the report of the AAF inspector general in Chief of Staff of Army, "Participation of Negro Troops in the Post-War Military Establishment," and, of course, in [Lyon,] "Training of Negro Combat Units by the First Air Force," unless otherwise cited. See also the account of a Maj. Richard Jennings, a participant, in Motley, ed., *The Invisible Soldiers*, 71–72. Lee, who pulled few punches, omits all reference to the Freeman Field incident.

"UNAUTHORIZED" STORY ON THE 477TH: Brig. Gen. R. L. Owens, Deputy Chief of Air Staff, to Assistant Chief of Staff, G-2, April 12, 1945 (President Roosevelt died suddenly on this day), Arnold Papers, 291.2, Box 72. See also Indianapolis *Recorder*, March 17, 1945, and Pittsburgh *Courier*, March 31, 1945. Memo from Col. John R. Harris, acting inspector general, to Air Inspector, Hdq. Army Air Forces, Washington, D.C., April 14, 1945, filed in Chief of Staff of Army, "Participation of Negro Troops in the Post-War Military Establishment."

128 "WE RESENTED THE HELL OUT OF SEGREGATION": Watson OAFH interview transcript. In Watson's words, "It was position and promotion, it wasn't that damn club at all" (p. 8).

129 EVIDENCE OF WHITE HOUSE INTEREST: Chief of Staff of Army, "Participation of Negro Troops in the Post-War Military Establishment."

130 "A STEP BACKWARD": McCloy Committee report found in ibid., and in NA RG 107, Decimal File 291.2, Assistant Secretary of War, 1940–47.

MAJORITY OPINION: Gropman, *The Air Force Integrates*, 28. See also General Giles's identical sentiments, Arnold Papers, 291.2, Box 72, May 29, 1945.

GENERAL HUNTER: Letter from General Hunter to Osur, November 30, 1974, in Osur, *Blacks in the Army Air Forces*, 200.

131 PACIFIC THEATER: See Arnold Papers, 291.2, Box 72, June 19, 1945. Also discussions on topic in Subject File, Civilian Aide to Secretary of War, NA RG 107, Decimal File 291.2, 1940–47, May 31, 1945.

BLACK FLIERS "COMPLICATE" WAR: General Kenney to General Arnold, July 19, 1945; General Eaker to Arnold, same date, Arnold Papers, 291.2, Box 72; Gropman, *The Air Force Integrates*, 29–30.

COLLAPSE OF 477TH: Osur, *Blacks in the Army Air Forces*, 108.

SEPARATION FROM MILITARY: "Documented History of First Air Force," 3–4.

Chapter 7. Climax and Victory

133 ROTATION OF 302ND: Material not found in 332nd and component records is found in XV Fighter Command (Prov.), "History of XV Fighter Command," unless otherwise cited.

GIBSON AT RAMITELLI: It was during this tour that Gibson made his much-resented remark about some units of the 92nd "melting away." See Arnold, *Buffalo Soldiers;* Lee, *The Employment of Negro Troops*, 576–79.

134 FIGHT OVER BERLIN: Purnell interview, June 17, 1978; "XV Fighter Command, Special Intelligence Reports," OAFH, 672.01.

136 LUFTWAFFE FLIGHT TRAINING: Boog, "Higher Command and Leadership," 142; Suchenwirth, *Historical Turning Points*, 119–26; Overy, *The Air War*, 81, 145.

138 THE ME 163: Ethell and Price, *German Jets in Combat*, 100–135; Suchenwirth, *Historical Turning Points*, 119–26.

Chapter 8. Aftermath

141 RETURN HOME: Captain Louis Purnell volunteered to re-enter combat in the Pacific, rather than face Walterboro AAFB again (Purnell interview).

142 COLOR-CODED MAP: Arnold Papers, 291.2, Box 72, March 13, 1945.

BOYCOTT: War Department, "Report of Board of Officers on Utilization of Negro Manpower in the Post-War Army," Supplemental Report, General Eaker, Gillem Board Supplemental Reports Comments, Tab H, 2.

COLONEL ROBERTS: Francis, *The Tuskegee Airmen*, 163.

"I DO NOT BELIEVE": Ibid., 163–64.

ELITE OUTFIT: Watson claims that "it was a matter of pride, pride, pride" (Watson OAFH interview transcript, 26).

GODMAN ARMY AIR FIELD: Parrish tartly termed such postwar black outfits as the 332nd "colored waiting room units" (Parrish, "The Segregation of Negroes in the Army Air Forces," 55; data from 332nd postwar unit history).

143 REJECTION IN RESTAURANTS: Gropman, *The Air Force Integrates*, 75–76. Parrish, "The Segregation of Negroes in the Army Air Forces," 91; Watson OAFH interview transcript, 29; [Lyon,] "Training of Negro Combat Units by the First Air Force," 1:163; Parrish before Gillem Board, p. 8.

145 "A MILLION NEGROES": Wynne, *Afro-Americans and the Second World War*, 122.
UTILIZATION OF BLACKS: War Department, "Report of Board of Officers on Utilization of Negro Manpower in the Post-War Army," November 1945, Air Adjutant General Mail and Records, 291.2, Box 348 (looseleaf binder).

146 NO NEED FOR BLACK OFFICERS: "Training of Negroes within the First Air Force," 420.04C, HRC. This document should not be confused with Captain Lyon's sympathetic and daring "Training of Negro Combat Units by the First Air Force." Hunter quote in Gropman, *The Air Force Integrates*, 39.

147 NEED TO KEEP BLACK UNITS SMALL: Memo to the Chief of Staff, Subject: "Participation of Negro Troops in the Post-War Military Establishment," September 17, 1945, Arnold Papers, 291.2, Box 72.
"THERE CAN BE NO *CONSISTENT* SEGREGATION POLICY": Parrish opinions in letter to Brig. Gen. W. E. Hall, quoted in Gropman, *The Air Force Integrates*, 281.

148 "IT'S INEVITABLE": Parrish oral history, 10.
"AMALGAMATION" OF THE RACES: "Recommendations for Organization, Command, and Utilization of Negro Soldiers in a Future Emergency," July 17, 1945, NA RS. Lee File. Other, more "liberal," sentiments are found in "Training and Performance of Negro Troops in Fourth Air Force," July 24, 1945, OAFH 45a, 765. The Second Air Force history concluded that utilization of blacks had been unsuccessful, but still called for their better employment ("History of Second Air Force," September 2, 1945).
POLITICAL PRESSURE: Vandenberg to Assistant Chief of Air Staff, October 16, 1945, Arnold Papers, 291.2, Box 72.
BLACK COMBAT TROOPS: The Gillem Board and its recommendations are extensively reviewed by Gropman, *The Air Force Integrates*, 46–71.

149 "I AGREE THAT THE PRACTICABILITY": Marshall to McCloy, August 25, 1945. Filed with "Gillem Report Papers," in Memo for Chief of Staff, Subject: "Participation of Negro Troops in the Post-War Military Establishment."
"THAT THE BASIC ARMY POLICY BE CHANGED": Gibson to McCloy, August 8, 1945, filed with "Participation of Negro Troops in the Post-War Military Establishment" memo; Gibson to Secretary of War, November 28, 1945, NA RG 107, Assistant Secretary of War, 291.2, Box 40.
IMPETUS FOR CHANGE: War Department, "Report of Board of Officers on Utilization of Negro Manpower in the Post-War Army," November 1945, NA RG 18, 291.2, Box 348.

150 BREAK WITH SEGREGATION: The conclusions of the Gillem Board were published almost without change as War Department Circular 124 (1946). The Board's recom-

mendation of an extensive racial education program resulted in *Army Talk 170.* Gropman, *The Air Force Integrates,* 59.

"CONSERVATIVE" RECOMMENDATIONS: Parrish, "The Segregation of Negroes in the Army Air Forces," 98.

EVENTUAL ENDING OF SEGREGATION: Gibson to Robert P. Patterson (Secretary of War), November 28, 1945, NA RG 107, Assistant Secretary of War, 291.2, Box 40.

SOMETHING OUT OF THE ORDINARY: McCloy memo to Patterson, November 24 and 28, 1945, in "Supplemental Report of War Department, Special Board on Negro Manpower," 1, in Gillem Papers, dated January 26, 1946.

"JUST ANOTHER STUDY": Evans interview, OAFH, 4; *Army Talk 170,* 1.

"THE ALL NEGRO AIR CORPS": Parrish, "The Segregation of Negroes in the Army Air Forces," 92–93. See Wilkins, "Still a Jim Crow Army."

"THE ARMY'S ULTIMATE AIM": See "Supplemental Report of War Department, Special Board on Negro Manpower," 4; *Army Talk,* 170, 1.

151   LIMITED NUMBER OF SEPARATE UNITS: MacGregor and Nalty, eds., *Blacks in the United States Armed Forces,*   409.

FORRESTAL: Gropman, *The Air Force Integrates,* 89; Evans interview.

INTEGRATION OF THE MILITARY: McCoy and Ruetten, *Quest and Response.*

152   TRUMAN'S GOAL OF EQUALITY OF TREATMENT: "President's Committee on Equality of Treatment and Opportunity in the Armed Services," March 28, 1949, NA RG 341, Box 782; published as *Freedom to Serve: Equality of Treatment and Opportunity in the Armed Services: A Report of the President's Committee* (Washington, D.C., 1950). President Truman's instructions to the four service secretaries and the members of the Fahy Committee exemplify the man: he informed them that he was not interested in fair or better treatment, just equal treatment (Gropman, *The Air Force Integrates,* 114–15).

24TH INFANTRY REGIMENT: Wynne, *Afro-Americans and the Second World War,* 45; Dalfiume, *Desegregation of the U.S. Armed Forces,* 47, and *passim*; MacGregor and Nalty, eds., *Blacks in the United States Armed Forces,*   409; R. Appleman, *South to the Naktong, North to the Yalu: The U.S. Army in the Korean War* (Washington, D.C.: Government Printing Office, 1961). In all fairness, it should be pointed out that the record demonstrates clearly that in the first weeks of the Korean War, although there was enough individual bravery to go around, few if any U.S. units put up very strong or effective resistance to the enemy.

153   SYMINGTON: Gropman, *The Air Force Integrates,* 89–90, 296, 298; Nichols, *Breakthrough on the Color Front,* 75, 76, 78; Dalfiume, *Desegregation of the U.S. Armed Forces,* 77, 78.

"CORRECTIVE ACTION": MacGregor and Nalty, eds., *Blacks in the United States Armed Forces,* 5398, 401, 407.

154   ELIMINATION OF SEGREGATION: Gropman, *The Air Force Integrates,* 86–90. In the words of the best authority on the subject, "Air Force integration was one of the great success stories of the civil rights movement" (ibid., 90). See also Francis, *The Tuskegee Airmen,* 167. It should further be noted that the Army and the Navy did not fully comply with President Truman's directives until just after the Korean War.

EVANS SUCCEEDS GIBSON: Evans, "Counselor to SECDEF."

GENERAL VANDENBERG: Gropman, *The Air Force Integrates*, 85.

"OUR PLAN": Ibid., 115.

BALANCE OF TEST SCORES: Ibid., 120–23; Watson OAFH interview transcript.

WATSON: Watson OAFH interview transcript, 44. Watson might have felt even worse had he known that Colonel Davis had told the Giles Air Force Board that only about 30 percent of the 332nd officers were worth retraining (Ulysses Lee File, vol. 2, Box 513, "Miscellaneous Data" and "General" tabs). Eugene Zuckert, who was involved in Air Force desegregation as assistant secretary of the Air Force, and who later became Air Force secretary, remarked later that the 332nd "was not an effective operation from the standpoint of the Air Force" at that time (Zuckert OAFH oral interview, K239.0512-674, April 1973).

"NOW TAKE AN ORDINARY CAPTAIN": NAACP Papers, Library of Congress, container 405, March 15, 1949. Spann Watson, of Walterboro notoriety, was undoubtedly one of the officers (Gropman, *The Air Force Integrates*, 306). Air Force Secretary Zuckert later conceded that the screening boards probably had been a mistake (ibid., 307).

155 TWENTY-FOUR UNITS SEGREGATED: "History of the 332nd Fighter Wing," January 1– March 31, 1948, and June 1949, 41. MacGregor and Nalty, eds., *Blacks in the United States Armed Forces*, 404.

NEGATIVE RACIAL INCIDENTS: MacGregor and Nalty, eds., *Blacks in the United States Armed Forces*, 400–401. See also Kenworthy, "Taps for Jim Crow in the Services." Contemporary black reaction can be found in "Armed Services Jim Crow Policy Ends"; "The Air Force Goes Interracial"; and Defense Department report on final abolition of military racial segregation, New York *Times*, October 31, 1954; Parrish interview.

SERIOUS RACIAL TROUBLE: Gropman, *The Air Force Integrates*, 169ff.

"OBSERVING ANCIENT CUSTOMS": Evans, "Counselor to SECDEF," 4.

Chapter 9. Summary and Retrospect

157 NUMBER OF BLACK OFFICERS: "National Defense Conference on Negro Officers," 71, NA RS; Air Force Headquarters, Lee File, Box 383.

158 STATISTICAL CONTROL DIVISION: Long after wartime and postwar tensions had presumably faded, General Eaker, who had been senior AAF commander in the Mediterranean, conceded that "the 332nd performance was on a par with the average of all pursuit squadrons under my jurisdiction" but went on to add that "I believe that all black fighter squadrons were happier, more confident and, therefore, rendered better service under their own black officers and as a homogeneous unit" (letter to Osur, quoted in Osur, *Blacks in the Army Air Forces*, 165).

332ND GOOD AVERAGE GROUP: Parrish oral history, 27.

159 "LESS MECHANICAL TROUBLE": Comparative data on combat performance of the 332nd and its component squadrons is drawn from AAF Office of Statistical Control, "USAAF Statistical Digest, World War II"; letter from James Eastman, Jr., Chief Research Branch, HRC, to L. Paszek, OAFH, July 21, 1977.

Bibliography

Primary Sources

Records and Papers

Alabama Archives and History, Montgomery, Ala. Contains some material on military racial situation and white reactions during World War II.

Army Air Forces Records, HRC. Unit records of the 99th, 100th, 301st, and 302nd Pursuit Squadrons, 79th and 332nd Fighter Groups, and 477th Medium Bomber Group (Colored). Microcopies of the bulk of these records are in the OAFH.

Army Air Forces Records, and Army Adjutant General Decimal Files. NA RG 18, 291.2.

Henry Arnold Papers. LC.

Ira Eaker Papers. LC.

James Carmichael Evans Papers. AMHI.

Alva C. Gillem Papers. AMHI.

Alan Gropman Collection. HRC.

Lee File. NA. Material relating to Lee, *The Employment of Negro Troops* (1966).

Lee File (Ulysses Lee File). Box 512, NA, April 1944–June 1945. NA. Contains weekly summaries of military racial matters.

"Milestones"/Tuskegee Institute Presidential Archives. Tuskegee Institute, Ala. Some material on early black flying at the Institute.

Franklin D. Roosevelt Presidential Papers. Franklin D. Roosevelt Library, Hyde Park, N.Y. Contains material on General Davis and black civilians in World War II.

Secretary of War Records. Office of the Assistant Secretary of War, Civilian Aide to the Secretary of War. NA RG 107, 291.2, Secretary of War, Assistant Secretary of War, Civilian Aide to the Secretary of War.

———. Minutes of Meetings of Advisory Committee on Negro Troop Policies. NA RG 107 291.2, 1941–1945.

Carl Spaatz Papers. LC.

Spingarn and NAACP Papers. LC. Contain considerable material on blacks in the military during World War II, mostly letters of complaint from black service personnel of discriminatory or cruel treatment.

Official Reports and Studies

AAC/AAF/SEAACTC. "Clashes between Civil and Military Police in Tuskegee, Alabama." April 24, 1942. Alabama Archives and History 220.765, Montgomery, Ala.

AAF Office of Statistical Control. "USAAF Statistical Digest, World War II." December 1945. OAFH.

Army Service Forces. Morale Service Division. "The Adjustment of the Negro Soldier to the Army." First draft, January 29, 1944. OAFH.

Army Special Forces. Deputy Director of Intelligence. "Racial Situation in the United States." April 7, 1944. Army Intelligence Domestic File, 1941–48. NA RG 319, War Department, Deputy Director of Intelligence, 292.2.

"Attitudes of the Negro Soldier." Draft of July 26, 1943. Lee file, NA RG 18.

Avery, D. B. "The Negro and the Air Force." ACS College Research Study, MAFB, March 1949. OAFH.

Army War College. "The Use of Negro Manpower in Time of Emergency." Box 7, Tab H, Gillem Papers. 1936.

———. "The Colored Soldier in the U.S. Army." Historical Section, 1942.

———. "The Use of Negro Manpower in War." October 10, 1925.

Byers, Jean. "A Study of the Negro in Military Service." Department of Defense, Washington, D.C., June 1947.

Catington, James. "Sociological Factors Concerned with the Segregation of Negro Troops in the Armed Forces." ACS College Research Study, MAFB, May 1949.

Chief of Staff of the Army Air Forces. Memo to Chief of Staff of the Army: "Participation of Negro Troops in the Post-War Military Establishment." 1945.

Civil Aviation Administration, "Domestic Air News, Washington, D.C., 1926–1928." Washington, D.C., 1939.

"Classification and Assignment of Enlisted Men in the Army Air Arm, 1917–1946." USAF Historical Study No. 76, 1953.

"Colored Officers." March 17, 1944. OAFH 220.765.2. Unpublished typescript.

Department of the Census. "Negro Aviators." December 21, 1940. NA RG 107, Box 178, Entry 91.

Department of the Navy. Memo: "Naval Services of Negroes. United States Navy." 1924. Washington, D.C.

England, Merton, and Chauncey Sanders. "Legislation Relating to the AAF Training Program, 1939–1945." AAF Historical Study No. 7, April 1946.

Evans, James Carmichael. "MS. A Compilation Relating to the Negro Citizen and Minority Affairs in General vis-à-vis the War Department." July 1970. Department of Defense, Washington, D.C.

Gaffney, John B. "Application of Personnel Management as Applied to Negro Troops in the Air Forces." ACS Research Study, October 1948.

Grant, C. L. "The Development and Function of AAF OCS and OTS." USAF Historical Study No. 99, 1953. Simpson Center, MAFB.

Greer, Allen J. "Extract from Reports of Officers on Subject of Negro Manpower, Responses of LTC Allen J. Greer, Infantry, Chief of Staff, 92nd Division." April 13, 1924. AMHI.

Jones, R. L., and Chauncey Sanders. "Personnel Problems Relating to AAF Commissioned Officers, 1939–1945." USAF Historical Study No. 11, 1951.

Klein, Phillip B. "Utilization of Negro Personnel in the Air Force." Air War College Research Study, MAFB, March 1949.

Kunish, Lester L. "Utilization of Negro Airmen on Air Force Bases." Air War College Research Study, MAFB, February 1949.

Link, Fidelis A. "Determination of Policies for Utilization of Negro Manpower in the U.S. Air Force." ACS College Research Study, MAFB, November 1949.

McCloy, John J. Memo: "Supplemental Report of War Department, Special Board on Negro Manpower." January 26, 1944. Gillem Papers.

"Morale in the AAF in World War II." USAF Historical Study No. 78, MAFB, 1953.

"National Defense Conference on Negro Officers." April 26, 1948. USAF Headquarters, Washington, D.C.

"Negro Units at Godman Field and Walterboro Army Air Base." May 29, 1944. NA RG 18 AAF, Box 104.

Nelson, Dennis D. "The Integration of the Negro in the U.S. Navy, 1776–1947." 1948. Bureau of Personnel, U.S. Navy, NAVEXOS-P-526. Washington, D.C.

[Nippert, Eugene.] "A Statement of Policies Followed by the Army Air Forces during World War II with Respect to the Training and Utilization of Negro Troops." September 17, 1945.

Operations Division. Memo to Brig. Gen. Dwight D. Eisenhower: "Colored Troop Problem." April 2, 1942. NA RG 107, Assistant Secretary of War, Box 124.

"Participation of Negro Troops." Summer 1945. Looseleaf folder containing reports from numbered air forces and other units, plus a summary report. The original of this file is in the Arnold Papers, the OAFH, and the National Archives, as well as the author's files.

Paszek, L. "Brief History of the 99th Fighter Squadron, 1939–1949." n.d. Typescript, OAFH.

[Paszek, L.] "Negro Airmen of the A.A.F.: The History of the 99th Fighter Squadron." n.d. HRC.

Pesch, John J. "Should Negroes and Whites Be Integrated in the Same Air Force Units?" ACS College Research Study, MAFB, April 1949.

Report of the Special Board on Negro Manpower. "Policy for Utilization of Negro Manpower in the Post-War Army with Recommendations for Development of Means Required and a Plan for Implementation of the Same." November 1945.

Schuman, B. "Role of the NAACP in the Integration of the Armed Forces According to the NAACP Collection in the Library of Congress." 1971. Typescript, Center of Military History, Washington, D.C.

U.S. Congress. "Hearings before Subcommittee of the Committee on Appropriations on H.R. 9209." 76th Cong., 3rd sess., 1941.

War Department. "Colored Soldiers in the U.S. Army." 1942. In MacGregor and Nalty, eds., *Blacks in the United States Armed Forces.*

————. "Report of Board of Officers [Gillem Board] on Utilization of Negro Manpower in the Post-War Army." 1945. NA RG 18, 291.2, Box 40.

————. Research Bureau. "Attitudes of Enlisted Men toward Negroes." November 30, 1942. Assistant Secretary of War Decimal File 291.2, 1940–45.

————. Special Services Division, Research Branch. "What the Soldier Thinks." August 2, 1943. NA RG 330, 2.

War Department/Department of the Army. "Organization and Training of Negroes." Army General Staff College, Washington Course, Confidential Conference, April 21, 1920; untitled 1923–24 AWC course, File 127-23. AMHI.

Wiley, Bell I. "The Training of Negro Troops." Army Ground Forces Study No. 36, 1946.

Young, Hugh D. "Effective Utilization of Negro Manpower in the United States Air Force." ACS School Research Study, December 1948.

Unit Histories

Unless otherwise indicated, these histories are found in the USAF HRC.

"The Composite History of the 477th Composite Group, Godman Field, Kentucky." January 1944–September 1945. GP-477-HI, 14–18.

XV Fighter Command (Prov.). "History of the XV Fighter Command (Prov.) for Quarter Ending 31 March." 1945.

XV Fighter Command (Prov.). "Medical History, Headquarters, XV Fighter Command (Provisional)." January 1–March 1, 1945. 672.01.

"History of 66th AAF Flying Training Detachment."

"Historical Record of the 99th Fighter Squadron." n.d.

"History of Southeastern Army Air Corps/Air Forces Training Command." OAFH.

"History of Southeastern Army Air Force[s] Training Detachment, Moton Field, Tuskegee Institute, Alabama." OAFH.

"History of the 99th Pursuit/Fighter Squadron." 1941–1945.

"History of the 332nd Fighter Group (SE)." July 1944–November 1948.

"History of the 332nd Fighter Wing." January 1–March 31, 1948, and June 1949.

"History of the 477th Bombardment Group (Medium)." January 15, 1944–July 15, 1945.

"History of the 477th Composite Group." September 15, 1945–June 30, 1947.

"History of the 2143nd AAF Base Unit Pilot School, Basic Advanced and Tuskegee Army Air Field, Tuskegee, Alabama." January 1945–April 1946.

"History of the 2164th AAF Base Unit Tuskegee Institute." May-June 1945.

"History of the Mediterranean Allied Air Force." Eaker Papers.

"History of the Second Air Force, September 2, 1945–March 30, 1946."

"History of Tuskegee Army Air Field." OAFH.

[Lyon, Earl D.] First Air Force. "The Training of Negro Combat Units by the First Air Force." n.d. 2 vols., 420.04C. Also contains "Plans for the Activation of the Colored Bombardment Group (M)." December 1943 and May 1946.

"Official History of the 79th Fighter Group," GP 79–HI, microframe 1301, OAFH.

"Training and Performance of Negro Troops in Fourth Air Force." July 24, 1945.

"Training of Negroes within the First Air Force." 1945.

Woodward, Elon A. "The Negro in the Military Service of the United States—A Compilation of Official Records, State Papers, Historical Extracts, etc., Relating to His Military Status and Service from the Date of His Introduction into British North America—1639–1886." Washington, D.C., 1888; typescript, NA, 1963.

Public Documents

AAF. Letter 35-100. "Utilization of Negro Personnel." March 1, 1946.

———. Letter 35-101. "Utilization of Negro Manpower in the Postwar Army Policy." April 27, 1946.

———. Letter 35-130. "Enlistments and Reenlistments in the Regular Army." June 21, 1946.

———. Office of Statistical Control. *Army Air Forces Statistical Digest: World War II.* Washington, D.C., December 1945.

———. Statistical Control Division. *Army Air Forces Statistical Digest, 1946.* June 1947.

Assistant Secretary of Defense. *Integration and the Negro Officer in the Armed Forces of the U.S.A.* Washington, D.C., 1962.

Department of the Army. *Utilization of Negroes in the Post-War Army.* Washington, D.C., 1948 (text of Gillem Report).

Link, M. M., and H. A. Coleman. *Medical Support of the Army Air Forces in World War II.* New York, 1955.

Owen, Chandler. *The Negroes and the War.* Washington, D.C., 1942.

USAF. Letter 39-8. *Assignment of Air Force Enlistees, Reenlistees, and Returnees.* February 14, 1949.

———. Regulation 35-78. *Air Force Personnel Policies.* September 14, 1950.

———. Statistical Services. *United States Air Force Statistical Digest: 1948, January 1949–June 1950, Fiscal 1951, 1952, 1953, 1954.*

Executive Branch

Department of the Navy. *Guide to the Command of Negro Naval Personnel.* Washington, D.C., 1944.

Evans, James C. *The Negro in the Army: Policy and Practice.* Department of the Army. Washington, D.C., 1948.

Fair Employment Practices Committee. *First Report, July 1943–December 1943.* Washington, D.C., 1945.

Office of War Information. Survey Division, Bureau of Special Services. *The Negro's Role in the War.* Washington, D.C., 1943.

Pearson, Paul F. *The Development of National Policy Regarding Black Combat Soldiers in the U.S. Army, 1912–1925.* U.S. Army War College Study. March 3, 1972.

President's Committee on Civil Rights. *To Secure These Rights.* Washington, D.C., 1947.

President's Committee on Equality of Treatment and Opportunity in the Armed Services. *Freedom to Serve.* Washington, D.C., 1950.

Selective Service System. *Special Groups.* Monograph No. 10, vol. 1. Washington, D.C., 1953.

Strickland, Patricia. *The Putt-Putt Air Force.* Washington, D.C., 1971.

U.S. Senate, 67th Cong. *Hearings Before a Special Committee on Charges of Alleged Executions Without Trial in France.* Washington, D.C., 1923.

War Department/Department of the Army. Pamphlet 20-6. "Command of Negro Troops." Washington, D.C., February 29, 1944.

———. "Army Talk, 170." April 12, 1947.

———. Army Services Manual M-5. "Leadership and the Negro Soldier." Washington, D.C., October 1944.

———. "Prejudice!—Roadblock to Progress." "Army Talk, 70." May 5, 1945.

———. Special Services Division. Research Branch. *Attitudes of White Enlisted Men toward Sharing Facilities with Negro Troops.* Washington, D.C., July 30, 1942.

———. Special Service Division. Research Branch. Services of Supply. *Attitudes of Enlisted Men toward Negroes for Air Force Duty.* November 30, 1942.

———. U.S. Army Center of Military History. *Special Bibliographic Series, Number 2: The U.S. Army and the Negro.* Carlisle Barracks, Pa., 1971.

———. U.S. Army Center of Military History. *Order of Battle of the United States Land Forces in the World War.* Zone of the Interior, vol. 3, pt. 1. 1948; rpt.: Washington, D.C., 1988.

Theses and Dissertations

Adams, T. R. "The Houston Riot of 1917." M.A. thesis, Texas A&M University, 1972.

Cook, L. H. "The Brownsville Affray." M.A. thesis, University of North Carolina, 1948.

Flemming, William F. "American Negro Combat Soldiers in World War I." Ph.D. diss., Western Reserve University, 1975.

Gill, G. R. "Religious, Constitutional, and Racial Objections to United States Involvement in World War II, 1939–1945." M.A. thesis, Howard University, 1974.

Green, R. E. "Colonel Charles Young, Soldier, Diplomat." M.A. thesis, Howard University, 1972.

Gropman, Alan. "The Air Force Integrates: Blacks in the Air Force from 1945 to 1965." Ph.D. diss., Tufts University, 1975.

Hadley, James Stiles. "The Social Attitudes of Negro Servicemen." M.A. thesis, Atlanta University, 1945.

Leggett, Edwin S. "Racism in Commercial Aviation, 1946–1972." M.A. thesis, Howard University, 1972.

McGuire, P. "Black Civilian Aides and the Problems of Racism and Segregation in the U.S. Armed Forces, 1940–50." Ph.D diss., Howard University, 1975.

Murray, Paul T. "Blacks and the Draft: An Analysis of Institutional Racism, 1917–1971." Ph.D diss., Florida State University, 1972. Condensed and edited version published in *Journal of Black Studies* 2 (September 1971).

Park, Phocion Samuel, Jr. "The Twenty-Fourth Infantry Regiment and the Houston Riot of 1917." M.A. thesis, University of Houston, 1971.

Parrish, Noel F. "The Segregation of Negroes in the Army Air Forces." Diss. for the ACS School, MAFB, May 1947.

Tinsley, James A. "The Brownsville Affray." M.A. thesis, University of Colorado, 1942.

Film

[AAF.] Silent film, primarily gun camera. Unedited. NA 18, CS, 27 6; 1059, 2; 18 CS, 122, n.d.

Democracy, or a Fight for Right and Loyal Hearts. 1928.

Department of Agriculture. *Henry Browne, Farmer.* NA 59, 53. 1943.

Office of War Information. *Negro Colleges in Wartime.* NA 208-7 PPC. 1943.

Paramount Pictures newsreel. NA 200, PN 156, PPCA. 1942.

——. NA 208, PN 344. 1944.

Universal Studios newsreel. NA 208, UN 88. 1944.

War Department. *From Harlem to the Rhine* (twelve two-reel episodes), n.d.

——. *Our Hell Fighters Return.* 1918.

——. Signal Corps. *Training of Colored Troops.* NA 11 1H-1 SA-1. n.d. (c. 1917).

——. *The Negro Soldier.* NA 111F. 1944. (Print also in Franklin D. Roosevelt Presidential Library.)

——. *Welcome to Britain.* NA GI-33 (c. 1944).

——. *Westward Is Bataan.* NA OF-27 (c. 1944).

——. *Wings for This Man.* NA SFP-151. 1945.

Sound Recordings

"Elmer Davis on Meeting of Negro Newspaper Editors." March 10, 1943. NA.

President Franklin Roosevelt meeting with black leaders, September 27, 1940. NA.

Secondary Sources

Books

Allen, R. *Port Chicago Mutiny: The Story of the Largest Mass Mutiny in U.S. Naval History.* New York, 1989.

Arnold, Thomas St. John, O.B.E. *The Buffalo Soldiers: The 92nd Infantry Division and Reinforcements in World War II, 1942–1945.* Manhattan, Kan., 1989.

Barbeau, A. E., and F. Henri. *The Unknown Soldiers: Black American Troops in World War I.* Philadelphia, 1974.

Benedict, Ruth, and Gene Weltfish. *The Races of Mankind.* New York, 1943.

Boog, Horst. "Higher Command and Leadership in the German Luftwaffe, 1935–1945." In A. Hurley and R. C. Ehrhart, eds. *Air Power and Warfare.* Proceedings of the 8th Military History Symposium, USAF Academy, Colorado Springs, Colorado. October 1978. Washington, D.C., 1979.

Brown, Earl, and George R. Leighton. *The Negro and the War.* New York. 1942.

Bullard, Robert Lee. *Personalities and Reminiscences of the War.* New York, 1925.

Caidin, Martin. *The Ragged, Rugged Warriors.* New York, 1966.

Capra, Frank. *The Name above the Title.* New York, 1971.

Carisella, P., and James Ryan. *The Black Swallow of Death.* Boston, 1972.

Carroll, J. M., ed. *The Black Military Experience in the American West.* New York, 1971.

Chew, Abraham A. *A Biography of Colonel Charles Young.* Washington, D.C., 1923.

Coffman, Edward. *The War to End All Wars.* New York, 1968.

Craven, Frank Wesley, and James Lea Cate, eds. *The Army Air Forces in World War II.* Vol. 2, *Europe: TORCH to POINTBLANK, August 1942 to December 1943.* Chicago, 1949.

———. *The Army Air Forces in World War II.* Vol. 3, *Europe: ARGUMENT to V-E Day, January 1944 to May 1945.* Chicago, 1951, 1965.

———. *The Army Air Forces in World War II.* Vol. 7, *Services around the World.* Chicago, 1958.

Dalfiume, Richard. *Desegregation of the U.S. Armed Forces: Fighting on Two Fronts, 1939–1953.* Columbia, Mo., 1969.

Davis, Benjamin O., Jr. *Benjamin O. Davis, Jr., American: An Autobiography.* Washington, D.C., 1991.

Davis, Benjamin. *The Negro People and the Communist Party.* New York, 1943.

Davis, Lenwood, and George Hill. *Blacks in the American Armed Forces, 1776–1983: A Bibliography.* Westport, Conn., 1985.

Ethell, Jeffrey, and Alfred Price. *The German Jets in Combat.* New York, 1979.

Finkle, L. *Forum of Protest: The Black Press during World War II.* New York, 1975.

Fletcher, Marvin. *The Black Soldier and Officer in the U.S. Army, 1891–1917.* Columbia, Mo., 1974.

———. *America's First Black General: Benjamin O. Davis, Sr., 1880–1970.* Lawrence, Kan., 1989.

Foner, J. D. *Blacks and the Military in American History: A New Perspective.* New York, 1974.

Ford, James W. *The War and the Negro.* New York, 1942.

Fowler, A. L. *Black Infantry in the West, 1869–1891.* Westport, Conn., 1971.

Francis, Charles. *The Tuskegee Airmen: The Story of the Negro in the U.S. [Army] Air Force[s].* Boston, 1955.

Gatewood, W. B. *"Smoked Yankees" and the Struggle for Empire: Letters from Negro Soldiers, 1898–1902.* Urbana, Ill., 1971.

Ginker, R. R., and J. P. Spiegel. *Men under Stress.* Philadelphia, 1945.

Gropman, Alan. *The Air Force Integrates, 1945–1964.* Washington, D.C., 1978.

Guzman, J. *The Negro Yearbook: A Review of Events Affecting Negro Life, 1941–1946.* Tuskegee, Ala., 1947.

Hastie, William. "On Clipped Wings: The Story of Jim Crow in the Army Air Corps." Washington, D.C., 1943.

Haynes, R. V. *A Night of Violence*. Baton Rouge, 1976.

Johnson, Charles S. *To Stem This Tide: A Survey of Racial Tension Areas in the United States*. Chicago, 1943.

Johnson, J. R. *Why Negroes Should Oppose the War*. n.d. (c. 1939).

Jones, Claudia. *Jim Crow in Uniform*. New York, 1940.

Kendrick, Douglas B. *The Blood Program in World War II*. Washington, D.C., 1974.

Koppes, C. R., and Gregory D. Black. *Hollywood Goes to War: How Politics, Profits, and Propaganda Shaped World War II Movies*. New York, 1987.

Lane, Anne J. *The Brownsville Affair: National Crisis and Black Reaction*. Port Washington, N.Y, 1971.

Leckie, W. H. *The Buffalo Soldiers: A Narrative of the Negro Cavalry in the West*. Norman, Okla., 1967.

Lee, Ulysses. *The Employment of Negro Troops: The U.S. Army in World War II*. United States Army in World War II, Special Studies, Office of the Chief of Military History, Department of the Army. Washington, D.C., 1966.

McCoy, Donald, and Richard T. Ruetten. *Quest and Response: Minority Rights and the Truman Administration*. Lawrence, Kan., 1973.

MacDonald, Nancy, and Dwight MacDonald. *The War's Greatest Scandal! The Story of Jim Crow in Uniform*. March on Washington Movement. New York. n.d. (c. 1943).

MacGregor, Morris J., and Bernard C. Nalty, eds. *Blacks in the United States Armed Forces: Basic Documents*. Vol. 5. Wilmington, Del., 1977.

McGuire, P. *Taps for a Jim Crow Army: Letters from Black Soldiers in World War II*. Santa Barbara, Calif., 1983.

———. *He, Too, Spoke for Democracy: Judge William Hastie, World War II, and the Black Soldier*. Westport, Conn., 1988.

Mandelbaum, David G. *Soldier Groups and Negro Soldiers*. Berkeley, Calif., 1952.

Maurer, Maurer, ed. *Air Force Combat Units of World War II*. New York, 1963.

———. *Combat Squadrons of the Air Force[s], World War II*. Washington, D.C., 1969.

Merrill, Francis E. *Social Problems on the Home Front*. New York, 1948.

Mets, David R. *Master of Airpower: General Carl A. Spaatz*. Novato, Calif., 1988

Miller, Kelly. *Kelly Miller's Authentic History of the Negro in the World War*. 1919.

Millet, Alan R. *General Robert L. Bullard and Officership in the United States Army, 1881–1925*. Westport, Conn., 1975.

Moon, H. L. *The Emerging Thought of W.E.B. Du Bois: Essays and Editorials from "The Crisis."* New York, 1972.

Morison, Elting. *Turmoil and Tradition: A Study of the Life and Times of Henry L. Stimson*. New York, 1960.

Motley, Mary, ed. *The Invisible Soldiers: The Experience of Black Soldiers, World War II*. Detroit, 1975.

Murray, Florence, ed. *The Negro Handbook, 1944*. New York, 1944.

Myrdal, Gunnar. *An American Dilemma: The Negro Problem and Modern Democracy*. New York, 1944.

Nankivell, John. *History of the 25th Regiment, U.S. Infantry, 1869–1926.* Denver, 1927.

National Association for the Advancement of Colored People (NAACP). *Burnings at the Stake in the United States.* Washington, D.C., 1919.

Nelson, Dennis. *The Integration of the Negro into the United States Navy.* New York, 1951.

Nichols, Lee. *Breakthrough on the Color Front.* New York, 1954.

Northrup, Herbert. *The Negro in the Air Transport Industry.* Philadelphia, 1971.

Osur, Alan. *Blacks in the Army Air Forces during World War II.* Washington, D.C., 1977.

Ottley, Roi. *New World A-Coming: Inside Black America.* Boston, 1943.

Overy, R. J. *The Air War, 1939–1945.* New York, 1980.

Patton, Gerald W. *War and Race: The Black Officer in the American Military, 1915–1941.* Westport, Conn., 1981.

Peck, James. *Armies with Wings.* New York, 1940.

Powell, W. J. *Black Wings.* Los Angeles, 1934.

Quarles, Benjamin. *The Negro in the Civil War.* Boston, 1953.

Record, Wilson. *Negroes and the Communist Party.* Chapel Hill, N.C., 1951.

Rose, Robert A. *Lonely Eagles: The Story of America's Black Air Force in World War II.* Los Angeles, 1976. (Originally published as "Lonely Eagles" in the *Journal of the American Aviation Historical Society.* Pt. 1, Summer 1975; pt. 2, Winter 1975.)

Schoenfeld, Seymour. *The Negro in the Armed Forces: His Value and Status—Past, Present, and Potential.* Washington, D.C., 1945.

Scott, Emmett J. *The American Negro in the World War.* Chicago, 1919.

[79th Fighter Group.] *The Falcon: Combat History of the 79th Fighter Group, United States Army Air Force[s].* Munich, 1946.

Smithsonian Institution. *Black Wings.* Washington, D.C., 1983.

Stimson, Henry L., and McGeorge Bundy. *On Active Service in Peace and War.* New York, 1947.

Stouffer, Samuel, et al. *Studies in Social Psychology in World War II.* Vol. 2, *The American Soldier: Combat and Aftermath.* Princeton, 1949.

———. *Studies in Social Psychology in World War II.* Vol. 4, *Measurement and Prediction.* Princeton, 1950.

Suchenwirth, R. *Historical Turning Points in the German Air Force War Effort.* MAFB, 1959; rpt.: New York, 1968.

Utley, R. M. *Frontier Regulars: The U.S. Army and the Indian Wars.* New York, 1973.

Villard, Oswald Garrison. *The Story of the Negro.* New York, 1909.

Wagner, Ray. *American Combat Planes.* Garden City, N.Y., 1982.

Ware, Gilbert. *William Hastie: Grace under Pressure.* New York, 1984.

Washburn, P. S. *The Federal Government Investigation of the Black Press during World War II.* Miami, Ohio, 1986.

Weaver, J. D. *The Brownsville Raid: The Story of America's First Black Dreyfus Affair.* New York, 1970.

Weiss, Nancy. *Farewell to the Party of Lincoln: Black Politicians in the Age of FDR.* Princeton, 1983.

White, Walter. *A Man Called White: The Autobiography of Walter White.* New York, 1948.

————. *How Far the Promised Land?* New York, 1956.

Williams, Charles. *Sidelights on Negro Soldiers.* Boston, 1923.

Wolseley, R. E. *The Black Press and the U.S.A.* Ames, Iowa, 1971.

Wynne, Neil A. *Afro-Americans and the Second World War.* London, 1970.

Articles

"Air Corps." *The Crisis,* February 1942.

"The Air Force Goes Interracial." *Ebony,* September 1949.

"American Negro in World War I and II." *Journal of Negro Education* 12 (Summer 1943).

Amidon, Beulah. "Negroes and Defense." *Survey Graphic* (June 1941).

Aptheker, H. "Negro Casualties in the Civil War." *Journal of Negro History* (January 1947).

"Armed Forces Jim Crow Policy Ends." *The Crisis,* May 1949.

"Army Air Corps Smoke Screen." *The Crisis,* April 1941.

"Army Can Have Jim Crow in Selective Services Act." *The Crisis,* January 1941.

Billington, Monroe. "Freedom to Serve: The President's Committee on Equality of Treatment and Opportunity in the Armed Forces 1949–1950." *Journal of Negro History* (October 1966).

Blum, John M. "United Against: American Culture and Society during World War II." *The Harmon Memorial Lectures in Military History 1959–1987,* ed. H. R. Borowski. Washington, D.C., 1988.

Bombardier [pseud.]. "The Story of the 477th Bombardment Group." *Politics,* June 1944.

Bond, H. M. "Should the Negro Care Who Wins the War?" *Annals of the American Academy of Political and Social Sciences* (September 1942).

————. "The Negro in the Armed Forces of the United States prior to World War I." *Journal of Negro Education* 12 (Summer 1943).

"Brigadier General Benjamin O. Davis." *Opportunity,* November 1940.

Brown, Nugent. "Tuskegee, World's Only Army Flying School for Negroes." *Service,* September 1942.

Brown, Warren. "A Negro Looks at the Negro Press." *Saturday Review of Literature,* December 19, 1942.

Brunson, W. T. "What a Negro Soldier Thinks About." *Social Service Review* (December 1944).

Bullard, Robert Lee. "The Negro Volunteer: Some Characteristics." *Journal of the Military Service Institution of the United States* (July 1901).

Butow, R. C. "The FDR Tapes." *American Heritage,* February/March 1982.

Carter, Art. "With Colonel Davis' Flyers in Italy." *This Is Our War,* 1945.

Carter, E. A. "A Negro Pursuit Squadron." *Opportunity,* April 1941.

————. "Pilots for 99th Pursuit Squadron Begin Training at Tuskegee." *Opportunity,* August 1941.

Centurion [pseud.]. "Kitchen Soldiering." *Infantry Journal,* May-June 1936.

Clark, Kenneth. "Morale among Negroes." *Second Yearbook of the Society for the Psychological Study of the Social Sciences,* ed. Goodwin Watson. New York, 1942.

———. "Morale of the Negro on the Home Front: World Wars I and II." *Journal of Negro Education* (Summer 1943).

Clayton, H. R. "Fighting for White Folks?" *The Nation,* September 26, 1940.

Cripps, Thomas, and David Culbert. "The Negro Soldier (1944): Propaganda in Black and White." *American Quarterly* (Winter 1979).

Dalfiume, Richard. "The 'Forgotten Years' of the Negro Revolution." *Journal of American History* (June 1968).

———. "The Fahy Commission and Desegregation of the Armed Forces." *The Historian,* November 1968.

Davis, Arthur P. "Will a Long War Aid the Negro?" *Negro Digest* (November 1943)

Day, Jack. "The Inside Story of Tuskegee." *Pittsburgh Courier,* September 1945.

DeBow, Charles, as told to W. A. H. Binie. "I Got Wings." *American Magazine,* August 1942.

Du Bois, W. E. B. "Close Ranks." *The Crisis,* July 1918.

Eastland, J. O. "Are Negroes Good Soldiers?" *Negro Digest* (December 1945).

"Experiment Proved?" *Time,* September 20, 1943.

"First Negro Officer Commissioned in U.S. Air Corps." *Opportunity,* April 1942.

Flynn, G. Q. "Selective Service and American Blacks during World War II." *Journal of Negro History* 69 (1984).

"The Fort Dix Straw." *Amsterdam News,* March 28, 1942.

Gatewood, Willard B., Jr. "John Hanks Alexander of Arkansas: Second Black Graduate of West Point." *Arkansas Historical Quarterly* (Summer 1982).

Granger, Lester. "Negroes and War Production." *Survey Graphic* (November 1942).

Hall, E. T. "Race Prejudice and Negro-White Relations in the Army." *American Journal of Sociology,* March 1947.

Hasdorff, James. "Reflections on the Tuskegee Experiment." *Aerospace Historian,* September 1977.

Hastie, William. "The Negro Soldier Is the Negro Youth of Today." *Annals of the American Academy of Political and Social Sciences* (April 1942).

———. "The Negro in the Army Today." *Annals of the American Academy of Political and Social Sciences* (September 1942).

———. "Negro Officers in Two World Wars." *Journal of Negro Education* 12 (Summer 1943).

———. "The Negro in the Army Today." *Journal of Negro Education* 12 (Summer 1943).

"Hate Rules at Tuskegee Base Charged to Colonel Frederick Kimble." *Pittsburgh Courier,* January 2, 1943.

Head, H. "The Negro as an American Soldier." *World Today,* March 7, 1907.

Heinl, N. G. "Colonel Charles Young: Pointman." *Army,* March 1977.

Hershey, Lewis B. "They're in the Army." *Negro Digest,* December 1942.

High, Stanley. "How the Negro Fights for Freedom." *Readers' Digest,* July 1942.

Hinkson, De Haven. "The Role of the Negro Physician in the Military Services from World War I through World War II." *Journal of the National Medical Association* (January 1972).

Janeway, Eliot. "Fighting a White Man's War." *Asia*, January 1943.

Jones, Lester. "The Editorial Policy of Negro Newspapers of 1917–1919 Compared with That of 1941–1942." *Journal of Negro History* (January 1944).

Kenworthy, E. W. "Taps for Jim Crow in the Services." *New York Times Magazine*, June 11, 1950.

———. "The Case against Army Segregation." *Annals of the American Academy of Political and Social Sciences* (May 1951).

Lee, Alfred. "Subversive Individuals of Minority Status." *Annals of the American Academy of Political and Social Sciences* (September 1942).

Lee, H. "He Thinks Air Force." *Aerospace Historian* (Autumn 1969).

Lee, Ulysses. "Letters from the Jim Crow Army." *Twice a Year* (Fall-Winter 1946–47).

———. "The Draft and the Negro." *Current History*, July 1968.

"The Lynching Record for 1918." *Outlook*, January 22, 1919.

McGuire, P. "Judge William Hastie: Confronting the Social Military Status of Blacks in the U.S. Army, 1940–1942." *The Oracle*, Spring 1977.

———. "Judge William Hastie, Civilian Aide to the Secretary of War 1940–1943." *Negro History Bulletin* (May-June 1977).

———. "Judge William Hastie, World War II and Army Racism." *Journal of Negro History* (October 1977).

———. "Judge William Hastie and Army Recruitment 1940–1943." *Military Affairs* (April 1978).

———. "Judge Hastie, World War II, and the Army's Fear of Black Blood." *Review of Afro-American Issues and Culture* (Summer 1979).

———. "Judge Hastie, World War II and the Army Air Corps." *Phylon*, June 1981.

———. "Desegregation of the Armed Forces: Black Leadership, Protest and World War II." *Journal of Negro History* (Spring 1983).

———. "Military Hemophobia." *The Researcher: A Journal of Interdisciplinary Studies* (Spring 1985).

Martin, Louis. "Fifth Column among the Negroes." *Opportunity*, December 1942.

Michael, William Burton. "Factor Analyses of Tests and Criteria: A Comparative Study of Two A.A.F. Pilot Populations." *Annals of the American Academy of Political and Social Sciences* (May 1951).

Milner, Lucille B. "Jim Crow in the Army." *New Republic*, March 13, 1944.

Mizrahi, J. "A Volunteer in Spain." *Wings*, April 1972.

Morrell, M. A. "A White Man's War." *The Crisis*, April 22, 1940.

Moton, R. R. "American Negroes and the World War." *World's Work*, May 1918.

Mueller, William R. "The Negro in the Navy." *Social Forces*, October 1945.

Murray, John Milne. "Accomplishments of Psychiatry in the Army Air Forces." *American Journal of Psychiatry* (March 1947).

Murray, Paul. "Blacks and the Draft: An Analysis of Institutional Racism, 1917–1971." *Journal of Black Studies* (September 1971).

"Myth of Race Equality in the Army." *The Nation*, August 23, 1941.

"The Negro as a Soldier and Officer." *The Nation*, August 1, 1901.

"Negroes at War: All They Want Now Is a Fair Chance to Fight." *Life*, June 15, 1941.

"The Negro in the AAF." *Flying*, June 1945.

"The Negro Officer." *New York Evening Post*, April 4, 1919.

"Negro Pilots Got Wings." *Life*, March 23, 1942.

"Ninety-Ninth Squadron." *Time*, August 3, 1942.

"99th Pursuit Squadron, All Negro." *Time*, September 15, 1941.

Oak, V. V. "What about the Negro Press?" *Saturday Review of Literature*, March 6, 1943.

Osur, A. "Black-White Relations in the U.S. Military, 1940–1942." *Air University Review* (December 11, 1981).

Ottley, Roi. "The Negro Press Today." *Common Ground*, Spring 1943.

———. "A White Folks' War." *Common Ground*, Spring 1942.

Padover, Saul. "Japanese Race Propaganda." *Public Opinion Quarterly* (1943).

Paszek, L. "Negroes and the Air Force, 1939–1949." *Military Affairs* (Spring 1967).

Peck, James. "When Do *We* Fly?" *The Crisis*, December 1940.

"Pilots for 99th Pursuit Squadron Begin Training at Tuskegee." *Opportunity*, August 1941.

Powell, Adam Clayton. "Is This a White Man's War?" *Common Sense*, April 1942.

Prattis, P. R. "The Morale of the Negro in the Armed Forces of the United States." *Journal of Negro Education* 12 (Summer 1943).

———. "The Role of the Negro Press in Race Relations." *Phylon* (1946).

Reddick, L. S. "The Negro Policy of the United States Army, 1775–1945." *Journal of Negro History* (January 1949).

———. "The Negro Policy of the American Army since World War II." *Journal of Negro History* (April 1953).

Reynolds, Grant. "What the Negro Thinks about the War Department." *The Crisis*, September-November 1944.

Robert, Harry. "The Impact of Military Service upon the Racial Attitude of Negro Servicemen in World War II." *Social Problems* 1 (October 1952).

Roosevelt, Eleanor. "My Day." March 3, 1941.

———. "Race, Religion and Prejudice." *New Republic*, May 11, 1942.

———. "Abolish Jim Crow." *New Threshold*, August 1943.

Rose, R. R. "Art and the Airman." *Journal of the American Aviation Historical Society* (Fall 1974).

Schuler, Edgar. "The Houston Race Riot, 1917." *Journal of Negro History* (July 1944).

Schuyler, George S. "A Long War Will Aid the Negro." *The Crisis*, November 1943.

Service. Tuskegee Institute, Tuskegee, Ala., 1936–45.

Sitkoff, Harvard. " Racial Militancy and Interracial Violence in the Second World War." *Journal of American History* (December 1971).

"Snow Clearers, Cotton Pickers." *The Crisis*, March 1943.

Steele, Matthew F. "The 'Color Line' in the Army." *North American Review* (December 21, 1906).

Stevensonberg, George. "Negroes in the Navy." *Army and Navy Journal* (January 19, 1907).

Strother, R. S. "The Cadet Who Refused to Quit." *Readers Digest*, September 1965.

Taylor, H. A. "Flying the Curtiss P-40 (Tomahawk), Viewed from the Cockpit." *Air International*, August 1974.

Thompson, C. H. "The American Negro and the National Defense." *Journal of Negro Education* (October 1940).

Thornborough, L. "The Brownsville Episode and the Negro Vote." *Mississippi Valley Historical Review* (December 1957).

Villard, Oswald Garrison. "Negroes as Soldiers." *The Nation* 63 (1906).

———. "The Negro in the Regular Army." *Atlantic Monthly,* June 1903.

———. "Shall It Be a War of Color?" *Christian Century,* April 2, 1942.

Watson, Goodwin, ed. *Second Yearbook of the Society for the Psychological Study of the Social Sciences.* New York, 1942.

Weiss, Nancy. "The Negro and the New Freedom: Fighting Wilsonian Segregation." *Political Science Quarterly* (March 1969).

Welliver, Wellman. "Report on the Negro Soldier." *Harper's Magazine,* April 1946.

Werrell, Kenneth. "Mutiny at Army Air Forces Station 569: Bamber Bridge, England." *Aerospace Historian* (December 1975).

White, Walter. "A Negro Enlisted Man: Jim Crow in the Army [Air] Corps." *The Crisis,* December 1940

———. "Air Pilots, But Segregated, Army Air Corps Smoke Screen." *The Crisis,* February 1941.

———. "It's Our Country Too." *Saturday Evening Post,* December 14, 1940.

———. "Old Jim Crow in Uniform." *The Crisis,* February 1939.

———. "The Right to Fight for Democracy." *Survey Graphic* (November 1942).

———. "Too Dark for Army Air Corps." *The Crisis,* December, 1940.

———. "What the Negro Thinks of the Army." *Annals of the American Academy of Political and Social Sciences* (September 1942).

"White House Blesses Jim Crow." *The Crisis,* September 1940.

"White Man's War." *Time,* March 2, 1942.

"A White Man's War." *Common Ground,* Spring 1942.

"A White Man's War?" *The Crisis,* January 1942, April 1942.

Wilkins, Roy. "Still a Jim Crow Army." *The Crisis,* April 1946.

Wynne, Neil. "The Impact of the Second World War on the American Negro." *Journal of Contemporary History* (July 1971).

Miscellaneous.

Department of the Army. "Employment of Negro Troops. U.S. Army in World War II." 23.7 CJ 5. Pt. 13, Boxes 86–87. Ulysses Lee material. AMHI.

Department of the Navy. "The Negro in the Navy." Bureau of Personnel. Typescript, n.d. (c. 1945).

Douglas, Helen Gahagan. "The Negro Soldier. A Partial Record of Negro Devotion and Heroism in the Cause of Freedom, Gathered from the Files of the War and Navy Departments." U.S. Congress, House of Representatives. typescript from material appearing in the *Congressional Record,* January 24, 25, 28–31, and February 1, 1946.

Du Bois, W. E. B. "The Black Man and the Wounded World." Boxes 54–58, Special Collections, Fiske University, Atlanta. n.d. (c. 1918).

Lynn Committee to Abolish Segregation in the Armed Forces. Pamphlet, n.d.

Marchbanks, Vance. "Medical Disposition of Pilots." Private study transcript, n.d.

"The Negro Looks at the War." Schomburg Collection, New York Public Library, New York.

Washington, G. L. "The History of Military and Civilian Pilot Training of Negroes at Tuskegee, Alabama, 1939–1945." Typescript. Washington, D.C., n.d.

Index